What Design Can't Do
Essays on Design and Disillusion
Silvio Lorusso

Set Margins' #26

Set Margins' #26
What Design Can't Do:
Essays on Design and Disillusion
by Silvio Lorusso

ISBN: 978-90-833501-3-4
Graphic design: Federico Antonini
(www.federicoantonini.info)
Advisor: Freek Lomme
Copy-editing: Isobel Butters

Printed by Balto Print (Vilnius)
Reprints: 2nd (May 2025)
Print run: 4000
Typeset in: HAL Timezone
First edition: 2023

Unless otherwise credited, all images reproduced in this book are the property of their respective authors. Every effort has been made to trace copyright holders and to obtain their permission for the use of copyrighted material. In the event of any copyright holder being inadvertently omitted, please contact the publisher directly.

Cover and backcover illustration: details from *Melencolia I*, Albrecht Dürer (1514), engraving

The citations from Italian, French and Portuguese sources were translated by the author. All the links referenced in this book were visited on the 28th August, 2023.

This publication is licensed under a Creative Commons Attribution-NonCommercial-ShareAlike 4.0 International License (CC BY-NC-SA 4.0). To view a copy of this license, visit https://creativecommons.org/licenses/by-nc-sa/4.0/.

Set Margins'
www.setmargins.press

Praise for *What Design Can't Do*

"Are you a bit depressed about design? This book might help you understand why. It may also make you laugh. With a lightness of touch, Silvio Lorusso provides an unflinching but well-reasoned discussion as to how design has become so 'bigged up' and what this actually means for its practitioners. After reading this book, design will never look the same to you."
– Guy Julier, author of *Economies of Design*

"What happens once design is a smokescreen and can no longer claim to be a blueprint for change? This is the question Silvio Lorusso puts on the table. How did form, no matter how cool and disruptive, become so futile and tired? Read this with caution: we can no longer design ourselves out of this painful realisation."
– Geert Lovink, author of *Stuck on the Platform*

"The disillusion of design is the disillusion of the world. This book is an essential read, not only for specialists. Because design affects us all, and because understanding where design fails helps us understand where design succeeds."
– Emanuele Quinz, author of *Strange Design*

"Italo-pessimist design critique at its best."
– Clara Balaguer, cultural worker and grey literature circulator

TABLE OF CONTENTS

	Prologue: Starter Pack	p. 14
1.	In the Middle	p. 32

PART I. EXPECTATIONS

2.	Everything Everyone All at Once: On Design Panism	p. 72
3.	A Complex Relationship: On Synthesis and Autonomy	p. 96
4.	Flipping the Table: On Power and Impotence	p. 130

PART II. REALITY

5.	Form Follows Format: On Semi-Automation and Cultural Professionalism	p. 168
6.	Kritikaoke: On Ornamental Politics and Identity as a Skill	p. 208
7.	The School as Real World: On Aspirations and Compromise	p. 244

	Epilogue: Ragequit	p. 290
	Acknowledgements	p. 306
	Bibliography	p. 310
	Index of Names	p. 334

What Design Can't Do

Essays on
Design and Disillusion

Silvio Lorusso

Set Margins' #26

To my friends

"The challenge of modernity is to live without illusions and without becoming disillusioned."
– Antonio Gramsci, 1929–35[1]

"Until today, the history of design has remained a history of defeats, suffered by the high-flying aspirations of the designers in their battle against utilization by *Das Kapital.*"
– Hans Magnus Enzensberger, 1972[2]

---

[1] Antonio Gramsci. *Letters from Prison*. New York: Columbia University Press, 1994.
[2] Hans Magnus Enzensberger. "Remarks Concerning the New York Universitas Project." In *The Universitas Project: Solutions for a Post-Technological Society*, edited by Emilio Ambasz. New York: The Museum of Modern Art, 2006, p. 107.

Prologue:

Starter Pack

> "[...] a fantastic paradox [concerns] modern industrial society and the way people live and act in it. It is the contradiction between the apparent omnipotence of humanity over its physical environment (the fact that technique is becoming more and more powerful, that physical conditions are increasingly controlled, that we are able to extract more and more energy from matter) and, on the other hand, the tremendous chaos and sense of impotence concerning the proper affairs of society, the human affairs, the way social systems work, etc."
> – Paul Cardan (Cornelius Castoriadis), 1965[3]

> "Soon chaos will be our common denominator, we carry it within us and we will find it simultaneously in a thousand places, everywhere chaos will be the future of order, order already no longer makes sense, it is nothing more than an empty mechanism and we wear ourselves out to perpetuate it so that it can consign us to the irreparable."
> – Albert Caraco, 1982[4]

> "In practice, of course a designer's life is as muddled, informal, and accident-prone, as most people's lives manage to be; not only behind the scenes, but sometimes in front of them."
> – Norman Potter, 1969[5]

According to Victor Papanek, an early environmentalist, countercultural designer and outspoken critic of US consumerism, design is "the conscious and intuitive effort to impose meaningful order." Hence, tidying up a desk, curating a party playlist, structuring the chapters of a book... all of these activities can be understood as a design endeavour. It is distressing, however, to realise that very few human activities escape this definition. If this is the case, what specific kind of order are designers meant to

[3] Cornelius Castoriadis. *The Crisis of Modern Society*, Solidarity pamphlet No. 23, 1965. https://libcom.org/article/crisis-modern-society-cornelius-castoriadis.
[4] Albert Caraco. *Breviario del caos*. Milano: Adelphi, 1998, p. 93.
[5] Norman Potter. *What Is a Designer: Things, Places, Messages*. London: Hyphen Press, 2006, p. 19.

PROLOGUE

A particularly niche graphic design starter pack.
@screensaviors (2016).

impose? And is it in any way more stable than the fragile, provisional order that we all attempt to carve, like a horde of industrious archivists in the Tower of Babel?

As every parent entering their kid's room knows, if design is about order, its precondition is not void, but chaos.[6] The book you are reading locates itself within chaos. As such, it's a weird design book. It explores the disorder that can't be contained, the mess that overflows the dams of what we consider arranged and designed, including our mental models and subjectivities. Imposing a meaningful order begins with drawing the line that separates what is subject to the design effort from what it is not: the former is what designers generally call 'problem.' Design is a magic circle that produces an orderly inside and a chaotic outside. Designers safeguard and rework the circle's shifting border,[7] and place ideas, things and people either within it or without it. But the line is porous: our attempts at ordering are inevitably artificial and their outcome necessarily unstable: entropy corrodes the negentropic islands that we call our projects. Order is always under siege. Chaos seeps in, corrupts the magic circle, erodes its contour. This collection of essays traces such erosion. Whereas what's inside design's magic circle can be defined, the chaos that surrounds it can only be described. Hence, *What Design Can't Do* is about describing more than prescribing.

Nowadays, chaos appears to be more powerful than order. Global-scale logistic systems seem as flawed as our tiny life projects. This is why today, more than ever, design

6 This is something that novelist Mary Shelley already pointed out in 1831: "Invention, it must be humbly admitted, does not consist in creating out of void, but out of chaos." The quote comes from a preface to her novel *Frankenstein; or The Modern Prometheus*. The plot seems to suggest that traces of chaos reside in the order, or even that order is nothing but provisionally patched chaos, like the body-corpse of the monster. See Maria Popova. "'Frankenstein' Author Mary Shelley on Creativity." *The Marginalian* (blog), June 25, 2018. https://www.themarginalian.org/2018/06/25/mary-shelley-creativity-frankenstein-1831/.

7 The general tendency is toward the border's extension: "And so we have been forced to expand the boundaries of the systems we deal with, trying to internalize those externalities." Horst W. J. Rittel and Melvin M. Webber. "Dilemmas in a General Theory of Planning." *Policy Sciences* 4, no. 2 (June 1, 1973): 155–69, p. 159.

is polarised. It feels either all-encompassing, infrastructural, planetary, big, baffling – or improvisational, ad-hoc, tiny, volatile. "Today's design culture is an expression of our intense prototype lives – wails Geert Lovink – [p]recarity as an open and free lifestyle is getting stuck in a never-ending series of failures. Projects either fall through or never get finished. Life feels like an endless row of proposals."[8]

Every problem is a wicked problem:[9] its resolution is temporary, its paradigm ever-shifting, its focus evolving. How can one provide yet another abstract definition of the design process when the circumstances of a messy reality are so imposing? Design is left with only one option: staring chaos in the eyes, waiving the somewhat reassuring notion of 'complexity.'[10] For chaos is not complexity: complexity is a field where various forms of expertise compete; chaos is the repressed that returns when the experts fail. If, as James Bridle argues, "complexity is not a condition to be tamed, but a lesson to be learned,"[11] chaos is a grievance that has nothing to teach.

Things do not only appear intricate: they feel meaningless, alien, even to those of us who have devoted themselves to the cause of order. Designers are torn between having to believe, for professional and vocational reasons, in the modern promise of a harmonic, fluid orderliness and being caught in an absurd, glitchy reality. They are the ideal type of a hyper-modern subjectivity – disillusioned evangelists who are losing faith.

"Mess is the Law," declares architect Jeremy Till: "It has taken me this long to work out that maybe architecture

---

[8] Geert Lovink. "Precarious by Design." In *Entreprecariat: Everyone Is an Entrepreneur, Nobody Is Safe*, by Silvio Lorusso. Eindhoven: Onomatopee, 2019. pp. 10-12.

[9] A wicked problem is a problem that can't be unambiguously and definitively solved because its formulation is incomplete, shifting or even contradictory. The term was coined by design theorists Rittel and Webber, *op. cit.*

[10] Hardly surprisingly many design papers and essays begin by paying an introductory tribute to complexity.

[11] James Bridle. *New Dark Age: Technology and the End of the Future*. London: Verso, 2018, p. 138.

roses are red
violets are blue
PLEASE **Don't Study** PLEASE
Graphic Design

Kevin McCaughey (2015).

is a mess; not an aesthetic mess but a much more complex social and institutional mess."[12] Writing in the '70s, architect Giancarlo De Carlo was more hopeful: "The mere sound of the word disorder generally provokes irrepressible neurosis, so it must be made clear that disorder does not mean the accumulation of a systematic dysfunction, but on the contrary the expression of a higher functionality capable of including and making manifest the complex interplay of all the variables involved in a spatial event [...] The salvation of the world – in all fields, from politics to aesthetics – is in disorder as the alternative of a constricting and overwhelming order that can no longer be shared."[13] In a similar vein, Henri Bergson argued that chaos is an order that we cannot see.[14] What if, instead, we focus on order as a means to ignore chaos? Theodor Adorno believed that the task of art was to bring chaos into order.[15] Let's at least bring it into focus.

Talking of her book *Composing a Life*, anthropologist Mary Catherine Bateson wrote that the project "started from a disgruntled reflection on my own life as a sort of desperate improvisation in which I was constantly trying to make something coherent from conflicting elements to fit rapidly changing settings."[16] Here, I engage with a similar urgency, which I believe to be commonly felt. To do so, I explore the mechanisms that are put forward to maintain the illusion of order and the confidence in those who can bring it about. The goal is to shed light on the sense of disillusionment deriving from the distance between orderly expectations and a chaotic reality. A focus on this distance,

---

12 Jeremy Till. *Architecture Depends*. Cambridge, MA: MIT Press, 2013, p. XII.
13 Giancarlo De Carlo. *La piramide rovesciata: architettura oltre il '68*. Macerata: Quodlibet, 2018, pp. 112-4.
14 Quoted in Tomás Maldonado. *La speranza progettuale: ambiente e società*. Torino: Einaudi, 1997, p. 112.
15 Theodor W. Adorno. *Minima Moralia: Reflections from Damaged Life*. London: Verso, 1978, p. 222.
16 Quoted in Penelope Green. "Mary Catherine Bateson Dies at 81; Anthropologist on Lives of Women." *The New York Times*, January 14, 2021. https://www.nytimes.com/2021/01/14/books/mary-catherine-bateson-dead.html.

which might seem alien to the mission of design, is in fact at its core. After all, identifying a problem means nothing other than "knowing what distinguishes an observed condition from a desired condition."[17] The point is not to 'fix' disillusionment, but to understand its origin and the way it affects beliefs and behaviour. To do so, we must place ourselves *in the middle*, looking at how designers have to negotiate between management and execution, technics and humanities, autonomy and dependence, power and subjugation, bureaucracy and innovation, things and self.

* * *

What does the chaos surrounding the magic circle of design look like? Being unable to generalise, as chaos is always unique, I can only describe my own: a draconian series of InDesign paragraph styles, a lost Indexhibit site, a logo commissioned on Fiverr for a laugh, an absent-minded visit to the Dutch Design Week, a 404 error on a wrong jQuery URL in a static webpage, a bunch of risoprint zines, a student's expiring visa, a weak eduroam WiFi access point, a crowdfunded exhibition, a poster about the Anthropocene depicting mushrooms and bacteria, a Linmon-Lerberg IKEA desk travelling from one rented room to another, an unpaid internship report, a video essay featuring a North-American female voice-over, an Instagram ad followed by a @dank.lloyd.wright meme, some dusty mammoth Taschen volumes left at my dad's place, variable fonts, walking tote bags, people dressed like posters, hand-made protest signs, post-its, a dub DJ-set, Cinema 4D free assets, a Twitter hot take on the new CIA brand, a bachelor thesis on transhumanism, an urgent email from an obnoxious client, an alignment error on a 1200 print-run, two herniated discs, a MacBook Pro with Touch Bar, a pair of Lidl flip-flops, an expired

---

[17] Rittel and Webber, *op. cit.*, p. 159.

PROLOGUE

Adobe Creative Cloud subscription, the daily advice of Stefan Sagmeister, a coffee-stained funding application, the e-flux spinner pattern, a witty rip-off of the MAGA hat, 10-page portfolios (10mb max), a Unity-based exploratory "videogame," a Marcel Breuer tubular chair (tried once in a corporate office), this very Markdown file edited in dark mode.

Someone who is familiar with design in the Global North (and probably elsewhere too) might have some of these items in their personal design starter pack. "Starter pack" is the name of a meme in which the defining features of a certain profession, subculture or fandom are displayed against a white background.[18] They can be items, tools, books or even habits. Often, clothes and accessories are included, showing that much of our professional identity inevitably conforms to a certain stereotype and signals it. Many different starter packs for the designer category exist: "the graphic design student" starter pack, the "pretentious designer" one, the "pissing off a graphic designer" version… Their implicit message being that there is no fundamental difference between tools, devices, literature or accessories. Everything is an appendix of identity, something that contributes to a sense of belonging, and in some lucky cases, to the accumulation of prestige. The starter pack meme highlights something else as well, namely that identity formation combines consumption with professional production. Or even that profession is, at least in part, a form of consumption.[19] A chaotic assemblage of designerly stuff floating on a white canvas is supposed to alchemically generate personal character and personalised meaning. Mieke Gerritzen and Geert Lovink speak of "an aesthetic ambiance around your personality, filled with seductive ideas, things and experiences."[20] But this form of

---

18   See https://knowyourmeme.com/memes/starter-packs.
19   I expand on this point in chapter 5.
20   Mieke Gerritzen and Geert Lovink. *Made in China, Designed in California, Criticised in Europe: Design Manifesto*. Amsterdam: BIS Publishers, 2020.

High school friend: "My husband just got a promotion, I'm pregnant and we just bought our first house.

Me:

@screensaviors (2016).

aesthetic identification is fragile. Another recent memetic formula reads: "designer is not a personality." There is a growing feeling that both profession and consumption are insufficient means to build a solid, stable identity.

If we look specifically at graphic design, a dense, complex starter pack is the one built over three years in the Tumblr blog Critical Graphic Design.[21] There, one can scroll through a plethora of obscure inside jokes (some already outdated as the blog shut down in 2015), an obsession with avantgarde designers who are also cultural producers, especially from the Netherlands, the UK and the US (such as Experimental Jetset, Zak Keys, Michael Bierut), the parody of "criticality" as an attitude to display, some modified screenshots of the Photoshop interface, non-existing hyperstitional theory books.[22] Also noticeable is the mechanism of self-canonisation typical of small scenes, a fixation on ivy-league design schools such as Yale (but pictures of Yale forklifts are shown instead), an ironic indulgence in amateur design, a sensibility towards precarity and the hardships of the job market, a few rants on the hypocrisy of political design, an acute awareness of consumerism and profession as two intersecting domains ("Everything is stuff," a book by Metahaven along with a Nike pair of sneakers or a Guy Fawkes mask). Finally, some traces of disillusion ("roses are red violets are blue please please don't study graphic design").

Design critic Francisco Laranjo lamented the lack of coherence of the blog, but it was exactly its schizophrenic

---

Originally, the subtitle of the book was "Amsterdam Design Manifesto", an apt choice that situates the specific design chaos the authors describe. Having lived in the Netherlands for several years, I get their perspective. This is why their books will appear frequently in the following pages. But, whereas Gerritzen and Lovink focus mainly on the contemporary state of design, I concentrate on the state of *designers*, who are the first to be redesigned by it.

21 https://criticalgraphicdesign.tumblr.com.
22 Hyperstition is a term coined by writer and philosopher Nick Land. A portmanteau of the words "hyper" and "superstition," it suggests that ideas can be pushed into the cultural arena where they reinforce themselves, functioning as memetic self-fulfilling prophecies. See Delphi Carstens. "Hyperstition." *orphan Drift Archive* (blog), 2010. https://www.orphandriftarchive.com/articles/hyperstition/.

polyvocality that gave Critical Graphic Design its edge.[23] Critique is no less messy than affirmation. Furthermore, what the anonymous group behind the blog was suggesting, already more than eight years ago, is that next to the visible lifestyle and professional items of design personality, there is a hidden starter pack,[24] one made of silent, sometimes unconscious factors: nightmarish bureaucratic procedures, financial troubles, rich families, gender biases, shitty clients, unpaid internships, dynamics of micro or macro-celebrity, generous funding or lack thereof, networks of friends, circles of gossip and so on. These threaten or sustain the project of doing projects: the professional life project of becoming a cultivated designer, a cultural professional, and more crucially, of remaining one.

A more recent meme could have easily been featured on Critical Graphic Design. Here, someone brags about her achievements: "My husband got a promotion, I'm pregnant and we just bought our first house." Unlike the accomplished high-school friend, the meme protagonist is busy joining vector points in Adobe Illustrator, an infamously tedious process that disgracefully hasn't been automated yet. There is much to unpack in this low-resolution image. First, a traditional idea of success and the good life (only the SUV is missing). Then, a vivid expression of personal disorientation and self-doubt. The meme also speaks of the trivialisation of skills and the drabness of the design profession, which is, for the most part, littered with repetitive tasks.

Finally, it seems to suggest that the exchange is happening between two women. This is no coincidence. For women it is structurally more difficult to get to the top as a designer and reach a position that is either authorial or

---

23   Francisco Laranjo. "Critical Graphic Design: Critical of What?" *Design Observer*, April 16, 2014. http://designobserver.com/feature/critical-graphic-design-critical-of-what/38416.

24   The hidden starter pack refers to the notion of hidden curriculum theorised by, among others, John Dewey, Ivan Illich and Paulo Freire. See https://en.wikipedia.org/wiki/Hidden_curriculum.

PROLOGUE

GRMMXI (2014).
Source: https://grmmxi.fi/post/75583597164.

authoritative.[25] Women are more likely to be stuck with the tiny, menial aspects of the job. After all, one tactic to protect oneself from the chaos of life is to narrow one's project down, to make it as small as the distance between two zoomed-in vector points. The 'tiny' design project, with its controllable Bézier curves, can act as shelter from the life project, which often seems chaotic and meaningless – quite the opposite of the baby-boomer family image painted by the meme's accomplished friend.

* * *

Italian cultural critic Tommaso Labranca once listed two opposite artificial hells of art and design practitioners. On the one hand, the aseptic horror of the white cube; on the other hand, "the nightmare of chaos experienced in the always temporary and shaky dwellings of the artistic underworld."[26] In 2018, Airbnb launched a series of design talks entitled *When Chaos Is Your Creative Director*.[27] The choice of topic makes a lot of sense for a company which deals with people dressing up their room and apartments, often small and Escheresque, into pleasant, generic habitats for tourists and business visitors alike.[28] The people at Airbnb explain: "[...] while the fog of chaos leaves some of us frozen, there are rare talents who can see clearly enough to activate and create." That's the hope: to be one of the lucky few who not only build order, but protect it from seeping chaos.

They insist: "Because chaos is inevitable. Because we live in a world of political unrest, health crises, and

---

[25] Ruber Pater reports that while most graphic design students are women, the designers who run studios are predominantly male. *Caps Lock: How Capitalism Took Hold of Graphic Design, and How to Escape from It*. Amsterdam: Valiz, 2021, p. 294.

[26] Tommaso Labranca. *Vraghinaroda: Sopravvivendo a hipster situazionisti, santexuperine scalze e mistificatori deleuziani*. Milano: 20090, 2019, p. 84.

[27] https://airbnb.design/designed-chaos/ and https://airbnb.design/seasontwo/.

[28] Journalist Kyle Chayka dubbed this aesthetic style "airspace." See "How Silicon Valley Helps Spread the Same Sterile Aesthetic Across the World." *The Verge*, August 3, 2016. https://www.theverge.com/2016/8/3/12325104/airbnb-aesthetic-global-minimalism-startup-gentrification.

questionable ethical tech (*sic*), and design plays a critical role in addressing these global challenges." Even a behemoth company can't avoid admitting the inevitability of chaos, this blob-like material which is at the same time sublimely large and mundanely tiny, an agent whose indifference resists most organising efforts. Chaos precedes design and operates inside it: it is the manifestation of the Real beyond the designerly illusion of a stable and durable order. Given the chaotic qualities of design, one could appreciate the improvisational, almost absurdist illustration of designing provided by Enzo Mari, a legendary Italian designer who, growing up in the rubble of World War II, was first a vocal design utopianist, then a disillusioned realist, and finally a sort of Great Hater of the design world:

> We all design, every day, when we are forced to make our own decisions, even the seemingly trivial ones. For example, having to cook and finding in the fridge only a cup of yogurt and two onions.[29]

One way to look at design is by the capacity of its action, that is, the order it imposes. But design is also, more simply and fundamentally, yogurt and onions – what we are left with, the mess we're in.

---

29 Enzo Mari. *25 modi per piantare un chiodo: Sessant'anni di idee e progetti per difendere un sogno*. Milano: Mondadori, 2011, p. 5.

STARTER PACK

@dank.lloyd.wright (2022). A non-judgemental reading of this meme implies taking into account the reality of the kitchen sink, and thinking of utopian politics from the point of view of the kitchen sink.

PROLOGUE

Found image. Source unknown.

Chapter 1.

In the Middle

"And just as it is only the burning awareness of what we cannot be that guarantees the truth of what we are, so it is only the lucid vision of what we cannot, or can not, do that gives consistency to our actions."
– Giorgio Agamben, 2011[30]

"To reach this goal – to feel what we know and know what we feel – is one of the tasks of our generation."
– László Moholy-Nagy, 1947[31]

A TERRIBLE LIFE DECISION

The state of design in 2023. Gone are the days of the Apple craze, of design as a positive force of change and economic growth, a golden age in which not only designers but also managers and politicians would jump on the smooth and colourful bandwagon of design. The period ranging from the mid-80s to the late 2000s was a promising one: design went hand in hand with creativity, which wasn't just a skill or a quality, but a full sociopolitical project, that of individual autonomy and cheerful reinvention, freedom of choice, agile making and breaking, self-design. During this time, management guru Tom Peters's conviction that "design is everything, it's how you live in the world" became the default, the same Tom Peters who imagined a "world where the timid goal of 'improvement' (and the tendency to tinker) has given way to... an unabashed commitment to destruction."[32]

---

30   Giorgio Agamben. *Nudities*. Stanford: Stanford University Press, 2011, p. 45.
31   László Moholy-Nagy. *Vision in Motion*. Chicago: P. Theobald, 1947, p. 11.
32   2015 McKinsey interview, https://www.youtube.com/watch?v=K3i7x54mOyo. Tom Peters. *Re-Imagine!* London: DK, 2006, p. 31.

CHAPTER 1

Today, things are different. Creativity turned out to be not so emancipating: after the crisis of 2007 and 2008, we dwell in the debris of 'creative destruction.' What is constantly reinvented has no right to stability. A newer new is always impending. In fact, some time ago another keyword replaced design: *innovation*, a term which is itself now under scrutiny. Apple releases are still spectacular events, but the messianic aura around them has evaporated. The design field is still expanding, but it does so less boastfully than before. While change advances undaunted, a standstill is in place, an atmosphere of suspicion permeates the room. Needless to say, design is still employed to increase use value and exchange value (especially the latter), but there is a growing feeling that it has lost its transformative power. Or that design is not in control of this power. Or even that this power has *always* been out of control; as such, it is not power at all.

The "design culture turn" has run its course.[33] Design is not a buzzword anymore and today, more than ever, is ambiguously polarised. In this conjuncture, it is designers themselves, especially the young and not-so-young ones,[34] as well as those who inhabit the peripheries of the design citadels, who are starting to question the value and impact of such practice and its position within power structures. In a way, it is the very idea of design as an abstract and autonomous entity that is put into question: there is no Design, but designed artefacts, systems and processes, both material and immaterial; there are multiple influencing forces at play, and, in the middle of it all, there are

---

33 Guy Julier identifies a turn in design culture taking place between the '80s and the 2000s. This turn is linked to a new social and economic arrangement generated by neoliberal policies. *Economies of Design*. Los Angeles: Sage, 2017, p. 14.

34 Perhaps, especially not-so-young ones: "The disgruntlement seems to go up the longer someone has been in the field: The more seasoned and experienced a UX person is, the more likely they are to be asking whether realizing user-centered values is even possible under capitalism." Jesse Garrett. "Ux Design Is More Successful Than Ever, but Its Leaders Are Losing Hope. Here's Why." *Fast Company*, June 3, 2021. https://www.fastcompany.com/90642462/ux-design-is-more-successful-than-ever-but-its-leaders-are-losing-hope.

designers, stuck between the grand project of modernity and the 'smol' tactics of everyday life.

While 'the power of design' mantra is ecumenically reiterated during conferences, the daily life of most designers is mundane, structured around those "trivial purposes" that the First Things First manifesto already lamented in 1964.[35] The cult of design heroes survives, but a sense of bitterness pervades the crowd, as the kind of hagiographic praise and unanimous approval that makes a hero doesn't match the times. Design heroes, even those who are alive and well, are the vestiges of a dying religion. It's a post-heroic age. Of course, a lot of work is yet to be done to eradicate the double myth of design as a force of good and the designer as the hero who governs it, but the sentiment is clear.

Let's zoom in on this sentiment. Can the field's 'sad passions' be revealing of something we don't fully comprehend? According to cultural theorist Raymond Williams, "one generation may train its successor, with reasonable success, in the social character or the general cultural pattern, but the new generation will have its own structure of feeling, which will not appear to have come 'from' anywhere."[36] What does it mean to inhabit design's current structure of feeling, its *Stimmung*? Can a sentiment not just be the object of analysis but also its medium, its propeller? Neither a theoretical inquiry, nor a critique, a how-to manual or an activist pamphlet, this book is a passionate diagnosis. Much of it deliberately insists on sense, feeling, perception. This is because perceptions matter as much as knowledge, and emotion as much as reason, or to put it another way, reason is one of the many forms that emotion takes. We now know that "the designer's own mindset/posture [is] an essential component of the design process"[37] and, if we are to trust László

---

35 Ken Garland. "First Things First: A Manifesto," 1964.
36 Raymond Williams. *The Long Revolution*. London: Penguin Books, 1965, p. 65.
37 Terry Irwin, Gideon Kossoff, and Cameron Tonkinwise. "Transition Design Provocation." *Design Philosophy Papers* 13, no. 1 (January 2, 2015): 3–11. https://doi.

CHAPTER 1

Found image. Source unknown.

Picture taken by Marta Romanelli in 2018
near the Politecnico of Milan.

CHAPTER 1

Moholy-Nagy, we must see designing not as a profession, but as an attitude.[38] Today, design is an attitude that wants to be considered a profession, but this attitude is perturbed by individual and social turmoil.

Constant redesign can be exhausting. Like in the Gartner Hype Cycle, after a "peak of inflated expectations," we reach a "trough of disillusionment."[39] The signs pop up in unexpected places: design is often the butt of the joke. Some designers are doubtful and disoriented. Others are anaesthetised and disappointed. Some of them are plain angry and resentful. Disillusionment is palpable. How many disillusioned designers are there? What's the exact percentage of chagrin in the design field? Clearly, there is no objective way to measure this. What is certain is that the "slope of enlightenment" is not in sight. Some designers get stuck: they feel unable to produce meaning with the instruments provided by the their field. "The truth is we are the most iconic, lazy, useful idiots of our era." This is how designer Baptiste Fluzin commented the call to arms to counter the rise of Donald Trump.[40] All in all, it might be a good time: perhaps designers are suddenly realising that their relationship with their discipline has always been a form of Stockholm syndrome.

Luckily for us, disillusion is not just *disillusionment*, a passive feeling of dismay and disappointment. It is also *disillusioning*, the active lifting of illusions, an engagement with reality without at least some of the old veils. Thus, disillusion is a pendulum oscillating between lucidity and dismay. Who is more prone to this sentiment? Design disillusion is the 'feel' of those who have access neither to the reassurance of the centre nor to the effervescence of the

---

org/10.1080/14487136.2015.1085688.
38 Moholy-Nagy, *op. cit*, p. 42.
39 Marcus Blosch and Jackie Fenn. "Understanding Gartner's Hype Cycles." *Gartner*, August 20, 2018. https://www.gartner.com/en/documents/3887767/understanding-gartner-s-hype-cycles.
40 Baptiste Fluzin. "Designers, Designers, Designers." *Tumblr* (blog), October 11, 2016. https://bfluzin.tumblr.com/post/152990139318.

margin, those who feel stuck in some sort of pseudo-cultural, semi-professional suburbia. Those who can't seem to attune themselves to design's display of good sentiments and prescription of appropriate behaviours. Despite running the risk of generating even more of it, one needs to think *with* disillusion to measure the space that separates expectations from reality.

Where is such disillusion expressed and how can it be probed? For obvious reasons, design pessimism mostly manifests informally, in ephemeral chats and conversations, in memes and tweets, often deleted shortly after. While it is becoming a genre in itself, the public anti-design critical outburst is still an exception. If we turn our gaze from the official disquisitions of museums, magazines and galleries which acrobatically rip design apart while reassembling it, to the oral environment of social media, we witness an outpouring of doubts, reality checks and self-deprecating humour. Just innocuous jokes, one might say. But what if we take those jokes seriously? A popular design publication suggested that jokes could bring down governments.[41] More humbly, I believe they could disclose something worthy of our attention. Let's look at some of them.

According to a series of memes, graphic design is: no longer my passion / my burden / my prison. A Twitter user admits: "Every day I think about what a terrible life decision being a designer has been." Another one rebukes: "design is so unimportant in the grand scheme of things and I'm sick of seeing people kid themselves into thinking their contributions as a designer are some form of visual activism." On a wall, painted red, we find the statement "design ruined my life," while a sticker on a trash can yells in caps: "graphic design is shit / coding is shit / all I want is revenge."[42] Facetiousness, for sure. Designers' humour, no

---

41   Metahaven. *Can Jokes Bring down Governments?* Moscow: Strelka Press, 2014.
42   To be fair, there are also positive expressions, such as "Every day I remind myself of how lucky I am that I get paid for drawing rectangles."

doubt. Nothing other than understatement and self-deprecation as a bonding mechanism. After all, that's what social media are for. More rigorous sources would surely reassure us. Among them, are a few surveys on designers' conditions. Lucienne Roberts, Rebecca Wright and Jessie Price, editors, together with social scientist Nikandre Kopcke, of the book *Graphic Designers Surveyed* report that "[a]lthough 83% of respondents said they would recommend a career in graphic design, only 55% of respondents expressed satisfaction with their career – and 23% were actively dissatisfied."[43] Stefanie Posavec, who designed the book, concludes that "[...] while designers are an independent, opinionated (and, dare I say it, mouthy) bunch when it comes to how we feel about our practice and our chosen field, this strong will doesn't always translate into higher wages or shorter hours."[44]

From Flavia Lunardi's 2018 survey on Italian graphic design studios we learn that although 86.9% of the respondents don't want to change job, 71% of them are not appeased by the recognition of the graphic designer's role in Italy.[45] In this case, like in those of the UK and US, it seems that the majority like their job and yet they are unhappy with it. Is this an instance of what Lauren Berlant called "cruel optimism?" The theorist used the term to refer to a situation in which "the object/scene that ignites a sense of possibility actually makes it impossible to attain the expansive transformation for which a person or a people risks striving [...]."[46] The object/scene being, in this situation, a designer's career.

According to the design census of 2019 carried out by the American Institute of Graphic Arts (9,429 participants), one out of three designers is dissatisfied, and 7% of

---

[43] Lucienne Roberts, Rebecca Wright, and Jessie Price, eds. *Graphic Designers Surveyed*. London: GraphicDesign&, 2015, p. 456. The survey spans the UK and US. In the overall sample, 85% of the respondents were under 40 and predominantly white, pp. 50-51.
[44] *Ibidem*, p.18.
[45] Flavia Lunardi. "Grafica Italia 2018." ISIA Urbino, 2018.
[46] Lauren Berlant. *Cruel Optimism*. Durham, NC: Duke University Press, 2011, p. 2.

them are ready to call it quits. And this does not take into account the self-selecting bias of a professional association which plausibly includes practitioners who have obtained a certain degree of stability or success in their practice. What would be the dissatisfaction rate if designers at large were considered? Moreover, those surveys implicitly ask for a sort of definitive assessment of oneself, and therefore the respondent might be cautious when it comes to negative self-evaluation.

THE BIG SPLIT

Is this anything new? US sociologist C. Wright Mills diagnosed an uneasiness with the role of the designer already in the late 1950s. He highlighted two trends: first, the importance that distribution was gaining over production, thus that of status over subsistence; second, the subordination of activities to capitalism and nationalism. This is the nexus where designers operate:

> Designers work at the intersection of these trends; their problems are among the key problems of the overdeveloped society. It is their dual investment in them that explains the big split among designers and their frequent guilt; the enriched muddle of ideals they variously profess and the insecurity they often feel about the practice of their craft; their often great disgust and their crippling frustration.[47]

According to Mills, the designer is a "man in the middle" who cannot fully understand their position without considering the cultural and economic conjuncture they're

---

[47] C. Wright Mills. "Man in the Middle: The Designer." In *Power, Politics and People*, edited by Irving L. Horowitz, London: Oxford University Press, 1969, p. 374. This was part of Mills' talk at the 8th International Design Conference of Aspen in 1958. The same conference where, almost twenty years later, Saul Bass asked students "why do we have to assess capitalism? We're just trying to stage a design conference." See Alice Twemlow. "'A Guaranteed Communications Failure:' Consensus Meets Conflict at the International Design Conference in Aspen, 1970." In *Aspen Complex*, edited by Martin Beck. London: Sternberg Press, 2013.

CHAPTER 1

I'm too sad to tell you, a mixed media artwork created by conceptual artist Bas Jan Ader between 1970 and 1971. Luca Trevisani calls the work "a neat empathic trap": both liberatory and manipulative, Ader's weep shows the ambiguity of manifesting one's sad passions.

Bumper sticker by Freelance Studio, who found the original
image on Twitter.

in. One suspects that his words caused some stir. Designers are not used to seeing themselves in the middle: they place themselves at the top of cultural and decision-making processes. They portray themselves as in charge of the plan. But then, they are frustrated by the realisation that the plan and the design are two very different things.[48] Mills's diagnosis, however, might not fully apply today. Whereas in the past the designer's crippling frustration derived from the awareness of being an "organisation man," a cog in the cultural and economic machine, now, given the abundance of designers, the frustration has more to do with being a cog *outside* the machine, that is, being less and less able to shape its workings.[49] After all, Mills was speaking to a crowd of prominent representatives of the field many of whom, despite the "Aspen-style" informality,[50] were firmly embedded in the industrial and corporate world.

Mills explained that *White Collar,* one of his most popular books, was "about the new little man in the big world of the 20th century [...] for, in truth, who is not a little man?" Here, I propose to focus on the 'interscalar' gap between the personal tiny and the structural huge, to connect the vector points of individual life to the grand issues rooted in modernity and its crisis. The '60s white-collar worker was beginning to experience what would become the default torments of the no-collar professional worker, a category that the designer centrally represents: The "new little man [...] seems to have no firm roots, no sure loyalties to sustain his life and give it a center [...] Perhaps because he does not know where he is going, he is in a frantic hurry; perhaps because he does not know what frightens him, he is paralyzed with fear."

---

[48] See chapter 4.
[49] William H. Whyte. *The Organization Man*. Philadelphia: University of Pennsylvania Press, 2002.
[50] *International Design Conference in Aspen: The First Decade*, 1961. https://www.youtube.com/watch?v=8MxCGKicSfg.

This is how the magazine *Industrial Design* reviewed Mills's talk:

> Generally when a speaker addresses members of a profession not his own, he tells them what they want to hear. He can do it obviously, by telling them how good they are; or subtly, by telling them how bad they are, then making it all right at the end by exhorting them to be better. In either case, since he tells them only what they tell each other, he contributes only the illusion of a fresh perspective. An exception is this paper read to the Design Conference in Aspen this summer by sociologist and author (*The Power Elite*) C. Wright Mills. Neither lullaby nor mock attack, it is a hard analysis of the designer in our society.[51]

Neither lullaby nor mock attack. We can take this as a methodological principle to carry out an inquiry that is self-conscious of its own participation in the design discourse, a discourse which mostly welcomes what it can digest in utilitarian terms, be it criticism or praise.

Since Aspen, design's identity crisis has only worsened. In the '70s, Tomás Maldonado detected a dimming of the "designerly hope," brought about by a youthful nihilism that was leading to a pre-emptive renunciation of action. Maldonado was thankful to the youth "for waking us up from our drowsiness and reminding us without euphemism that ours is not an Arcadian age, but an agonizingly convulsive one."[52] And yet, he firmly believed in the necessity of hope, hence his essay on the topic. Although I agree with Maldonado, this book takes a different approach: it examines hopelessness *in itself*, resisting the urge of immediately rejecting it, for it is in hopelessness that hope sprouts.

---

51   In Javier A. Treviño. "C. Wright Mills as Designer: Personal Practice and Two Public Talks." *The American Sociologist* 45, no. 4 (December 1, 2014): 335–60. https://doi.org/10.1007/s12108-014-9196-y.

52   Maldonado, *La speranza progettuale, op. cit.*, p. 10.

"Only for the sake of the hopeless ones have we been given hope," wrote Walter Benjamin.[53]

THE EVERYDAY DESIGNER

Maldonado had the young in mind, Mills the professional class. What's the subject of this book, then? The designer in the real world, I'm tempted to say. Still, what reality? The question is not an easy one and has serious theoretical implications. "When I talk about reality – wrote Ursula Franklin – I'm not trying to be a philosopher. I think of reality as the experience of ordinary people in everyday life."[54] With this in mind, who do we call a designer? What particularities do we include in this definition? The more we categorise, the more our categories quiver. Shall we consider designers only people who studied design? What do we do, then, with those self-taught practitioners who have achieved professional recognition? How could we leave out the "legions of designers who work in-house for companies or as freelancers?"[55] Shall we break down designers by the type of service they provide? That won't work. Graphic designers craft products, product designers conceive services, service designers do performances, performers strategically call their activity choreographic design, strategic designers print posters and fliers, etc. Specialisms have detached themselves from products to become a sort of shared attitude and a common set of cultural and methodological references. More than with the things that they do, designers identify with the sensitivity they adopt when they do those very things. To a certain extent, the contemporary designer is a designer without qualities.

Radical openness is our last resort: trust the person who calls themselves a designer to be one. Trust the designer who makes some of her income designing logos for friends,

---

53 Walter Benjamin. *Selected Writings Vol. 1*, 1913-1926. Cambridge, MA: Belknap, 2004.
54 Ursula M. Franklin. *The Real World of Technology*. Toronto: Anansi, 1999, p. 27.
55 Julier, *op. cit.*, p. 5.

IN THE MIDDLE

Found image, photoshopped. In the original picture, taken
in London, the sticker reads "Growth is shit, jobs are shit,
all I want is revenge."

CHAPTER 1

as well as the design *auteur* who sell his designs as collectible NFTs to pay rent; trust the business student who started calling themselves a designer after having learned about design thinking, trust the art director and the service designer, trust the critical designer, the user-centred designer, the design catalyst, the metadesigner, trust the designer who makes 'actually existing design.' This stance goes against notions of quality, excellence and even expertise, notions that have been mobilised by the field to acquire status. We need to relativise these notions to be able to see how, and if, they still lead to status. Excellence has always been the rhetorical instrument of a winning elite. But in order to understand elitist aspirations, we need to picture a kind of designer who is not so much part of an elite. This designer is not taken into account by design literature, which mostly focuses on promoting and strengthening the field. I will call this figure the *everyday designer*. While this kind of practitioner might have cultural and political aspirations, a good portion of their time is spent in mundane tasks. Perhaps the everyday designer has just launched a small boutique studio and struggles to find the clients who could appreciate their research capabilities. Perhaps they just had a kid. The everyday designer might be simply a student, taking an undergraduate or master's degree, either a technical or more artistic one. Or a recent graduate, trying to practice what has been preached to them. They might be sitting in a small agency thinking up a campaign to enrich the portfolio of a small bank. The everyday designer is a Photoshop whiz, he's toying with Figma or Sketchup, she's banging her head against CSS rules or the settings of a 3D printer. The everyday designer is the designer caught up in daily, menial tasks beyond creation, while daydreaming about their role and career. They're good enough designers – yet they might even be contemplating the idea of quitting.

What the everyday designer is not: the design star at the top of their field, the universally recognised expert,

IN THE MIDDLE

Me in the middle of the night questioning my decision to become a designer

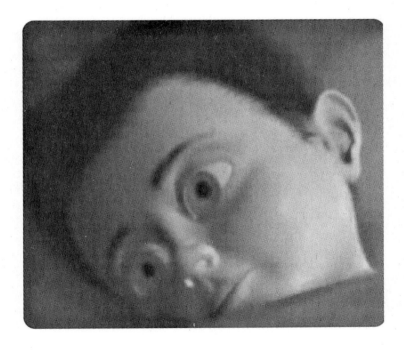

Found image. Source unknown.

the one everyone else looks at and emulates – in short, all those designers we hear tips and advice from, those who saturate the media sphere affirming their ideas and their role. It's not their fault: if asked, they answer. While the image of the design star is intrinsically iconic, that of the everyday designer is admittedly rather blurry, but its function is clear: to avoid exceptionalism. Or, more accurately, to isolate the exceptions that shape the rule and the deviations produced by the norm. In this sense, the everyday designer is seldom a resolved regularity, but more frequently a living discrepancy. That said, blurriness is part of the lens I adopt: many practitioners will readily recognise that they have acted as one or more of the 'personas' I just mentioned. Indeed, the everyday designer is not really a person, but a configuration. It's the personalisation of a semi-professional designing multitude at the edge of the design's field of vision.

In a similar vein, for his book *Economies of Design*, Guy Julier steered clear

> of the more senior, established end of the design career, not least because this is already much more represented through design media. These tend to focus on big success stories. We hear little of the designers who continue working the long hours for relatively low financial reward or those, indeed, who after a decade of so leave design altogether to do something else.[56]

Where is the everyday designer based? The answer is unavoidably partial. The practitioner I have in mind is generally active in the Global North: Europe and the US. This is of course a shortcoming, but I don't think it defeats my anti-exceptionalist purpose. A European designer is an exception, of course, but an exception that contains multiple normalities. Furthermore, Europe offers enough variety to highlight and compare stark differences in terms of

---

56   Julier, *op. cit.*, p. 55.

desires, aspirations and the possibility to realise them.[57] Finally, European design is not so European anymore. Go to design academies and you will find a substantial part of Chinese, Korean and Latin American students. Go to a final show in Amsterdam or Milan and you will see not only projects *on* the Middle East, but also projects made *by* Middle Eastern designers.

Most of my references and examples derive from graphic design. There are multiple reasons for this. First, a personal one: I trained as a graphic designer and therefore I'm more familiar with this context. Second, a methodological one: given the low access barrier of this field, the everyday designer is more likely to be a graphic designer than a more niche figure. Graphic design is a diluted practice, one in which professionals have to put increasing effort to assert their expertise to clients and society at large. Graphic design is where the necessity of radical openness becomes most obvious, since it's also where the pro/amateur binary abruptly collapses. Graphic design, one of those "rather inchoate professions" in and around design,[58] might even show the general trajectory of professions.

In 1995, design theorist Richard Buchanan proposed a model of design activities structured around four orders. In this model, graphic design is – controversially, one must say – the most limited one, as it deals particularly with symbols. The other three orders are industrial, interaction, and environmental design.[59] In contrast to this model, I propose to see graphic design as the widest of the orders, as it is more affected by technical, cultural and methodological democratisation: it is spread more diffusely

---

57 I think in particular of the gap between funding-rich countries like the Netherlands (where I used to reside) and funding-poor countries like Italy (where I come from). The designer is not just a "man in the middle" of cultural and economic trends, but also of cultural and economic contexts.
58 The expression is Mills's. Quoted in Treviño, *op. cit.*, p. 351.
59 Richard Buchanan. "Design Research and the New Learning." *Design Issues* 17, no. 4 (October 1, 2001): 3–23. https://doi.org/10.1162/07479360152681056.

across society. If we accept whoever professes themselves a designer to be one, we have to see design not just as an activity, but as a community of practice able to provide a sense of belonging. I would be tempted to speak of class, if it weren't for the abysmally different conditions among everyday designers. Many have argued that in a modern society everyone designs. While not denying this obvious fact, the lens chosen here is that of *consciousness*: everyday designers are conscious of their role and cultural context – they are self-conscious.[60] In this sense, the notion of everyday designer differs profoundly from the generalist claim that "everyone is a designer," a claim that can be either a defence of autonomy or a form of libertarian individualism. In other words, the everyday designer is explicitly a designer in a world where everybody designs.

I'M NO EXPERT

It is true for me what was true for Karl Kraus: "I do not like to meddle in my private affairs."[61] However, as much as I'd like to avoid entering the stage, a few words on 'who speaks' are due. Shortly put, I consider myself an everyday designer who, thanks to his partial, intermittent, but hopefully lasting professional belonging to the field, has had enough time to write about his condition and the condition of his peers. This is my personal discrepancy, the exceptional normality I represent. While this work emerges from my own doubts and uncertainties, it doesn't derive from an urgency to critique or celebrate but, to use an apt expression by graphic designer Jan van Toorn, from a "passion for the real." Once again, it's neither lullaby nor mock attack.

This is a design book without much design in it. Or to be more precise, the design we encounter is not so much the portfolio material of designers, but the designed

---

60 This point is slightly controversial, as I sense that the professionals of design discourse are abandoning the profession as a matter of concern. See chapter 7.
61 Harry Zohn. *Karl Kraus*. New York: Ungar, 1971, p. 17.

graphic design for cheap
graphic design for a few dollars
graphic design in a few minutes
graphic design in a few clicks
graphic design in an instant
graphic design that requires no effort
graphic design that just requires you to 'insert company name here'
graphic design that requires no graphic designing skills whatsover
graphic design that is easy
graphic design that is easily disposable
graphic design that is pre-determined
graphic design that is imitative
graphic design that is repetitive
graphic design that doesn't make sense
graphic design in the form of stock images
graphic design in the form of $5 logos
graphic design in the form of mixing and matching friendly styles
graphic design in the form of '18+ free attractive flyer templates for your business'
graphic design without the wait
graphic design without paying crazy prices
graphic design without the hassle
graphic design without the expertise
graphic design without thinking
graphic design without an idea
graphic design without a concept

graphic design without a graphic designer

Promotional (Mis)information by Adelia Lim (2018). A "collection of cheaply produced promotional materials that responds to the way graphic design is valued when design templates come into play."

environment that surrounds them, made of objects, services, but also institutions, protocols, values, myths. As discussed in the prologue, I'm more concerned with the 'mess we're in' than the projects we work on. Furthermore, this book is full of memes, a cultural form that exemplifies distributed agency and the attitude of the *bricoleur* – both aspects that challenge the compromised vocational image of the designer as planner. Memes also reflect the everyday designer's condition: disillusioned designers won't write papers to express their chagrin, they don't have time for that. They will make a meme instead.

For various reasons, several theorists have drawn a fairly clear line between professional designers and non-professional ones. Design historian Victor Margolin speaks of design with a capital 'd' and design with a small 'd,' the former being associated with the Industrial Revolution and the advent of mass communication, the latter being a broadly human activity.[62] Architect Ezio Manzini proposes a model in which "expert design" and "diffuse design" interact in various ways.[63] The everyday designer is located between these poles – not fully recognised as an expert, but also not a mere human being who plans ahead. The notion of the everyday designer sheds light on the fact that divides based on professionalism and expertise are nuanced, complicated and, more importantly, *dynamic*. The point is not only that these divides do not dignify practices that aren't traditionally recognised by the design field, but also that expertise and professionalism are categories in constant renegotiation. A professional skill might become a default one, and everyday designers might struggle to be considered expert. Furthermore, as with any profession, expert design is vampiristic: it sucks the vitality of diffuse

---

62 Steven Heller. "The Evolution of Design." *The Atlantic*, April 9, 2015. https://www.theatlantic.com/entertainment/archive/2015/04/a-more-inclusive-history-of-design/390069/.
63 Ezio Manzini. *Design, When Everybody Designs*. Cambridge, MA: MIT Press, 2015, p. 40.

design – the intelligence of the general intellect – to maintain its status. The crisis of the professions exacerbates vampirism: as expert designers lose prestige in the eyes of the public, they try to absorb diffuse design to reinstate their role and position.

LIFE PROJECT

In *The Politics of the Artificial*, Margolin warns us that "if designers are going to realize the full potential of design thought, then they should also learn to analyze how the situations that frame design practice are themselves constructed."[64] Similarly, anthropologist Lucy Suchman is in favour of "ethnographic projects that articulate the cultural imaginaries and micropolitics that delineate design's promises and practices."[65] In these words, we hear the echo of Mills: the process of professional negotiation, the oscillating reputation of the everyday designer, the kernel of their vocations and ambitions should be made explicit.

The construction of ambition and vocation is strictly linked to the era in which design with a capital 'd' emerged: modernity. And when modernity becomes relentless and more flexible, in the phase that coincides with what we call neoliberalism, ambitions and vocations follow suit. Guy Julier explains that during the '80s, "the professional environment and aspirations of design mirrored the increased flexibility and speed afforded by the Big Bang for the financial sector."[66] In this regard, Ezio Manzini raises a relevant issue: "How and to what extent modernity's promise of designability of one's own life has been fulfilled is obviously an open question." This is the question we are tackling here, however not in general terms – that

---

64 Victor Margolin. *The Politics of the Artificial: Essays on Design and Design Studies*. Chicago: University of Chicago Press, 2018, p. 241.
65 Lucy Suchman. "Anthropological Relocations and the Limits of Design." *Annual Review of Anthropology* 40, no. 1 (2011).
66 Julier, *op. cit.*, p. 25.

CHAPTER 1

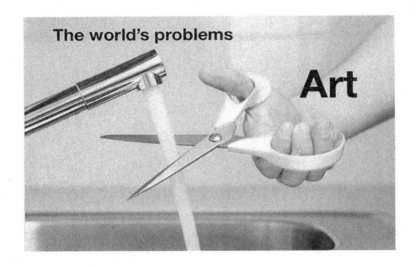

Found image. Source unknown.

would be exceptionally pretentious – but within design itself. Thus, the question becomes: what is the horizon of designability of one's own design practice? The protagonist of Manzini's story is

> a subject immersed in his everyday life, taking part in various conversations; a node in various networks and an actor in various social forms. From his point of observation and action, he designs and co-designs his action on the world operating as a *bricoleur*: he looks for usable materials around him (products and services, but also ideas and knowledge) and, adapting and reinterpreting them, he uses them to compose his life project.[67]

This is a good characterisation of the everyday designer. When talking of life projects, the distinction between design and bricolage becomes blurry. The everyday designer is always working with a set of constraints that do not only belong to the internal logic of the design, but to its presence in the world. Everyday designers design their life project from the rubble of what is already there – their activities and career included. This process is dynamic and contingent, as Julier points out: "Designers' responsiveness to changing commercial contexts results in rapid reinventions of the professional field – a constant redesign of design itself."[68] Their practice is inevitably *compromising*.

Designers readjust. In Manzini's words, "in order to adapt to what is required of them, they must redesign themselves and their way of operating. But then this is what is required of everybody today."[69] If the modern project does not fulfil its promises of identity, administration and prosperity, the designer, being one of its poster children, becomes a hypermodern post-professional figure,

---

67 Manzini, *op. cit.*, p. 4.
68 Julier, *op. cit.*, p. 38.
69 Manzini, *op. cit.*, p. 2.

located between autonomy and dependence. And, like everyone else, caught in endless projects:

> The weak, depressed, self-critical, virtual self is essentially that endlessly adaptable subject required by the ceaseless innovation of production, the accelerated obsolescence of technologies, the constant overturning of social norms, and generalized flexibility. It is at the same time the most voracious consumer and, paradoxically, the *most productive self*, the one that will most eagerly and energetically throw itself into the slightest *project*, only to return later to its original larval state.[70]

The figure of the everyday designer shows us a dire situation, one where it is not individuals who direct projects, but projects that direct individuals.

CRACKED UP ON CAPITALISM

This reversal begins just after the phase of education. The leap from the *vita contemplativa* of the design school to the *vita activa* of independent or studio work is seldom devoid of trauma. Furthermore, a series of structural forces loom over the possibility of designerly gratification. According to a Gallup survey, 85% of workers worldwide do not feel engaged with their job.[71] From this perspective, the previous statistics about designer dissatisfaction acquire the opposite meaning. As dire as it might sound, one third of dissatisfied practitioners is not so bad. Let's consider again *Graphic Designers Surveyed*. The editors refer to an overall job satisfaction in the US of 48%, against the 78% of the UK. In this scenario, graphic designers living the States would be relatively more satisfied than those

---

[70] The Invisible Committee. *The Coming Insurrection*. New York: Autonomedia, 2009, p. 31.

[71] Jim Clifton. "The World's Broken Workplace." *Gallup*, June 13, 2017. https://news.gallup.com/opinion/chairman/212045/world-broken-workplace.aspx.

active in Great Britain.[72] But even in some affluent strongholds of design culture things are not so rosy: "[...] when asked about their satisfaction a year or two after graduating, a consistently high share of former design students – approximately 40%; twice as many compared with other studies – would not choose the same field of study again," reports Paola De Martin from Switzerland.[73]

All things considered, a certain degree of cynicism is to be expected. This is nothing new. The position of designers within capitalist and consumerist enterprises makes them pessimistic and frustrated.[74] But it's not only that. Issues related to the changing world of work need also to be taken into account. To begin with, there is the feeling of a decreasing return of investment from higher education, with the subsequent idea that a study loan spent on rising fees and rent might not be a good deal. 'ROI resentment' becomes particularly justified if we examine the income generated by the activity of designers: 44% of the *Graphic Designers Surveyed* are economically "just getting by."[75] The income disparity between various design specialisations might fuel such resentment. Furthermore, the work itself is often unstable and unpredictable, particularly when it comes to freelancing. Then, there are strong disparities between countries. For instance, the 15% unemployment rate in Spain against the 3.3% of the Netherlands. These disparities can fuel ambitions – and then curb them. There is, as well, the issue of sexism and the gender gap[76] (and yet women are surprisingly slightly

---

72   Roberts et al., *op. cit.*, p. 456.
73   Paola De Martin. "Breaking Class: Upward Climbers and the Swiss Nature of Design History." In *Design Struggles: Intersecting Histories, Pedagogies, and Perspectives*, edited by Claudia Mareis and Nina Paim. Amsterdam: Valiz, 2021, p. 66.
74   "Being at the centre of the sales curve, it is logical that many graphic designers develop a 'cynical relationship to both consumerism and capitalism', writes Boehnert. Designers are frustrated with the discipline, but see no other ways of making money." Pater, *op. cit.*, p. 208.
75   Roberts et al., *op. cit.*, p. 296.
76   *Ibidem*, p. 118.

CHAPTER 1

Poster by Elliott Ulm (2021).

IN THE MIDDLE

Print-on-demand baseball hat by Stephanie Davidson.

more satisfied with their career).[77] A widespread sense of futurelessness can also not be ignored. Design, with its fast-paced trends, is instrumental to it. The feeling is also related to the unfolding climate crisis, in comparison to which everything pales, any action feels inappropriate, abstract, irrelevant. How can one speak about petty things like professional recognition when we are facing extinction?[78]

A TikTok user summarises some of these problems in a 30-second rant:

> Hi guys, ever just wonder how much of a scam everything in our life is? When I first went to college I was like: oh my god, I need to find a purpose. What am I gonna do that's gonna give me such life fulfilment? And my answer to that was USER EXPERIENCE DESIGN. I really thought the ANSWER to my LIFE was UX DESIGN. I'M CRACKED UP ON CAPITALISM![79]

As authors like Guy Julier, Ruben Pater and Matthew Wizinsky aptly demonstrate, design is tightly (if not inextricably) connected to capitalism.[80] But not everything can be reduced to this relationship. Or, more precisely, not everything should be reduced to this relationship in its most general sense. The risk here is to perform Capital's job of abstracting lived practices and treat them as generic, 'lo-res' instances of exploitation. This usually leads to sacrosanct but also interchangeable calls for unionisation, petitions to 'pay your interns,' etc. We

---

77 *Ibidem*, p. 134.
78 Recently, MoMA design curator Paola Antonelli made the provocative claim that humans should design "an elegant ending" of their race. In such statements urgency meets powerlessness. Antonelli's provocation can be interpreted as an intelligent move to annex design powerlessness to her curatorial interests. Augusta Pownall. "'We Don't Have the Power to Stop Our Extinction' Says Paola Antonelli." *Dezeen*, February 22, 2019. https://www.dezeen.com/2019/02/22/paola-antonelli-extinction-milan-triennale-broken-nature-exhibition/.
79 @suwuuuuu, post deleted.
80 Julier, *op. cit*. Pater, *Caps Lock*, *op. cit*. Matthew Wizinsky. *Design After Capitalism: Transforming Design Today for an Equitable Tomorrow*. Cambridge, MA: MIT Press, 2022.

shouldn't treat the designer (or any other kind of practitioner, for that matter) as an economically-determined stick figure who doesn't possess any specificity other than being a 'cultural worker.' We shouldn't miss the *specific* manifestations of design's liaison with capitalism. This oversight might be strategically valid from the point of view of 'praxis,' but it is less so when it comes to comprehend the designer's condition. Instead, the question we need to ask is: how does design differ from other activities entrenched in capitalism? Let's begin with design culture's default optimistic attitude.

THE UNCHANGEABLE

All the bad news won't affect design's standard stance. The fact that optimism is intrinsic to design emerges clearly in Herbert Simon's definition: "Everyone designs who devises courses of action aimed at changing existing situations into *preferred* ones."[81] More than focusing on the state of things, design pays attention to how things ought to be. And, of course, they ought to be better. So, from the point of view of design, pessimism appears vulgar and easy. Optimism, instead, is praised. But optimism can also be easy and vulgar, it can be mesmerised by abstract possibilities at the expense of a callous reality. Marco Petroni argues that "[t]oo often in the world of design the harshness of the *real* is accepted only when translated or rendered imaginative."[82] This translation, which is what we call a project, is also a way of projecting oneself outside reality.

Ultimately, design is terrified by what it is unable to change. It must systematically repress any manifestation of its impotence. The unchangeable is design's taboo. In this sense, it simply mirrors a broader condition which Italian philosopher Giorgio Agamben describes as follows:

---

81 Herbert A. Simon. *The Sciences of the Artificial*. Cambridge, MA: MIT Press, 2019, p. 111. The italics are mine.
82 Marco Petroni. *Il progetto del reale: il design che non torna alla normalità*. Milano: Postmedia Books, 2020, p. 10.

> Separated from his impotentiality, deprived of the experience of what he can not do, today's man believes himself capable of everything, and so he repeats his jovial 'no problem,' and his irresponsible 'I can do it,' precisely when he should instead realize that he has been consigned in unheard of measure to forces and processes over which he has lost all his control. He has become blind not to his capacities but to his incapacities, not to what he can do but to what he cannot, or can not, do.[83]

Agamben associates such positive, affirmative alienation, such perceived surplus of potential, to flexibility, instability and to the confusion between role and vocation. Along these lines, we can interpret design disillusion as a return of the repressed, the revenge of a reality that perturbs, with its constraints and limitations, the optimistic project of establishing the preferable.

A GENEALOGY OF DESIGN DISILLUSION?

Is it possible to assemble a genealogy of design disillusion? It's no easy task. Should one begin with the Radical Design movement of the '60s and '70s? Or with Le Corbusier, who in 1923 wrote that "[e]ngineers are healthy and virile, active and useful, moral and joyful. Architects are disenchanted and idle, boastful or morose. That is because they will soon have nothing to do."[84] Or with Charles Baudelaire, who prophesied an Americanisation brought about by "the mechanical?"[85] Instead of listing such expressions of disenchantment one by one, we can highlight instead certain recurring themes: mechanisation and rationalisation;

---

83   Agamben, *op. cit.*, p. 44.
84   Le Corbusier quoted in Beatriz Colomina and Mark Wigley. *Are We Human? The Archaeology of Design*. Zürich: Lars Müller, 2016, p. 114.
85   Baudelaire cited in Cornelius Castoriadis. *Postscript on Insignificance: Dialogues with Cornelius Castoriadis*. London: Bloomsbury, 2011, pp. 25-6.

division of labour with its dulling effects; exploitation of natural and human resources; lack of meaning, autonomy and legitimacy.

These themes are often intertwined. This is the case for instance in John Ruskin's interpretation of the nature of Gothic architecture. Ruskin differentiated between "servile ornament" (typical of Greek and modern architecture) and "constitutional ornament" (typical of Gothic and medieval architecture). Servile ornament is about perfection. Here, the tasks assigned to tradespeople are so simple that they cannot be executed incorrectly, but they curb the labourers' inventiveness. On the other hand, constitutional ornament acknowledges a hierarchical relationship between the master and tradespeople, but allows the latter to invent, make mistakes and therefore be gratified with what they do. What Ruskin didn't like of servile ornament was basically the division of labour that such a style implied. This division of labour causes a 'mechanisation' of the labourers' work, so they lose autonomy, and therefore meaning in what they do. Nowadays, this sense of mechanisation feels bigger and more absurd: while there is room for imperfection, while the 'soul' seems to have found its place within work, no coherent whole emerges. There's no Gothic cathedral in sight. The 'whole' looks like a flawed socio-technical machine which is often jammed like an office printer.

MELANCHOLY

A legendary engraving by Albrecht Dürer shows an allegory of melancholy, a 'humour' almost obsessively discussed in the philosophical treatises of the Renaissance.[86] The allegory shows a winged figure surrounded by an untidy accumulation of scientific equipment and tools of various trades: scales, an hourglass, a saw, some nails. Instead of employing them, the figure is cloistered, thoughtful, a cheek resting on a clenched fist, her sad eyes shining on a

---

86 Jacques Le Goff, ed. *L'uomo medievale*. Roma, Bari: Laterza, 2013, p. 305.

CHAPTER 1

Melencolia MMXXIII by @young_agamben (2023).

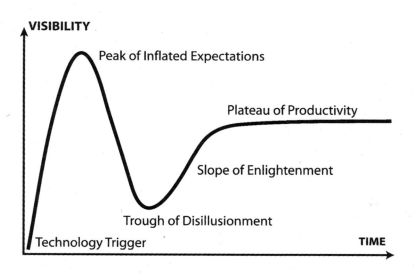

Gartner Research's Hype Cycle diagram.

shadowed countenance.[87] These thoughtful eyes, staring at the distance, betray the realisation that whatever one could craft will always be imperfect. Some believe *Melencolia I* to be the spiritual portrait of Dürer himself:

> Despairing of the limits of human knowledge, she is paralyzed and unable to create, as the discarded and unused tools suggest. Ironically, this anguished representation of artistic impotence has proved a shining and enduring example of the power of Dürer's art.[88]

Melancholy is a disposition shared by scholars and artists. Dürer himself was divided between these two worlds, to the extent that his wife disapproved of his affinity with Italian humanists.[89] Dürer's engraving is a good representation of disillusioned everyday designers. Surrounded by a chaotic profusion of technological and methodological possibilities, they ponder their inability to achieve in their projects (their life being one of them) an ideal of perfection – or at least meaningfulness.[90] Too focused on thinking, they detach from a practice that has unrecognised limits and boundaries. As a result, practice itself becomes a process of introspection, a *recherche*. Christopher Lasch's theory of narcissism, summarised by Anthony Giddens, points towards something similar: "Exclusion of the majority from the arenas where the most consequential policies are forged and decisions taken forces a concentration upon the self; this

---

87 See Raymond Klibansky, Erwin Panofsky, and Fritz Saxl. *Saturn and Melancholy: Studies in the History of Natural Philosophy, Religion and Art*. Nendeln: Kraus Reprint, 1979, pp. 284-366.

88 The National Gallery of Washington. "Albrecht Dürer, Melencolia I, 1514." https://www.nga.gov/collection/highlights/durer-melencolia.html/.

89 Le Goff, *op. cit.*, p. 226.

90 "The idea behind Dürer's engraving, defined in terms of the history of types, might be that of Geometria surrendering to melancholy, or melancholy with a taste for geometry. [...] Geometria's workshop has changed from a cosmos of clearly ranged and purposefully employed tools into a chaos of unused things; their casual distribution reflects a psychological unconcern." Klibansky, Panofsky and Saxl, *op. cit.*, p. 317.

is a result of the powerlessness most people feel."[91] For designers, like for everyone else, the self becomes a refuge, but, more than everybody else, designers approach it as a project and a research area.

* * *

What Design Can't Do is divided in two parts. In the first part, entitled *Expectations,* I unpack the ambitions of design as a theoretical discipline, a field and a profession. In the second part, entitled *Reality,* I look at how these ambitions interact and clash with the activity of everyday designers as technologists, cultural professionals and students. In both parts I try to probe our extreme present by taking stock of an often obliterated past.

---

[91] Anthony Giddens. *The Consequences of Modernity*. Cambridge, MA: Polity Press, 2015, pp. 122-3.

Part I. Expectations

Chapter 2.

Everything Everyone All at Once: On Design Panism

> "The secret ambition of design is to become invisible, to be taken up into the culture, absorbed into the background. The highest order of success in design is to achieve ubiquity, to become banal."
> – Bruce Mau and Jennifer Leonard, 2004[92]

> "Design has gone viral. The word *design* is everywhere. It pops up in every situation. It knows no limit."
> – Beatriz Colomina and Mark Wigley, 2018[93]

ILUSIÓN

Design disillusion can go beyond lamentation, it can be more than chagrin, discontent, mere *disillusionment*. Hopefully, it can be a form of lucidity: one able to unveil a series of illusions, understood here not as false beliefs but as idiosyncratic, dysfunctional, or even contradictory notions. The Spanish term *ilusión* can refer to a reasonable hope and even joy! Design illusions include those fits of collective enthusiasm that influence and shape the design field. How did such illusions come about? How do they structure the minds of designers, their perception of the world and other people, as well as their relationship with them? Some of them seem now hard-coded into the design discipline – they've become platitudes. While others, maybe less explicit, blend with broader social configurations. In this part of the book, I will consider the illusions concerning the very essence of design; those that affect the way in which design positions itself among other domains; and, finally, those pertaining to design's

---

[92] Bruce Mau, Jennifer Leonard, and Institute without Boundaries. *Massive Change*. London, New York: Phaidon, 2004, p. 4.
[93] Colomina and Wigley, *op. cit.*, p. 46.

CHAPTER 2

Mitch Goldstein (2022).

God is a Designer by Alix Gallet (2020), oil on canvas, 60x92cm.

capacity to act in the world. The first kind allows us to reconsider what design is, the second how design relates to other disciplines, the third what design can do. In three words: being, autonomy, power.

DESIGN HAUNTS

Two oft-heard assertions inform today's understanding of design: 'everyone is a designer' and 'everything is design.'[94] This all-embracing view of design can be named *design panism*. It is within the realm of design panism that designers (struggle to) articulate their role and position. But more than being a mere descriptor of a reality, design panism is an interpretative framework, a rhetorical instrument and a semi-conscious expansion agenda. Breaking down the conflicting meanings of these two common statements allows us to discern their consequences on the designer's identity and sense of realisation.

In a not-so-distant past, delimiting design was easy: whereas the mass-produced Moka pot hissing on the stove was unmistakeably design, the handmade ceramic cups used to drink its coffee weren't. Design began with the factory and ended with it: it was *industrial* design. Nowadays, things are more difficult: design escaped the assembly line to become a mentality, which is to say that our mentality has become industrialised.[95] The few handmade objects still surrounding us owe their aura to design. Design *haunts* them.

Whatever we make or encounter – a thing, an arrangement of things, a procedure to arrange such things – is haunted by design. Even if design is not there, it is already there. Thus, the ontological status of design is a ghostly one. As Bruce Mau and Jennifer Leonard put it, "for most of

[94] Similar statements can be found in the field of art (Joseph Beuys's "everyone is an artist") and architecture (Hans Hollein's *"Alles Ist Architektur"*). For the latter see Hans Hollein. "Alles Ist Architektur." *Bau*, 1968. https://socks-studio.com/2013/08/13/hans-holleins-alles-ist-architektur-1968/.

[95] Presumably, this industrialised mindset started to emerge in the West in the 16th century, with the appearance of the first mechanically reproduced books.

us, design is invisible. Until it fails."[96] But design is a peculiar ghost, one that craves the tangible world of the living. Design is like Slimer, the gluttonous spectre from *Ghostbusters*: one that enjoys ingurgitating as much food as it can.

Slimer's interactions with the material world are not seamless: they leave slime wherever they go. We can interpret such gelatinous secretions as design's ability to reconceptualise things within its mode of comprehension: suddenly, a pebble starts having a form and a function, it gets liable to a process of improvement, a process that is itself subject to a method. What has happened? Design has digested the thing: the pebble is now an *artefact*, a designed object.[97] This is the ultimate phase of the "extraordinary career" of the term 'design' noticed by Bruno Latour, a term that grew in "extension" (the typologies of products it is applied to) and "comprehension" (the parts of a thing design can comprehend):

> Today everyone with an iPhone knows that it would be absurd to distinguish what has been designed from what has been planned, calculated, arrayed, arranged, packed, packaged, defined, projected, tinkered, written down in code, disposed of and so on. From now on, "to design" could mean equally any or all of those verbs.[98]

But design's metabolism has gone further and left its muculent mark on what it couldn't process, namely, the thing's symbolic and ritual aura, its culture; substituted by design culture, with its own equalising symbols and rituals. The thing is apparently the same, but it is in fact completely different.

---

96 Mau et al., *op. cit.*, p. 2.
97 "The stone becomes an object only when it is given the function of a paperweight." Abraham A. Moles. "Objet et communication." *Communications* 13, no. 1 (1969): 1–21, p. 5.
98 Bruno Latour. "A Cautious Prometheus? A Few Steps Toward a Philosophy of Design (with Special Attention to Peter Sloterdijk)." Proceedings of the Annual International Conference of the Design History Society, edited by Fiona Hackne, Jonathan Glynne, and Viv Minto, 2–10. Falmouth: Universal Publishers, 2009.

CHAPTER 2

ORANGES, PEAS AND ROSES

In 1963, Italian design polymath Bruno Munari amused himself by describing an orange, peas and a rose as industrial objects. Whereas the orange is "an almost perfect object," the rose is deemed completely useless and complicated. Munari's innocent divertissement, a sort of lesson in design thinking and perhaps a subtle critique of mass production, exemplifies the *actual* way in which design comes to reinterpret and thus change reality. Once such reinterpretation has happened it is very hard to think reality otherwise, that is, beyond functionality and efficiency.[99]

With such a mindset in place, the designer might well be in charge of everything. According to design curator Paola Antonelli, designers are "respectful, curious, generous, and hungry for other fields' bodies of knowledge and expertise, designers invade without colonizing. Who can we trust more? They should run the world."[100] Ruha Benjamin might disagree. Asked, during a workshop, to offer a definition of design, the sociologist suggested that "design is a colonizing project."[101] By that she meant that design is used to describe everything. *Description* is indeed the form that design's slimy digestion takes.

As Paul Rodgers and Craig Bremner declare, "design is neither a product nor a service. Design occurs in relationship to everyone and everything – it describes and shapes relationships."[102] Design proceeds through formalisation. Focusing on one of today's most successful design currents, design thinking, Benjamin points out its capacity to

---

[99] Peas are described as "food pills of various diameters, packed in double valve cases, very elegant in form, colour, material, semi-transparent and easy to open." Bruno Munari. 2010. *Good design*. Mantova: Corraini.

[100] Paola Antonelli "Foreword." In Alexandra Midal. *Design by Accident: For a New History of Design*. Berlin: Sternberg Press, 2019.

[101] Ruha Benjamin. *Race After Technology: Abolitionist Tools for the New Jim Code*. Cambridge, UK: Polity, 2020, p. 176.

[102] Paul A. Rodgers and Craig Bremner. "The Design of Nothing: A Working Philosophy." In *Advancements in the Philosophy of Design*, edited by Pieter E. Vermaas and Stéphane Vial, 549–64. Design Research Foundations. Cham: Springer International Publishing, 2018. https://doi.org/10.1007/978-3-319-73302-9_25, p. 550.

> MY BODY IS A MACHINE THAT TURNS the dumbest fucking ideas INTO "this project investigates..."

@blank_gehry (2023).

CHAPTER 2

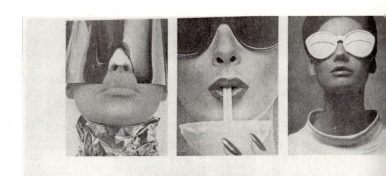

Spread from Hans Hollein's "Alles Ist Architektur," *Bau*, 1/2 1968.

EVERYTHING EVERYONE ALL AT ONCE

RCHITEKTUR

Aus einem Inserat der B. F. Goodrich Company.

encapsulate any form of activity, from the organisation of a protest to the user journey of a banking app (an uncommon etymology of the word 'design' links it to the Latin *designare*, which also means delimiting[103]). For Benjamin, the problem is that design thinking is forgetful, not unlike design in general: it neglects histories.[104]

> If one needs to "subvert" design, this implies that a dominant framework of design reigns – and I think one of the reasons why it *reigns* is that it has managed to fold any and everything under its agile wings.

Benjamin identifies a series of risks associated with design thinking, an "umbrella philosophy" that diminishes broader forms of human activity, erasing the genealogies from which they emerged in the first place, effacing tradition. It's a matter of hegemony: "Whether designspeak sets out to colonize human activity, it is enacting a monopoly over creative thought and praxis." Benjamin's concerns are specifically related to racial issues. From this vantage point she is able to see the way in which design depletes empowerment: "Maybe what we must demand is not liberatory *designs* but just plain old liberation. *Too retro*, perhaps?"[105]

THE LAST AVANTGARDE

A sense of disillusion partly derives from the realisation that design can be, like money, a general equivalent: something that severs the links between things and thus estranges them. It can devour contexts. Practitioners suspect that the umbrella is too small, that design is lacking the conceptual and practical means of encompassing

---

103 Tomás Maldonado. *Disegno industriale: un riesame*. Milano: Feltrinelli, 2008, p. 9.
104 Susan Stewart puts it in more systematic terms: "the excision of history from design thinking isolates the understanding that informs the design act from any understanding of the temporal trajectories in which it participates." "And So to Another Setting...". In *Design and the Question of History*, edited by Tony Fry and Clive Dilnot, 275–301, 2020. https://doi.org/10.5040/9781474245890.
105 Ruha Benjamin, *op. cit.*, pp. 174-180.

human activity, and that, by attempting to do so, it is actually making *tabula rasa*.[106] Design might be the last successful avantgarde: a deliberate repudiation of histories. Designers who come to terms with such awareness logically develop an impostor syndrome, an urge to resist design's reductive assimilation.

This can be the joint cause of many personal exoduses, dreamed of or executed: former designers decide to engage with the fullness of a certain human activity within its specific and historically-rich domain: farming, writing, cooking… all activities that resist reduction to "rural hacking," "content design," or "food design." More rarely, however, the act of design description provides an enrichment: the selectivity of design allows for the inclusion of forgotten voices, for the light-hearted reshuffling of austere practices, for a novel bridging of contexts. In these rare cases, design's 'ignorance' truly becomes its bliss.[107] At worst, design flattens a multiplicity of worlds into a one-dimensional, aseptic one; at best it nurtures them.[108]

It's hard to deny that "the logic of the world is the logic of

---

[106] If we are to consider 'progressive' policy making as a form of design, we recognise a similar impetus for erasure, in brutally explicit terms: "There is a sense in which rapid economic progress is impossible without painful adjustments. Ancient philosophies have to be scrapped; old social institutions have to disintegrate; bonds of caste, creed, and race have to burst; and large numbers of persons who cannot keep up with progress have to have their expectations of a comfortable life frustrated." United Nations, Department of Social and Economic Affairs. "Measures for the Economic Development of Under-Developed Countries," 1951. http://digitallibrary.un.org/record/708544.

[107] See chapter 3.

[108] The field of creative coding provides a good example of non-flattening design. Processing, one of the main programming languages deliberately conceived with artists and designers in mind, is part of a rich history of experiences where design bridges diverse fields of knowledge. Emerging from the MIT 'lab' culture, in which Muriel Cooper, a graphic designer, had a leading role, Processing gave rise to a broad community of makers and thinkers who go beyond the drive towards efficiency of much computation culture. See Golan Levin and Tega Brain. *Code As Creative Medium: A Handbook for Computational Art and Design*. Cambridge, MA: MIT Press, 2021. For a counterargument based on Processing's blindness to its own materiality cf. Michael Murtaugh. "Torn at the Seams: Considering Computational Vernacular." In *Vernaculars Come to Matter*, edited by Cristina Cochior, Sofia Boshat-Thorez, and Manetta Berends, 93–110. Rotterdam: Everyday Technology Press, 2021.

the description of the world."[109] If so, the describing entity is inevitably revealed in the description, together with its limits. This is how the formalisation that design provides betrays design's own amorphousness: "design today feels like a vast formless body – or in the parlance of contemporary architecture, a 'blob' – able to absorb any blows delivered to it – lacking coherency and increasingly dispersed," observed Andrew Blauvelt in 2003.[110] This doesn't seem to be just an isolated impression: when a group of researchers employed data mining techniques to examine two decades' worth of conversations on the PhD-Design discussion list, an established platform for specialised exchange, they discovered that there had been minimal advancement in defining design.[111] Today, the doubtful designer asks: how can something so indefinite *define* the world? Recognising the reductive appropriation of pre-existing practices through design as a bureaucratic cultural instrument, they nevertheless cling to their authority, real or perceived, sensing that it is ineffective, provisional – if not illegitimate.

BUSY BEE

As we learn that design is everywhere (and thus nowhere), we are also convinced that everyone is a designer. As an activity, design is often placed, so to speak, in the mind of the beholder, framed as an integral component of human capabilities. Design is presented as a "universal human life-skill,"[112] it is "all that we do, almost all the time,"[113] until the whole human race is characterised as a

---

[109] Francisco Varela. "Introduction." In Heinz von Foerster. *Observing Systems*. Systems Inquiry Series. Seaside CA: Intersystems Publications, 1984, p. XVI.

[110] Andrew Blauvelt. "Towards Critical Autonomy or Can Graphic Design Save Itself?". *Emigre*, 2004.

[111] Alethea Blackler, Levi Swann, Marianella Chamorro-Koc, Wathsala Anupama Mohotti, Thirunavukarasu Balasubramaniam and Richi Nayak. "Can We Define Design? Analyzing Twenty Years of Debate on a Large Email Discussion List." *She Ji: The Journal of Design, Economics, and Innovation* 7, no. 1 (March 1, 2021): 41-70. https://doi.org/10.1016/j.sheji.2020.11.004.

[112] Rick Poynor. "First Things Next." In *Obey the Giant: Life in the Image World*. Boston, MA: Birkhauser Verlag AG, 2007, pp. 141-2.

[113] Papanek, *op. cit.*, p. 3.

"designing species."[114] The list could continue endlessly.[115] In fact, "everyone is a designer" is a truism so common, both in and out of the design world, as to cause suspicion. Is this a marketing ploy to sell design books to a larger public?

To understand more clearly what this life-skill is about, we can consult an unlikely source, Karl Marx's *Das Kapital*. In the first volume, he famously compared an architect to a bee:

> A spider conducts operations that resemble those of a weaver, and a bee puts to shame many an architect in the construction of her cells. But what distinguishes the worst architect from the best of bees is this, that the architect raises his structure in imagination before he erects it in reality. At the end of every labour-process, we get a result that already existed in the imagination of the labourer at its commencement.[116]

Here, we gather that design is the exclusively human capacity to *prefigure*,[117] to imagine a structure before it is built.[118] Nobody can deny that humans have this imaginative ability, but is there any point in lumping it together with a historically specific practice consolidated during the Industrial Revolution? In this process, not only is design (our contemporary, Western idea of design)

---

114 Victor Margolin interviewed by Max Bruinsma in 2015, https://vimeo.com/133073827.

115 On my blog, I assembled a chronology of "design panism", from 1962 to 2022, later collated in a zine made together with the students of the Information Design Department at Design Academy Eindhoven: https://networkcultures.org/entreprecariat/design-panism-a-timeline/.

116 Karl Marx. *Capital*. Vol. 1. Marx/Engels Internet Archive, 1999. https://www.marxists.org/archive/marx/works/1867-c1/index.htm.

117 Of course, we find earlier examples of this idea, for instance in the concept of *disegno interno* (inner design) of the Italian architect and painter Federico Zuccari. See *L'Idea de' pittori, scultori ed architetti*, 1607.

118 It seems, however, that animals like rats are also capable of prefiguration, imagining alternative paths before they take them. So, prefiguration might not be the fundamental difference between humans and other animals, but our capacity/necessity to shape our environment and externalise survival functions to it. See Thomas Hills. "Can Animals Imagine Things That Have Never Happened?" *Psychology Today*, October 22, 2019. https://www.psychologytoday.com/intl/blog/statistical-life/201910/can-animals-imagine-things-have-never-happened.

CHAPTER 2

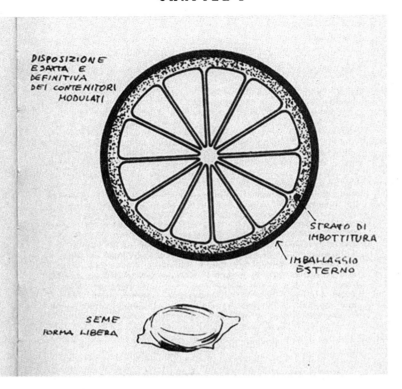

Spread from the book *Good Design* by Bruno Munari (1963).

naturalised, but also, as Beatriz Colomina and Mark Wigley remind us, the human reinvented.[119] In their writings, many architects and designers go back to the genesis of an archetypal artefact (a spear, a bridge, a nook) to justify their particular design philosophy, not unlike startup founders with their origin stories. A move that can be considered "an attempt to gain status for the profession by evoking a specious historical precedent," warns Papanek. Already in the '70s, he made the distinction clear: "In the beginning was Design, of course, but not industrial design."[120]

DESIGNED BY DESIGN

Proponents of an ontological idea of design like Tony Fry and Anne-Marie Willis add another element to design panism by suggesting that not just everything is design, and not only everyone is a designer, but also everyone is in turn *designed* by design, a point resonating with the formulation of Marshall McLuhan's friend Father John M. Culkin: "We become what we behold. We shape our tools and then our tools shape us."[121] In their view, design is a double movement: from the designer to the environment, but also, and more importantly, from the environment to the designer. Design is thus circular and bidirectional, one might say. Willis openly disassociates her idea of "ontological designing" from other forms of design panism, which can be found in "populist texts" such as Papanek's.[122] A lowbrow, demagogic idea of design panism corresponds to the perhaps wishful claim that anyone can, at least partially, design their own environment. On the contrary, highbrow design panism sees design as a sort of force field of intentionality investing both human

---

119   Colomina and Wigley, *op. cit.*
120   Papanek, *op. cit.*, p. 29. Interestingly, Papanek reverses Margolin's capitalisation.
121   To be fair, this aphorism should be formulated inversely: first, we are shaped by the designed world and then, perhaps, we design it back.
122   Anne-Marie Willis. "Ontological Designing." *Design Philosophy Papers* 4, no. 2 (June 1, 2006): 69–92. https://doi.org/10.2752/144871306X13966268131514.

and non-human agents. Here, 'everyone is a designer' and 'everything is design' are the same statement.

Both Willis' vertiginous conception of ontological designing and the apparently common-sense distinctions of Papanek and Margolin have their limits. The circularity of ontological designing clashes with the necessarily heuristic quality of design in practice, one that is based on a shared operational consensus: the belief that the agency lies in the designer, who is a synecdoche of the human. It is through this functional reduction that design operates, even when it supervises processes. Design intervenes by eschewing a full understanding of the world, in order to optimise its transformation. For a tree to grow healthily, it needs to be pruned. The alternative is apophenia: panic derived from the sense of total interrelation. The fact that Willis complains about designers' ability to comprehend ontological ramifications is, therefore, hardly surprising.

Anthropologist Lucy Suchman is careful when it comes to adopting the word 'design' in a broad sense. She suggests keeping "an eye to the tensions inherent in articulating projects in transformational change as 'small d' design, without reproducing the supremacy of Design with that initial capital letter." What is this supremacy about? She identifies four historical tendencies in the professional field of design: grandiosity, which is another word for universalism; progressivism, a standard development pattern "from them, to us, to a new us;" parochialism, that is, "the tendency to engage in conversations with each other, on behalf of everyone;" the predominance of ethics and values over politics.[123]

AUTHORITARIAN AND ANNOYING

Often, however, useful distinctions get lost in the fumes of design discourse. The result: a general idea of design

---

[123] Lucy Suchman. "Keywords for Ethnography and Design: Design." *Society for Cultural Anthropology*, March 29, 2018. https://culanth.org/fieldsights/design.

activity where everything we do or is done to us is design. At this point, one could ask for specificity through precise definitions. As we have seen though, this doesn't work. So, let's keep it general to get a better understanding of the dysfunctions of design panism. If design is a universal human feature, why are there humans who call themselves designers? Why is the prefigurative function delegated to a specialised congregation of people? And what is then left to the others? The matter is in fact not new to debate. In 1994, Ivan Illich and Carl Mitcham gave a sermon against design:

> Contra the widely promoted belief that design is something all human beings do and have done throughout history, but now must do more consciously and thoroughly than ever before, design is something that has had a history. Its beginnings can be traced to the rise of modernity, and it will almost certainly come to an end with the modern project. Indeed, we have an obligation not so much to promote designing as to learn to live without it, to resist its seductions, and to turn away from its pervasive and corrupting influence.[124]

In 2009, Italian mass culture theorist and cyberpunk expert Antonio Caronia expressed his hostility to design:

> Personally, I would like to outlaw design. Design is one of the most authoritarian and annoying practices that modernity has created. Design is one of the most striking consequences at the level of properly human activities – which are activities of creation [and] have been killed by the separation between the activities of planning and realization. This is design.[125]

---

124 Carl Mitcham. "In Memoriam Ivan Illich: Critic of Professionalized Design." *Design Issues* 19, no. 4 (October 1, 2003): 26–30. https://doi.org/10.1162/074793603322545037, p. 29.

125 Caronia quoted in Salvatore Iaconesi and Oriana Persico. *Angel_F. Diario Di Una*

In theory, the question of design expertise could be put in very simple terms: the existence of design experts doesn't prevent non-designers to exercise the broadly human activity of designing. Norman Potter puts that succinctly: "Every human being is a designer. Many also earn their living by design [...]."[126] However, the self-evident recognition that there are, in every field, experts and non-experts, people who are paid for their expertise and people who aren't, conceals a fundamental predicament of modern society, that of *being run* by expertise. Most facets of everyday life – not just work – are organised, scrutinised and assessed by what US sociologist Anthony Giddens calls "expert systems."[127] Those systems prefigure and configure. Here, the dominance of prescriptive technologies fosters a culture of compliance.[128] Individual autonomy is thus reduced, a problem that the very Norman Potter, explicit in his leftist libertarianism, was very conscious of.

More balanced in his judgement, Gui Bonsiepe admits the necessity of expertise while, at the same time, warning against all-encompassing claims on designing:

> There is a risk of falling into the trap of vague generalizations like "everything is design." Not everything is design, and not everyone is a designer. The term 'design' does refer to a potential to which everyone has access and which is manifest in everyday life in the invention of new social practices. Every one can become a designer in his special field, but the field that is the object of design activity always has to be

---

Intelligenza Artificiale. Roma: Castelvecchi, 2009, p. 276.

126 The extended quote: "Every human being is a designer. Many also earn their living by design – in every field that warrants pause, and careful consideration, between the conceiving of an action and a fashioning of the means to carry it out, and an estimation of its effects." Potter, *op. cit.*, p. 10.

127 "Systems of technical accomplishment or professional expertise that organise large areas of the material and social environments in which we live today." Anthony Giddens. *The Consequences of Modernity*. Cambridge, UK: Polity Press, 2015, p. 27.

128 Franklin, *op. cit.*, pp. 18-9.

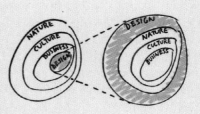

Screenshot of the massivechange.org website, including Bruce Mau's napkin sketch in which design becomes all-encompassing.

> identified [...] Design is a basic activity whose capillary ramifications penetrate every human activity. No occupation or profession can claim a monopoly on it.[129]

This idea is reminiscent of Antonio Gramsci's popular assertion that "all men are intellectuals, but not all men have in society the function of intellectuals." Here, the emphasis might seem on "all men," but it is actually on the intellectual's function. In fact, elsewhere Gramsci argues that

> The intellectual is a 'professional,' a skilled worker who knows how his own specialized 'machines' function. He has an 'apprenticeship' and a 'Taylor system' of his own. It is childish and illusory to attribute to everyone this acquired and not innate ability, just as it would be childish to believe that any unskilled worker can drive a train.[130]

"EVERYONE CAN DESIGN, EVEN DESIGNERS"

Whereas Illich and Mitcham were issuing a warning about the pervasiveness of design, critics like Caronia lamented the asymmetry that it creates between planners and executors. Today, such asymmetry appears to have evened up as design systems no longer offer just a singular product but an array of options. Intuitive graphic tools, customisation features, design methods, a do-it-yourself ethos... they all contribute to this shift.[131] The emergence of such design sandboxes could be understood as a democratisation of the ability to prefigure: designers design systems for non-designers to be able to design. This is the

129 Gui Bonsiepe quoted in Fernando Secomandi and Dirk Snelders. "Interface Design in Services: A Postphenomenological Approach." *Design Issues* 29, no. 1 (January 1, 2013): 3–13. https://doi.org/10.1162/DESI_a_00192,
130 Antonio Gramsci. *The Antonio Gramsci Reader: Selected Writings, 1916-1935*. Edited by David Forgacs. New York: New York University Press, 2000, pp. 389-90.
131 An example among many: IKEA distributes prefigurative ability offering online planning tools to its clients. See https://www.ikea.com/nl/en/planners/.

meaning of *Everyone is a Designer!*, Mieke Gerritzen and Geert Lovink's prosumerist manifesto written in 2000 and updated in 2010.[132] But while the designing ability, albeit limited, trickles down, a sense of powerless entrapment *trickles up*: designers, who are almost never in charge of the systems' system, lose their imagined *raison d'être*: their prefigurative know-how dissolves into the execution of someone or something else's high-level prefiguration: a manager, an engineer, an algorithm. With prefiguration sandboxes readily available, designers begin to perceive their relatively humble position.

'Everything is design' and 'everyone is a designer,' these ubiquitous truisms about the ubiquitousness of design, reflect the fact that designing agency has spilled out of the designer figure in various ways, to the point that common hierarchies of expertise can be overturned, as Cuban artist and designer Ernesto Oroza does when he quips that "everyone can design, even designers."[133] Design expands, while the designer shrinks. Designing capabilities are no longer just a feature of individuals but also of collective subjects like organisations.[134] When design starts to be conceived in terms of agency, it is reasonable to wonder whether it can be an impersonal agent in (or even for) itself. Design is then conceived as a force that surrounds designers, more than one that they exert: design designs them like it designs everyone else. More than being design's main subjects, designers are subjected to design: the designer becomes a condition more than a role. What kind of force is design? Tomás Maldonado speaks of a productive one: "Like all design activities that, in one way or another, intervene in the production-consumption

[132] Mieke Gerritzen and Geert Lovink. *Everyone Is a Designer in the Age of Social Media*. Amsterdam: BIS, 2010 and *Everyone Is a Designer! Manifest for the Design Economy*. Amsterdam: BIS, 2001.

[133] This is the title of a research unit led by Oroza within the Cité du design initiative, https://www.citedudesign.com/fr/a/everyone-can-design-even-designers-778.

[134] "In a world in rapid and profound transformation, we are all designers. Here, 'all' obviously includes all of us, individuals but also organizations, businesses, public entities, voluntary associations, and cities, regions, and states." Manzini, *op. cit.*, p. 1.

relationship, industrial design acts as a true productive force. What's more, it is a productive force that contributes to the organization (and hence socialization) of the other productive forces with which it comes into contact."[135] In this sense, design is not just a dependent part of other, larger systems, but a system in itself, able to interact with other ones, affecting them.

The Massive Change program, initiated in 2004 by renowned architect and designer Bruce Mau with the Institute without Boundaries, shows the ambiguous relationship between design as a productive force and the designer. Mau deliberately speaks of design as "one of the world's most powerful forces." A 'napkin sketch' made in the back of a cab postulates that design is no longer a mere subset of business but the broadest superset, one that includes nature, culture and business. Far from being intimidated by this realisation, he places a generic "we" (designers? policy makers? humanity as a whole?) in charge of the power of design, in order to "minimize unintended consequences and maximize positive outcomes." The project shows an optimism, at times cautious but more often untamed, about the (broadly understood) designer's ability to harness the force of design: "We have an unprecedented capacity to plan and produce desired outcomes through good design." Before unleashing wildly cheerful future predictions, the book resulting from the project, a kaleidoscope of technical and scientific innovations seen from a globalist view, introduces a sense of foreboding reminiscent of the work of Paul Virilio: "Accidents, disasters, crises. When systems fail we become temporarily conscious of the extraordinary force of design, and the effects it generates."[136] The optimism of Mau lies in the belief that disasters happen only when design fails, and not when – and this is becoming increasingly clear – design acts as intended. Design

---

135 Maldonado, *Disegno industriale: un riesame, op. cit.*, p. 14.
136 Mau et al., *op. cit.*, p. 10.

disillusion reacts instead to the fact that design, one of the main features of modernity, is not akin to a "carefully controlled and well-driven motor car," but to a juggernaut.[137]

* * *

Design panism is plural. 'Everything is design' doesn't only imply that everything in our environment is artificial, but also that our very gaze has been artificialised. There is no nature for us, only culture. What culture, specifically? A reductive one that erases histories, or a respectful one that welcomes careful innovation? The game is still on, but the first option is broadly felt and generates impostor syndrome. Affirming that everyone is a designer can mean many things. Design panism can be a matter-of-fact recognition that humans have an innate prefigurative ability. It can also be driven by a professionalist propaganda which characterises designers as *the* experts of such general ability. Furthermore, design panism can be used to justify a particular design philosophy. But it can also lead to an admission of the cultural limitations of design as a mode of comprehension. Design panism may be in line with a demand for autonomy against the prescriptive and bureaucratic structure of modern life, as it is run by experts who detain, in various fields, the monopoly on planning and implementing. What level of prefiguration should a designer aim for? Who should be in charge of design as an impersonal force? These remain open questions.

---

137 Giddens, *op. cit.*, p. 53.

Chapter 3.

A Complex Relationship:
On Synthesis and Autonomy

"Any discipline or generated system for the organization of reality faces the problem of having to exceed the scope of its object of inquiry, but since it, too, must be part of that object (if it is to be something as grand as reality), it must contain itself in a logical relationship to all it is trying to contain, which expands the initial problem of inclusion. There is, in other words, always *more* to and of reality."
- Lewis Gordon, 2011[138]

"As a generalist, [the designer] has made a specialty out of his lack of specialization."
- Gui Bonsiepe, 1974[139]

Design's ubiquity makes it hard to pinpoint. I'm reminded of a famous definition of deity offered by theologian Alain de Lille, a definition which almost sounds like a design brief: "God is an infinite sphere, whose centre is everywhere and whose circumference is nowhere."[140] With an indeterminate centre, design can easily reveal itself in between, and link, other disciplines and cultural domains. For instance, Walter Gropius, founder of the Bauhaus, understood design as "a new unity" of art and technics.[141] While they remain two distinct realms, design emerges amid them, producing a novel understanding of both.

As design becomes a cultural phenomenon under constant restructuring, it aspires, more and more consciously, to be the whole that exceeds the sum of its parts. That is, the very relationship between them. As design events

138 Lewis R. Gordon. "Shifting the Geography of Reason in an Age of Disciplinary Decadence." *Transmodernity* 1, no. 2 (2011). https://doi.org/10.5070/T412011810.
139 Gui Bonsiepe. "Design e Sottosviluppo." *Casabella*, 1974, p. 43.
140 Paolo Lucentini, ed. *Il libro dei ventiquattro filosofi*. Milano: Adelphi, 1999.
141 Herbert Bayer, Ilse Gropius and Walter Gropius, eds. *Bauhaus 1919-1928*. New York: The Museum of Modern Art, 1938. https://www.moma.org/documents/moma_catalogue_2735_300190238.pdf, p. 82.

show, any domain, any practice can be plugged into it: not just art and technics but also journalism, craftsmanship, obscure traditions, witchcraft... We can legitimately talk of design hyperconnectivity. Distinct phenomena appear to the design mindset as an assortment of equivalent nodes, with design itself acting as a *paranode*, "the conceptual space that lies beyond the borders of the node."[142]

BOTH FISH AND WATER

What are the consequences of hyperconnectivity on how designers view themselves? In 2006, Gui Bonsiepe called for an integration of the design perspective into higher education, lamenting the predilection for discursive results over projects, and insisting on the necessity for novel institutions:

> So far, design has tried to build bridges to the domain of the sciences, but not vice versa. We can speculate that, in the future, design may become a basic discipline for all scientific areas. But this Copernican turn in the university system might take generations, if not centuries. Only the creation of radically new universities can shorten this process.[143]

Here, Bonsiepe describes design's reasonable but not entirely successful attempt to build a bridge to another field. Victor Papanek had a more ambitious idea. In his seminal book *Design for the Real World,* he advocated a cross-disciplinary team where the designer acts as "the bridge between the disciplines." Notably, he saw the designer as a *synthesist*, a producer of wholes, one might say. For him, designers would have the epistemic last word, that is, the problem's formulation.[144]

---

142 Ulises A. Mejias. "The Limits of Networks as Models for Organizing the Social." *New Media & Society* 12, no. 4 (June 1, 2010): 603–17. https://doi.org/10.1177/1461444809341392, pp. 612-3.
143 Gui Bonsiepe. "Design and Democracy." *Design Issues* 22, no. 2 (2006): 27–34, pp. 28-9.
144 Papanek, *op. cit.*, pp. 187-8.

The US polymath Buckminster Fuller might have been the ultimate design synthesist: some of his most majestic plans, such as the 1959 proposal for a geodesic "Dome Over Manhattan" (a spherelike structure, unsurprisingly), reflect design's ambition to be an all-encompassing suprasystem.[145] However, it also manifests the limits of design's hyperconnectivity: as every problem is chased by another problem, the synthesist would end up enveloping "spaceship Earth" in its entirety. This, according to German philosopher Peter Sloterdijk, is simply not possible: while we live under modernity's vast dome, we tend to take for granted its life supports, which come invariably from an outside.[146] Italian theorist Raffaele Alberto Ventura employs an analogy close to Sloterdijk's ideas – the air conditioner:

> [It] consumes material resources to produce cold air, and in the meantime throws out hot air. That is, it solves one problem, but in doing so it creates another. Actually, more than solving it, it moves it from one subsystem to another.

Synthesis can never be complete. For Ventura, "every attempt to bring order to the world produces a certain amount of disorder."[147] Furthermore, one thing is to acknowledge the ambiguous planetary impact of modernity, and another one is to believe that designers can plan on that scale. Like technology, design is "both fish and water"[148] and it is crucial to specify whether we are referring to the former or the latter. Today, however, the passion for wholeness takes a different form: whereas Fuller's

---

145 A controversy exists regarding who actually designed this project as well as the other domes generally attributed to Fuller only. This issue of attribution casts a light on the politics of synthesis and its interactions with mechanisms of recognition. See https://archive.nytimes.com/cityroom.blogs.nytimes.com/2014/05/07/50-years-later-questions-over-who-designed-a-worlds-fair-dome/, and http://www.domerama.com/tc-howard-trying-to-understand-his-anonymity/.
146 Latour, *op. cit.*, p. 9.
147 Raffaele Alberto Ventura. *Radical choc: ascesa e caduta dei competenti*. Torino: Einaudi, 2020, p. 103.
148 Franklin, *op. cit.*, p. 6.

CHAPTER 3

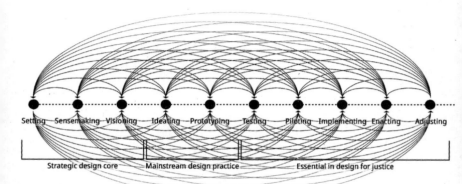

Diagram by Mauricio Mejía (2023) where each and every phase of the design process is linked to each and every other. An apt instance of the aesthetics of complexity. According to Mejía, "[m]ainstream design practices still focus on ideating and prototyping. The whole design process in complex situations includes a lot more activities."

craving for totality was rooted in an engineering mindset (a dream echoed by the '60s 'total design' agencies), contemporary design is an all-encompassing *cultural* sphere, one that emphasises comprehension, that is, understanding plus assimilation.

YOU KNOW NOTHING

To comprehend a wide range of phenomena, a cross-disciplinary approach is often invoked. But cross-disciplinarity is not exclusively a design virtue.[149] Cybernetics, for instance, was a successful bridge between scientific domains which built its own vocabulary pilfering terminology from disparate fields: homoeostasis, feedback, cognition...[150] We can also position the cross-disciplinary ethos within a prolonged criticism of specialisation. Inaugurated by Adam Smith,[151] it reached a peak with the '60s anti-bureaucratic counterculture. In 1973, sci-fi author and aeronautical engineer Robert Heinlein had one of his characters, Lazarus Long, assert that "specialization is for insects." Many designers and design theorists would agree, but only on the condition that design would provide the foundations of general activity. It is thus worth looking at the larger context of the quote:

> A human being should be able to change a diaper, plan an invasion, butcher a hog, conn a ship, *design* a building, write a sonnet, balance accounts, build a wall, set a bone, comfort the

---

[149] According to Wikipedia, "Cross-disciplinary knowledge is that which explains aspects of one discipline in terms of another." It is a form of translation. https://en.wikipedia.org/wiki/Academic_discipline. For an extensive list of the various forms of relations among disciplines, see Craig Bremner and Paul A. Rodgers. "Design Without Discipline." *Design Issues* 29 (July 1, 2013): 4–13. https://doi.org/10.1162/DESI_a_00217, pp. 11-12.

[150] Klaus Krippendorff. "A Dictionary of Cybernetics." *Departmental Papers* (ASC), 1986. https://repository.upenn.edu/asc_papers/224. Of course, design itself has borrowed from cybernetics. As an example, the Studio at the Edge of the World recently proposed a practice of "second order design fiction," which draws from the idea of second order cybernetics. See https://www.thestudioattheedgeoftheworld.com/news.html.

[151] Adam Smith. *The Wealth of Nations. Books 1-3*. London: Penguin, 2003.

dying, take orders, give orders, cooperate, act alone, solve equations, analyse a new problem, pitch manure, program a computer, cook a tasty meal, fight efficiently, die gallantly. Specialization is for insects.[152]

The emphasis is mine. In this list, designing is not a prism of each and every human endeavour but simply one of its manifestations. Here, design does not provide total synthesis, it is not presented as a placeholder for human activity at large. Instead, it is humbly connected to a specific typology of artefact. *Design is a part, not the whole*.

Papanek believed that design could contribute a form of meta-knowledge deriving from the interpretation of various scientific and social languages. But this possibility rests on what we could call meta-ignorance. According to Don Norman, "the trouble with experts is that they know too much and they think the same way other experts think. Designers, on the other hand, know nothing, they ask stupid questions, and that's exactly why they're brilliant."[153] This is a pretty common idea: designers can be candid, devoid of preconceptions, free from the past. Their naivety being an asset, designers are able to elude the narrow precincts of expertise. However, designerly candidness is itself a preconception which simply displaces what is known, believed or assumed. The risk is evident: instead of developing a productive non-knowledge, designers might just turn a blind eye to their own biases. As a result, their 'unknown knows,' what they don't know that they know, might act in the world in ways they can't determine or even perceive. The past still casts its invisible shadow on the present. Given these premises, can there be actual design synthesis? Sure, but it would be shaped by the personal and cultural point of view of designers. Their "stupid

---

152 Robert A. Heinlein. *Time Enough for Love: The Lives of Lazarus Long*. New York: Ace, 2003, p. 248.
153 Don Norman. Opening speech at Koç University, October 4, 2012. https://www.youtube.com/watch?v=z_7G053Zc-Y.

questions" will inevitably be sophisticated. Design can't be innocent.[154] Designers can frame problems, but as soon as these get slightly complex, 'designerly stupidity' becomes better at concealing rather than revealing.

THE EM DASH-SHAPED DESIGNER

In a scathing review of Papanek's bestseller for the Italian magazine Casabella, Gui Bonsiepe recognised the conservative and technocratic impulse implicit in his idea of synthesis:

> [Papanek] tasks the designer with the role of a filler for the weaknesses of other specialists in the design team: that of an interpreter, of a generalist, essentially exercising, alongside his normal function which Papanek never discusses, a mediating function. [...] The de-specialisation of the designer is ultimately reduced to a regression of the designer to the function of having-a-finger-in-every-pie.

Bonsiepe accused Papanek of turning design into "the only decisive and common-sense activity remaining to human beings." He was baffled by his conviction that designers should contribute to setting the goals for society at large, without negotiation or mediation: "The technologist throws the politician out [...] But for that you don't need a designer, you need a revolution."[155]

Specialisation or generalism? A typographic metaphor seems to offer a fruitful balance between the two. Circulating already in the late '70s in engineering circles, the idea of a T-shaped set of skills – meaning a deep, vertical specialisation accompanied by a horizontal breadth of

---

154 This is something Don Norman himself has recognised: "Designers who live in Western (including Western-influenced) societies inhabit a reality where everyone learns from the same books and universities and attends the same conferences. Consequently, everyone tends to think the same way: a dangerous thing." See "What Is Humanity-Centered Design?" *The Interaction Design Foundation*, 2022. https://www.interaction-design.org/literature/topics/humanity-centered-design.

155 Bonsiepe, "Design e sottosviluppo," *op. cit.*, pp. 43-4.

CHAPTER 3

Critical Graphic Design (2015). One could read this fictional book as a take on real-world interdisciplinarity.

knowledge – was popularised by David Guest in 1991.[156] What the T-shaped professional knows is both broad and deep. Needless to say, the metaphor was followed by a plethora of variations, including not only letters but diacritics and pictograms. Following Bonsiepe, the shape deriving from the skill set of the designer, as portrayed by Papanek, would be purely horizontal – a hyphen, or perhaps an em dash.

For Arturo Escobar, design culture has contributed to manufacture a uniform, ever-expanding "One-World World." This, in turn, threatens to eradicate what's left of what he calls, following decolonial theorist Walter Mignolo, the pluriverse, which is where "things and beings *are* their relations [and] do not exist prior to them."[157] To sustain the pluriverse (whatever that is), designers might have to relinquish the ambition of a synthetic monopoly on ideas through a singular mode of comprehension. It wouldn't be a big loss, since most of them didn't actually hold such monopoly in the first place: rarely are designers given room to truly reframe the problem, that is, to take into account more of its relationships, to expand the magic circle. To maintain the wealth of pre-existing relationships – be they historical, political or cultural – design should resist the temptation to formalise, to abstract, to be *the* relation.

And yet, a solution is always a formalisation, one that mirrors the problem's formulation. Designers' discomfort with synthesis might have to do with the fact that designed artefacts can only go so far when it comes to incarnating different, if not opposite, worldviews. More than in use, a synthesis of disparate goals and desires is found in narrative. Stories, more than things, are able to keep different ideas together. They are ambiguous by design. This might explain the current centrality of storytelling and the

---

156 See https://en.wikipedia.org/wiki/T-shaped_skills.
157 Arturo Escobar. *Designs for the Pluriverse: Radical Interdependence, Autonomy, and the Making of Worlds*. London: Duke University Press, 2018, pp. 70-1.

humanistic ascendancy over the technical in design as an all-encompassing sphere.

Relinquishing an alleged synthetic monopoly might also have a positive side-effect. Forgoing design synthesis doesn't mean giving up generalism – it means giving up *genericity*, a vagueness that makes practitioners feel groundless. Authentic generalism offers instead a solid, fertile ground, one that doesn't rest on design alone, but requires an engagement with things, beings and practices on their own terms. Generalism is the opposite of specialisation, but it thrives on specificity.

A KNACK FOR MISCHIEF

"The discipline without the discipline of another discipline." This definition – courtesy of David Reinfurt – refers to graphic design, but it can be well applied to design in general.[158] Both meanings of the word discipline are mobilised here: field of study and self-restraint. (Graphic) design might lack the acquiescence that permeates more established branches of knowledge – it has a knack for mischief. What does it mean for a discipline to disobey? It means escaping its own semi-rigidly defined confines, its own "provisional territorialisation."[159] From this perspective, design's disobedience appears liberating. A case in point is the prestigious MIT Media Lab. Former director Joi Ito proudly spoke of the lab's *anti*disciplinarity:

> An antidisciplinary project isn't a sum of a bunch of disciplines but something entirely new – the word defies easy definition. But what it means to me is someone or something that doesn't fit within traditional academic discipline – a field of study with its own particular

---

[158] David Reinfurt. *A *New* Program for Graphic Design*. Los Angeles: Inventory Press, 2019, p. 16.
[159] Jacques Rancière. *Et tant pis pour les gens fatigués*. Paris: Éditions Amsterdam, 2009, p. 478.

words, frameworks, and methods.[160]

The target of Ito's criticism was the hyper-specialisation and gatekeeping of disciplinary experts who become incapable of communicating with the outer world and even among themselves. Furthermore, he rightly pointed out that reality is not organised around disciplines: they are artificial compartments of knowledge. If disciplines are the little dots on the map of knowledge, Ito explained, antidisciplinary space, the space of design, is the white area in between.

While antidisciplinarity is a clear attempt to provide a space for the "misfits," an emphasis on uniqueness and novelty might lead to the disregard of much of the slow, cementing work performed within the disciplines – the work of maintenance: "We shouldn't be doing something that someone else is doing. If someone else starts doing it, we should stop." Not only can design devour contexts, it can also ignore them.

Besides what is to be done, disciplines are normally busy with *how* things should be done, namely, methods. Nigel Cross recounts how design tried to pump up its reputation by presenting itself as a science.[161] This turned out to be an illusion: after endless debates, designers and theorists alike realised that design is not a science exactly because its processes can't be turned into a formula. Unlike science, which is based on a single method, design has *methods* that are plural, ad hoc and often non-replicable – to the extent that speaking of methods might already be a stretch. Donald Grant, writing in 1979, sententiously concluded:

> Most opinion among design methodologists and among designers holds that the act of designing itself is not and will not ever be a scientific activity; that is, that designing is itself a

---

160   Joi Ito. "Antidisciplinary." Joy Ito's Web (blog), October 2, 2014. https://joi.ito.com/weblog/2014/10/02/antidisciplinar.html.
161   Nigel Cross. "Designerly Ways of Knowing: Design Discipline versus Design Science." *Design Issues* 17, no. 3 (2001): 49–55.

nonscientific or ascientific activity.[162]
Whereas the attempt to mimic the epistemology and methodology of science is doomed to fail, it is possible to turn design, a concrete set of "techniques of the artificial," into an object of study. This is what philosopher Donald Schön calls reflective practice.[163] In this way, design can finally achieve its status of discipline. Again Cross:

> Design as a discipline, therefore, can mean design studied on its own terms, and within its own rigorous culture. It can mean a science of design based on the reflective practice of design: design as a discipline, but not design as a science. This discipline seeks to develop domain-independent approaches to theory and research in design. The underlying axiom of this discipline is that there are forms of knowledge special to the awareness and ability of a designer, independent of the different professional domains of design practice.[164]

The design discipline becomes therefore the investigation of "designerly ways of knowing, thinking and acting." Such definition runs the risk of sounding circular, if not tautological. The idea of the "designerly," taken to its extreme, is that nothing precedes the designing act: it is this very act that forms its own understanding. Since a general design method akin to the scientific one cannot be established, design might then become whatever designers do.[165] If a designer were to propose using a pierced let-

---

162 Donald P. Grant. 'Design Methodology and Design Methods'. *Design Methods and Theories* 13, no. 1 (1979). See also Henrik Gedenryd, who adds that not only do designers disregard prescribed methodologies, but they also believe these simply don't work. "How Designers Work - Making Sense of Authentic Cognitive Activities." Lund University Cognitive Studies. Doctoral thesis, Lund University, 1998. http://lup.lub.lu.se/record/18828, p. 1.
163 Donald A. Schön. *The Reflective Practitioner: How Professionals Think in Action*. London, New York: Routledge, 2016.
164 Cross, *op. cit.*, p. 54.
165 This doesn't mean of course that certain replicable methods aren't employed by designers. For instance, the use of personas, paper prototyping or procedures like MoSCow are commonly used within design teams (See, for example, https://

tuce leaf as a face mask as protection from an aggressive virus, that would be a legitimate designerly approach.[166]

Schön's effort to systematise the design process is undoubtedly precious as it distils its underlying principle, namely, "a reflective conversation with the situation." But the form of this conversation is not, of course, set in stone. Given design's cultural expansion, it might be that a special form of knowledge, previously based on an intimate relationship with a set of materials, a technique or a category of products, is simply lost. The philosopher himself warns that, given the tendency "to think of policies, institutions, and behaviour itself, as objects of design, [we] risk ignoring or underestimating significant differences in media, contexts, goals, and bodies of knowledge specific to the professions."[167] When designers are integrated into a problem-solving chain, the validation of their results retrospectively includes their approach: if the product is good, the process must also be good. But things differ when the designerly approach becomes the focus, when the process itself is the product, when the production of meaning (what Manzini calls "sense-making") becomes prominent: the designerly attitude appears at the same time fully legitimate – and completely random.[168]

---

toolkits.dss.cloud/design/). But, as any designer will admit, those methods are limited or even detrimental to a genuine understanding of the issue at hand.

166   This is indeed what German-Namibian artist Max Siedentopf came up with. Of course, it was something between art project and provocation, but the very attention given to it by *design* platforms like Dezeen and the wave of indignation that followed (Siedentopf later apologised) signal the ambiguity of design methodologies: the way they lead to a result, as well as their very result, are dubious. See Amy Frearson. "Max Siedentopf Suggests Alternative Masks to Protect Against Coronavirus." *Dezeen*, February 17, 2020. https://www.dezeen.com/2020/02/17/alternative-coronavirus-masks-max-siedentopf/. During the first months of the Covid-19 pandemic, this was no isolated case. Architecture critic Kate Wagner called Coronagrifting the phenomenon of "cheap mockups of COVID-related design 'solutions.'" A phenomenon that seems to imply that the 'designerly' approach has some sort of immunity against serious scrutiny. "Coronagrifting: A Design Phenomenon." *McMansion Hell* (blog), May 23, 2020. https://mcmansionhell.com/post/618938984050147328/coronagrifting-a-design-phenomenon.

167   Schön, *op. cit.*, p. 77.

168   In the case of Coronagrifting, the product, being mostly an idea, coincides with the process, and it is deemed good, as long as it generates online engagement.

CHAPTER 3

Rendering of the Dome Over Manhattan by Buckminster Fuller (1960). Black and white photograph on board with dome overlay, 12.75in x 18.38in.

A COMPLEX RELATIONSHIP

Found image. Source unknown.
Original artwork: *Metamorphosis* by Herbert Bayer (1936).

CHAPTER 3

Design scholars Craig Bremner and Paul Rodgers react conservatively in the journal Design Issues. For them, the discipline of design is simply dissolving. This is the result of a three-fold crisis: professional, economic and technological. Bremner and Rodgers notice how "[p]ractice shifts from being 'discipline-based' to 'issue- or project-based.'" As a consequence, "design now finds itself in a position of not knowing what to project." Not unlike Ito, they recognise the non-disciplinary character of design, which is what they call undisciplinarity. Interestingly, they connect a disciplinary modus operandi to the character of the designer who adopts it.

> "Undisciplined" research straddles the ground and relationships between different idioms of distinct disciplinary practices. Here a multitude of disciplines "engage in a pile-up of jumbled ideas and perspectives. Undisciplinarity is as much a way of doing work as it is a departure from ways of doing work." It is an approach to creating and circulating culture that can go its own way without worrying about what histories-of-disciplines say is "proper" work. In other words, it is "undisciplined."[169]

Bremner and Rodgers commend the worry-free attitude of the undisciplined designer. But the chaotic quality of undisciplinarity might resemble pure relativism. In the pile-up of jumbled ideas and perspectives, one might feel dispirited. A tweet by Celeste Labedz aptly summarises the feeling: "Yeah, my work is interdisciplinary; I'm confused by *multiple* fields at the same time."[170] There may be a sense of being a Jack of all trades, master of none.[171] How can we prevent disorientation? The scholars' proposal is to hook up the act of designing to something stable, be

---

[169] Bremner and Rodgers, "Design Without Discipline," *op. cit.*, p. 12.
[170] https://twitter.com/celestelabedz/status/1391770429514190850.
[171] This is, in fact, Bruce Archer's *positive* suggestion. Archer quoted in Potter, *op. cit.*, p. 165.

that either disciplinarity (hence, design as "disciplined and irresponsible") or responsibility ("undisciplined and responsible"). Otherwise, insecurity might prevail.[172]

According to Danah Abdulla, the undisciplinarity of design is connected to the specialisation of the designer, or lack thereof. She considers the following conversation:
>What do you do?
>I'm a designer.
>What kind? Graphic? Fashion? Furniture? Interior?

Pressured for a specific answer, the designer feels anxious and, instead of simply adopting a general, interdisciplinary label, ends up finding shelter in a specialised discipline. However – Abdulla argues – disciplines are constrictive, bureaucratic, myopic: they are mainly concerned with administering their own rules and regulations. This is what Lewis R. Gordon calls "disciplinary decadence."[173] Quoting Moholy-Nagy, Adbulla points out that the urge to specialise isn't new in design, where vocational education "breeds specialists with a rather narrow horizon." Finally, she argues for "border-thinking," which consists in locating the inquiry at the very edge of a system of thought in order to break disciplinary boundaries.[174]

However, it is important to realise that, in the real world of work, inhabiting disciplinary borders has become the default. The widespread diffusion of 'multi-hyphenated' professional profiles is proof.[175] The everyday designer might opt for a specialisation to signal their affiliation to a certain cultural group, but in practice, their work is likely to span various lines of work, if not various jobs! This is

172 Bremner and Rodgers, "Design Without Discipline," *op. cit*, p. 13.
173 Gordon, *op. cit.*, p. 229.
174 Danah Abdulla. "Disciplinary Disobedience." In *Design Struggles: Intersecting Histories, Pedagogies, and Perspectives*, edited by Claudia Mareis and Nina Paim. Amsterdam: Valiz, 2021.
175 See Nikki Shaner-Bradford. "What Do You Do? I'm a Podcaster-Vlogger-Model-Dj." *The Outline*, November 25, 2019. https://theoutline.com/post/8301/everyone-you-know-is-a-multi-hyphenate. Artist Brad Troemel refers to this phenomenon as "polyemployment."

why a designer could end up feeling a certain repulsion towards multiplicity: "I don't want to have to know every software and skill. I just want to be a graphic designer – not a motion designer, 3D artist, UX strategist."[176]

It seems, then, that undisciplinarity (which somehow includes antidisciplinarity), understood here as an implosion of disciplines from the perspective of those who practice them, is to be found either at the high end of the workforce (e.g. the art director) or at the bottom (the occasional web designer-barista). In any case, the incentive is primarily financial: "The evasion of normative procedures and professional identities by the design industry is in no small part the result of its constant adherence to 'following the money' by inventing new specialisms to exploit technological and business opportunities."[177] This shows that undisciplinarity, rather than a mission, is *a destiny* of the so-called creative class. This was already clear in the '90s to graphic designer Rudy VanderLans:

> In a sense, everything can be learned on the job, even critical thinking, exploration, introspection, offset printing, intellectual development, bookkeeping, French literary criticism, programming, [and] contract writing... It can all be learned as you slowly develop into the all-around professional you're *supposed* to be.[178]

The emphasis, which is mine, highlights the necessity of this condition. J. Dakota Brown associates the role of all-around professional to the "zany," a frenetic character type who does it all, but struggles to keep it all together.[179] Paradoxically, the contemporary creative profes-

---

176   "Design Thread 2 – Excess of Everything," 2022. https://www.designthreads.report/thread2.
177   Julier, *op. cit.*, 24.
178   VanderLans quoted in J. Dakota Brown. "American Graphic Design in the 1990s: Deindustrialization and the Death of the Author." *Post45*, January 10, 2019. https://post45.org/2019/01/american-graphic-design-in-the-1990s-deindustrialization-and-the-death-of-the-author.
179   Brown, "American Graphic Design in the 1990s", *op. cit.*

sional is an amateur, someone "who dabble[s] in a range of activities without dedicating or committing themselves to any one field."[180] For everyday designers, antidisciplinarity, rather than making it possible to escape the constriction of disciplines, means entering a frenzied state of insecurity.

GOOD DOUBT, BAD DOUBT

Designer Michael Rock maintains that such insecurity produces anxiety: "Designer anxiety is rooted in a fear that what we do is not respected, worthwhile, important. This anxiety is fuelled by a business world that, in general, neither respects nor considers design particularly worthwhile or important. [...] Thus design activity is fraught with a desperate quality."[181] Designer and educator Brian LaRossa agrees:

> Graphic designers are insecure. This is understandable; design lacks defensible boundaries. It is ubiquitous and absorbent, everywhere and everything. It is never itself, always its subject. It is diffused evenly across our lives to such a low concentration that we often doubt its worth.

LaRossa, saying something that can be said of design at large, goes on, describing precisely the idiosyncrasies – the 'magic,' one could say – of the design process: "Our inquiries compound, narrowing options until we're left with something real."[182] Designers are asked to 'trust the process,' to have faith in a liturgy that acquires meaning only in hindsight. LaRossa, however, is positive about persistent doubt: he sees it as a fundamental component of the design craft. But, for designers to merrily linger in a

---

180 Gerry Beegan and Paul Atkinson. "Professionalism, Amateurism and the Boundaries of Design." *Journal of Design History* 21, no. 4 (2008): 305–13, p. 309.
181 Michael Rock. "On Unprofessionalism." *2x4* (blog), August 5, 1994. https://2x4.org/ideas/1994/on-unprofessionalism/.
182 Brian LaRossa. "Design as a Third Area of General Education." *Medium* (blog), January 23, 2021. https://brianlarossa.medium.com/design-as-a-third-area-of-general-education-80bc59875e45.

state of doubt, they need not only self-confidence, but the confidence of their peers, be they fellow practitioners or clients. Desirable doubts require certainties.

How can we take advantage of this inherent and productive insecurity without sinking into 'bad doubt,' that is, crippling self-doubt? How can we maintain conviction in spite of indifference or even hostility without having to have a kind of *Fountainhead* me-against-the-world cockiness? Undisciplinarity requires legitimacy and recognition to be practised. In a time when a proper balance between specialisation and generalism is yet to be found, undisciplinarity requires a social act of faith. Clients, users and journalists have to be convinced that the designer's 'stupid questions,' awkward methods (often pretentiously called 'methodologies') and hardly explicable connections will spark innovation in the end and, therefore, generate value.

According to Umberto Eco, "[t]echnique is administered by the artist or by the technician, who acts like a shaman."[183] This is not just about design: any kind of expert knowledge is esoteric. Ettore Sottsass believed that "design begins where rational processes end and magic begins." At times, the magic reference goes beyond analogy. Here's how Kursat Ozenc describes the "design shaman":

> A shamanesque designer doesn't stop in just reacting (*sic*) what's asked of her. She knows the friction in the world, and entropy embedded in human kind to derail from what's right and important. With that in mind, she works hard to create myths around sustainability. She creates micro-visions for a harmonious future, mixes the spiritual with the functional without hesitation. At times of hardship, she infuses light superstitions for the greater good.[184]

---

183 Umberto Eco. "Critical Essay." In *The Universitas Project: Solutions for a Post-Technological Society*, edited by Emilio Ambasz. New York: The Museum of Modern Art, 2006, p. 130.
184 Kursat Ozenc. "The 3 Most Unconventional Designers of 21st Century – Starting

However, if the expert or the designer is denied the trust to exercise their magic, the spell breaks.[185] Thus, productive insecurity requires a safe space to be exercised. Societal trust makes insecurity productive; without it undisciplinarity becomes mere disorientation. Design schools and labs can be seen as spaces that allow for a suspension of disciplinary disbelief toward design methods and practices. But what happens outside these enlightened post-disciplinary institutions? Annelys de Vet, director of the Design Department of the Sandberg Instituut of Amsterdam for a decade, recognises that "although design students remain some of the most forward-thinking individuals, designers are occupying rather fragile positions in society. As a department, we hope to provide a space for young people to prepare for a practice within a profession that is increasingly hard to define."[186]

Here, de Vet speaks of profession rather than discipline. According to Donald Schön, a professional is someone who "claims extraordinary knowledge in matters of human importance, getting in return extraordinary rights and privileges."[187] This definition clearly shows why someone might want to be considered a professional: a profession is not just a job, but a prestigious social position: "the image of The Professional; respect, high pay, beautiful lovers."[188] So, we can say that designers are considered

with Design Shaman." *Ritual Design Lab* (blog), April 4, 2016. https://medium.com/ritual-design/a-new-breed-of-21st-century-designers-b73712963b4.

[185] Here is a tangible example of a broken spell. Some years ago, I attended the XY summer school, organised by the soon-to-be Scuola Open Source in Castrignano De' Greci, in the deep south of Italy. There, some of the tutors insisted on the value of rituals and encouraged us to perform one every day. Journalists then came to visit. Later, in order to discredit the political party that indirectly funded the school, they wrote a vitriolic article where they labelled the whole event as 'shamanic' to denounce the waste of public money. Sergio Rame. "Gli sprechi di Vendola: un corso per formare gli sciamani (digitali)." *ilGiornale.it*, July 18, 2014. https://www.ilgiornale.it/news/politica/sprechi-vendola-corso-formare-sciamani-digitali-1038689.html.

[186] Annelys de Vet, ed. *Design Dedication: Adaptive Mentalities in Design Education*. Amsterdam: Valiz + Sandberg Instituut Design Department, 2020, p. 31.

[187] Schön, *op. cit.*, p. 4.

[188] Rock, *op. cit.*

CHAPTER 3

Poster designed by Herbert Bayer in 1923 to promote the first major exhibition of the Bauhaus. It includes Walter Gropius's new motto for the school: "Art and Technics: A New Unity".

professionals when society recognises the added value that their particular mixture of disciplines provides.

The increasing difficulty to define the design profession can be situated within a more general crisis of the professions. Schön draws a trajectory of the social role of the professions characterised by triumphalism during the '60s and scepticism during the '70s and '80s. Given the current debate around the crisis of competence, it is fair to assume that such scepticism never went away. This timeline almost perfectly coincides with the parable of design recognition, with a jubilant culmination of good design in the '60s and the growing doubt and antagonism during the '70s (with the politically engaged Radical Design and the sensuous Anti-Design), followed by the emergence of deconstructionism and post-modernism in the '80s.[189]

OWNING COMPLEXITY

The traditional justification for an expansion of professional domains is the growing complexity of our world. It is a litany that has been repeated uninterruptedly at least since the '60s. Not surprisingly, the design field insists on complexity and anchors itself to it, often arguing that the conventional scientific approach fails to grasp it.[190] Complexity, from this point of view, is not just matter of fact, but also an instrument for professional lobbying. Here, an interesting reversal ensues. What worries and disorients the general public becomes a reassuring design trope: with the increase in complexity, the need for professional designers increases too. Guy Julier, with a hint

189 Along these lines, we can think of the popularity of Critical Design (which is itself critical of design's role in society) at the turn of the millennium as a semi-conscious attempt to professionalise disciplinary self-doubt.

190 "Design is a way of behaving that approaches complexity in a different way (and expecting a different type of outcome) than we have conventionally used. Designers work in a way (a conversation with the self via the medium of drawing) that allows them to deal with very complex, ill-defined and ambiguous situations that would probably be inaccessible using conventional approaches." Ranulph Glanville. "Designing Complexity." *Performance Improvement Quarterly* 20, no. 2 (June 2007): 75–96. https://doi.org/10.1111/j.1937-8327.2007.tb00442.x.

of controversy, remarks: "It has become an orthodoxy to talk of the growing complexity of design in our 'complex world.'"[191] Innovation experts like to speak about complexity, albeit in vague terms, such as when they state that "society is growing increasingly complex and will only be more complex in the future." Scholar Lee Vinsel asks:

> What does this claim even mean? Complex in what way? Increasingly complex with respect to what metric? I have asked many professional historians this question, and they believe this increasing complexity claim is unsupportable.[192]

On the other hand, 'complicating' an issue is increasingly deemed as a valuable activity, an attempt to look deeper. So, complexity is at the same time the illness and the remedy. The orthodoxy of complexity goes hand in hand with design's anthropological turn. David Graeber notices that "[a]nthropologists are drawn to areas of density. [Their interpretative tools] are best suited to wend our way through complex webs of meaning or signification."[193] Designers are increasingly attracted to such dense areas of meaning, because it is where their self-attributed role of synthesists can be, presumably, better performed.

But 'owning' complexity is not enough. The professional ambition of the design field clashes with the trend of deprofessionalisation, which can also be understood as a proletarianisation of the professions and, therefore, a proletarianisation of design. This structural crisis goes hand in hand with what Schön, writing in the '80s, calls an internal "crisis of confidence:"

> The crisis of confidence in the professions, and perhaps also the decline in professional self-image, seems to be rooted in a growing scepticism

---

191 Julier, *op. cit.*, p. 6.
192 Lee Vinsel. "Design Thinking Is Kind of Like Syphilis — It's Contagious and Rots Your Brains." *Medium* (blog), August 3, 2020. https://sts-news.medium.com/design-thinking-is-kind-of-like-syphilis-its-contagious-and-rots-your-brains-842ed078af29.
193 David Graeber. *The Utopia of Rules: On Technology, Stupidity, and the Secret Joys of Bureaucracy*. Brooklyn: Melville House, 2015, p. 51.

about professional effectiveness in the larger sense, a sceptical reassessment of the professions' actual contribution to society's well-being through the delivery of competent services based on special knowledge.

The philosopher adds that scepticism involves the very knowledge that the professions purportedly possess. Again, the changes he highlights in the professional context uncannily resemble the current state of design discourse: "The situations of practice are not problems to be solved but problematic situations characterized by uncertainty, disorder, and indeterminacy." It turns out that complexity is not just a fog surrounding the professional ivory tower, but a haze invading its chambers. A need for synthesis emerges:

> What is called for, under these conditions, is not only the analytic techniques which have been traditional in operations research, but the active, synthetic skill of "designing a desirable future and inventing ways of bringing it about."[194]

Like other professions, design actively tries to affirm and preserve its place in society. But, unlike many of them, the design field is particularly subject to professional pluralism, the proliferation of conflicting views around the discipline's aims, methods and goals. Donald Schön's motivation to write his book was to shed light on the qualities of the reflective practitioner, concluding that "we are bound to an epistemology of practice which leaves us at a loss to explain, or even to describe, the competences to which we now give overriding importance."[195] While his attempt to clarify the tacit ways of knowing afforded by practice is laudable, this feeling of being at a loss is ineradicable in the design field. Furthermore, it becomes harder to convince non-professionals of the adequacy of design knowledge

---

194 Schön, *op. cit.*, p. 16.
195 *Ivi*, p. 20.

beyond the exploits of design stars, the micro-evolutionary changes in consumer products and services, or even the software skills of execution now available to the masses. In this setting, professional pluralism, whose most obvious manifestation in design is a proliferation of labels,[196] reinforces the crisis of confidence and the sense that design's professional knowledge is either common sense or a clunky 'methodocracy,' a generic set of procedures that the Methods Movement itself has abjured.

THE PLATONIC TURN

As a partial response to a disciplinary and professional impasse, various designers began to think of design as an autonomous sphere. What they advocated was the idea that design could be disconnected from its traditional service-based role to gain the freedom to decide upon its own societal concerns, instead of tackling the narrow ones of those who commissioned the work. The designer's privileged interlocutor would not be a client anymore, but the transcendental idea of society as a whole. The goal was – to apply Manzini's categories – to put problem-solving aside and fully devote designers' efforts to sense-making. Unsurprisingly, this claim has been put forward with particular energy in those design subfields, such as graphic and product design, that have been more impacted by the threefold crisis pointed out by Bremner and Rodgers: economic, professional and technological. Given the growing supply of trained designers and the aspirational allure surrounding the profession, product design is deeply affected by economic pressure.[197] Graphic design, on the other hand, has suffered a crisis of legitimacy due to the general availability of desktop publishing software, which

---

[196] "Sometimes, one gets the impression that a designer aspiring to two minutes of fame feels obliged to invent a new label for setting her or himself apart from the rest of the professional service." Bonsiepe, "Design and Democracy," *op. cit.*, p. 27.

[197] See Justin McGuirk. "Designs for Life Won't Make You a Living." *The Guardian*, April 18, 2011. https://www.theguardian.com/artanddesign/2011/apr/18/designs-milan-furniture-fair.

has lowered the access bar of certain design tasks and therefore its prices. Furthermore, graphic design has partially failed to reinvent itself for the web, giving way to the more systematic and service-oriented areas of user interface and user experience design (UI, UX).

From this perspective, the call for cultural and professional autonomy seems more like a retreat from a hostile marketplace and an indifferent public than the actual fulfilment of disciplinary independence. Whereas the traditional service-based path could likely lead to a relatively small income and little agency, the autonomous road would at least guarantee the possibility to set the terms of one's own activity, a positive self-narrative that fits the imperative to be in control of one's own life project.[198]

In 2002, Andrew Blauvelt invoked "critical autonomy" in graphic design. The Japanese-American designer and curator wasn't encouraging the withdrawal from society or fine-art romantic genius individualism. Critical autonomy meant that design could be busy "generating meaning on its own terms without undue reliance on commissions, prescriptive social functions, or specific media or styles." Not without a dose of "self-awareness and self-reflectivity," designers would develop "a capacity to manipulate the system of design for ends other than those imposed on the field from without and to question those conventions formed from within." Furthermore, Blauvelt pointed out that critical autonomy would confer coherence to the discipline of graphic design (thus, confirming its crisis), a coherence which was under the attack of stylistic pluralism and the exogenous terms and conditions under which it operates.

[198] As identity is nowadays deeply rooted in one's job, the issue of a gratifying professional self-image becomes crucial. I tackled this issue in my previous book: "Many simply ignore or even reject the circumstances that determine their own story. In doing so they often create an idealized personal narrative to the detriment of the material reality that lies behind it. In other words, they claim to be artists, journalists or entrepreneurs regardless of the income these activities actually generate. In this sense, the issue of precarity seems to be linked not only to work but also to the need to build and maintain one's identity." *Entreprecariat, op. cit.*, p. 55.

However, what Blauvelt, as well as most proponents of design's autonomy, overlooks is the actual possibility for (graphic) design to become autonomous. Can design turn itself into something different alone? Can it radicalise its sense-making, meaning-generating activity without having to rely on its socially attributed role? And can one even clearly identify a "system of design" to manipulate? J. Dakota Brown suggests another way forward:

> Rather than pinning our hopes on bootstrapping ourselves out of design's social function, we should ask why certain possibilities have consistently been foreclosed in the history of the practice.[199]

A radically different view on autonomy might help frame these questions. Arturo Escobar speculates that design can foster the autonomy of communities. His idea of autonomy is not a generic one, but it is strictly connected to movements of liberation in Latin America, what he calls *autonomìa*. The anthropologist derives this concept from Chilean biologist Francisco Varela's notion of autopoiesis: an autonomous system is one that "finds its way into the next moment by acting appropriately out of its own resources."[200] The key aspect of Varela's autopoiesis lies in its independence from the environment of a system's identity: its defining logic is internal and, while it responds to changes in the environment, it maintains an inner coherence.

This understanding of autonomy can be fruitfully applied to communities because it allows them to maintain their identity while changing: it's a fertile combination of tradition and innovation. It is what makes it possible to change "traditions traditionally."[201] But the idea of an

---

199 J. Dakota Brown. *The Power of Design as a Dream of Autonomy*. Chicago, IL: Green Lantern Press, 2019, p. 20.
200 Francisco Varela. *Ethical Know-How: Action, Wisdom, and Cognition*. Stanford: Stanford University Press, 1999, p. 11.
201 Escobar, *op. cit.*, p. 172.

autonomous community rests on the premise that identity and coherence are there to be preserved in the first place. Is this the case for design? Blauvelt argues that graphic design is fundamentally about difference. So, while the community the designer works for can hopefully operate 'autopoietically,' the designer might perceive their field as heteronomous, that is, fundamentally shaped by its environment to the extent that it can't preserve any organisational coherence. One can sense such *allopoiesis* as the technological pressures that affect the design field. Innovation is often what attacks the core of a discipline.[202] The reversal is ironic: whereas design as an endeavour is traditionally about reshaping the environment, as a culture it is mainly *shaped* by it. This might be the fundamental lesson we learn from the perspective of ontological design.

A PEDANTRY OF THE SPIRIT

Blauvelt's critical autonomy, one of the many attempts at freeing design practices from their service status, seems to be more a matter of wishful thinking than a viable option for the majority of designers. Looking at the ethical claims of graphic designers, J. Dakota Brown notices how "[the] inflation of design's autonomy and power entails a corresponding inflation of the autonomy and power of its practitioners."[203] Critical autonomy implies that the ethical and critical impetus to affect the world, doesn't happen via *use-artefacts* but by means of *conversation pieces*, that is, texts and objects that intervene by "making people think," "raising awareness," etc.[204] In this sense, we can

---

[202] An example: according to Lorraine Wilde, "it's not clear that anything resembling the traditional role of the graphic designer is really necessary or desired in new media. If you surf the Web, you know that lots of visual 'things' have been produced without the participation of someone the profession would even call a graphic designer." "The Macramé of Resistance." *Emigre*, no. 47 (1998). Is the identity of graphic designers preserved while they make the jump to digital media? Is graphic design a tradition worth maintaining when it comes to laptops and smartphones?

[203] Brown, *The Power of Design...*, op. cit., p. 12.

[204] Cf. Anthony Dunne and Fiona Raby. *Speculative Everything: Design, Fiction, and*

argue that design has attempted to keep up its status by radically transforming its internal principle of being a service. It's no coincidence that a recent anthology of Swiss writings on design is entitled *Not at Your Service*.[205] When it comes to the design field, autonomy derives from a sort of dysfunctional autopoiesis: an internal coherence, built from scratch, impedes a healthy relation with the environment. Critical autonomy signals the rise of the designer who focuses on ideas rather than things – the Platonic designer. Contra Bonsiepe's emphasis on practicality, Platonic designers return to the contemplative mode of academia as the access to problem-solving (as well as authentic problem-framing) is barred to them. They promote theories, foster reflection and criticise positions. Instead of transforming the environment through products and services, Platonic design claims to sway public opinion. But it has often little interest in verifying such claim.

Speculative designers Anthony Dunne and Fiona Raby blatantly celebrate this shift when they state that "once designers step away from industrial production and the marketplace we enter the realm of the unreal, the fictional, or what we prefer to think of as conceptual design – design about ideas."[206] But while the step away from industrial production might actually take place, there is no outside the market, at least the labour market, as the designer still has to sell their ideas. Conceptual design might be an immaterial commodity, but it is still a commodity that needs a buyer to complete its cycle, otherwise it is pure consumption. From this perspective, critical autonomy is perhaps nothing more than a concealment of heteronomy:

> Designers have attempted, through sheer will, to reinvent themselves as theorists and critics. But as long as they are at work, they are

---

Social Dreaming. Cambridge, MA: MIT Press, 2013, p. 21.
205 Björn Franke and Hansuli Matter, eds. *Not at Your Service: Manifestos for Design*. Zurich, Basel: Zurich University of the Arts, 2021.
206 Dunne and Raby, *op. cit.*, p. 11.

constrained by social forces over which they have little control – and which they have, unfortunately, shown little interest in grasping.[207]

The elephant in the room is design's self-sufficiency at scale. Undoubtedly, a small minority of designers, assisted by the cultural structure of museums and enlightened state support are able to exercise critical autonomy, but for the rest, the ability to "manipulate the system of design" is a mere disciplinary smokescreen. Maldonado:

> One has to admit that industrial design, contrary to what its precursors imagined, is not an autonomous activity. Although its design choices may seem free, and perhaps sometimes they are, they are always choices made within the context of a system of very rigidly established priorities. Ultimately, it is this system of priorities that governs industrial design.[208]

In this chapter I have shown that looking at how design weaves its web of relationships might be the only way to nail down its essence, but design's intrinsic in-betweenness is not devoid of intricacies. Design professes a generalist attitude, but its cultural hyperconnectivity, together with the synthetic monopoly that it holds (or claims to hold), might reduce it to a generic and reductive pursuit. Furthermore, its undisciplined character, when it is not backed up by a social act of faith, can lead to disorientation and crippling self-doubt. Design is situated within a more general crisis of the professions, where the tacit contract that broadly defines a profession – legitimised expertise offered in exchange of prestige and recognition – vacillates. That of the profession is not an absolute, static category, but a relative one in constant renegotiation. Finally, through the decades, design has formulated a demand for autonomy: designers want to decide upon

---

207   Brown, *The Power of Design...*, *op. cit.*, p. 19.
208   Maldonado, *La speranza progettuale*, *op. cit.*, p. 12.

their own concerns, methods and outputs – they want to determine their own added value. However, design's "critical autonomy" might disguise the abdication of its specific social role, that is, contributing to the production of preferable conditions by transforming the artificial environment, or, more succinctly, solving problems. Instead of becoming masters of their own destiny, designers risk ending up retreating into a Platonic realm where their main concern is not artefacts any longer, but ideas and principles whose reception is uncertain. A pedantry of the spirit, in Norman Potter's formulation:

> For the social task we have fresh evidence all the time of man's fallibility, of his deepening technological commitment; of the nature of affluence divorced from the social or spiritual awareness. Yet there is a pedantry of the spirit in dwelling too much on these things.[209]

---

[209] Potter, *op. cit.*, p. 45.

Chapter 4.

Flipping the Table: On Power and Impotence

"But is there still room for design? Frankly, it is very small."
– Tomás Maldonado, 1970[210]

"In the way that we conduct ourselves as designers, we are as free as the marketplace allows us to be."
– Adrian Shaughnessy, 2005[211]

"[D]id it hurt? when they hired you for your design experience and then just ignored all of your advice and told you exactly what to design and where"
– @tiffanyton, 2021[212]

MASS-PRODUCED IMPACT

Conventionally, designers are thought of as changing the world through the things they design: products, services, systems, environments, tools, machines. By designing the artefacts that make up our artificial world, they contribute to make the world more and more artificial, and, it seems, inescapably so. At the beginning of the twentieth century, in the culminating phase of industrial production and mass communication, the link between cause (design) and effect (world changes) was particularly tangible since its scale was colossal. Armies of identical artefacts would enter the life of the masses for a relatively long time. The slightest design change would suddenly re-adjust the operations of this mechanically-reproduced battalion of things. As industrial designer Carroll Gantz explains, "[designers would] transform the process of design from an individual creative act that produced one artefact at a time into a complex industrial mass production system

---

210 Maldonado, *La speranza progettuale*, op. cit., p. 76.
211 Adrian Shaughnessy. *How to Be a Graphic Designer Without Losing Your Soul*. New York: Princeton Architectural Press, 2005, p. 25.
212 https://twitter.com/tiffanyton/status/1433067196712833034.

CHAPTER 4

that made millions of identical products."[213]

Designers could think of themselves as a commanders whose designerly 'orders' would be executed *en masse*, in line with traditional definitions of power, such as Carl Schmitt and Max Weber's, namely, "the possibility to find obedience to a command."[214] A modern perspective on production implied a modern understanding of design's power. "One design for all" wasn't just a technical necessity but a programmatic ambition. Consider, for instance, Henry Ford's faith in a universal car, the T model. In 1922 (the same year Weber offered his definition of power), Ford expressed his deliberate intention to "build a motor car for the great multitude."[215] As Hal Foster puts it, "the commodity was its own ideology, the Model T its own advertising: its chief attraction lay in its abundant sameness."[216]

The sun hasn't set on standardised production yet. Most of the things we purchase and use are still mass-produced. Furthermore, if we take digital services into account, we have to admit that an entirely new dimension of mass production has emerged. One where segments of this mass are relentlessly sieved by means of quick cycles of test and implementation, where an interface change on a platform used by the millions, instantly deployed, can have monumental consequences. But how common is it for a designer to work on such a level? Pretty rare. Only a handful of designers have access to the prototyping rooms of these massively used products.[217] The majority of them will likely

213 Gantz quoted in Wizinsky *op. cit.*, p. 59.
214 Max Weber. *Typen der Herrschaft*. Ditzingen: Reclam, 2019, p. 7. Weber uses the word *Herrschaft*, a term covering a vast semantic field including notions of authority, rule, dominion and power.
215 Henry Ford and Samuel Crowther. *My Life and Work*. Garden City, NY: Doubleday, Page & Co., 1922. https://college.cengage.com/history/primary_sources/us/henry_ford_discusses.htm.
216 Hal Foster. *Design and Crime*. London: Verso, 2002, p. 19.
217 Spotify is a case in point. In 2018 it was used by around 200 million monthly active users. At the time, it had only 200 designers. A ratio of one designer for one million users, more or less the population of Milan. See Shaun Bent, Marina Posniak, and Geerit Kaiser. "Reimagining Design Systems at Spotify." *Spotify Design*, September 2020. https://spotify.design/article/reimagining-design-systems-

work on projects whose impact is limited in time, space and reach. Big projects, perhaps, but hardly as gargantuan. This doesn't mean that their efforts have little or no effect, but that the effect doesn't match the modern *forma mentis* of power as vast scale standardisation. Mentions of the tremendous influence that designers possess will be met by most with some reasonable scepticism.

CAUSE AND EFFECT

The modern, 'scalar' idea of design power also tends to place too much emphasis on the single object, as if its transformative power weren't enhanced or hindered by the environment it inhabits. As if the object weren't caught in a network of interactions with other objects. A linear, almost mechanistic understanding of design power (designer > product > user)[218] masks the improvisational role that the object performs on the stage of everyday life. The leading role attributed to the isolated object reflects another leading role – that of the designer. A reassuring narrative of invention also plays its part: when we perceive a groundbreaking change in habit, we are tempted to look for a singular artefact that represents such change – a symbol. Then, we try to identify an individual who conceived it, possibly through a Eureka moment.

However, we shouldn't forget that while products and services affect the world, they are also affected by it, and not just after coming into existence. According to design historian Glenn Adamson, the commodity itself is a consequence of power more than a cause of it, as the commodity is shaped by power relationships *before* entering the everyday use stage. While discussing the formal similarity of two bookcases conceived by two politically antipodal designers

---

at-spotify and https://www.statista.com/statistics/367739/spotify-global-mau/.

218 The Greater Good Studio, for instance, proposes the following "theory of change:" "We believe that research changes design, design changes behavior, and behavior changes the world." See https://web.archive.org/web/20160918151937/http://www.greatergoodstudio.com:80/theoryofchange/.

CHAPTER 4

Saul Bass-inspired cover of *Designers in Handcuffs*, one of the few books which candidly focuses on the limitation of doing a project. Designed by Lisa Buchanan.

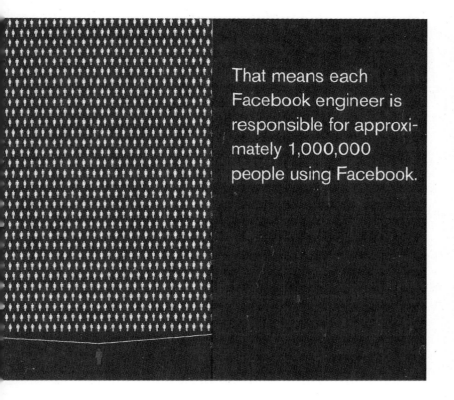

Spread from Facebook's "Little Red Book," distributed internally to employees. Designed by Ben Barry and Tim Belonax. Texts by J Smith.

CHAPTER 4

(the communist Enzo Mari and the Nazi sympathizer Ingvar Kamprad, founder of IKEA), he observes that "by the time something is designed, it is usually too late to determine its political effect. Commodities are principally the outcome of power relations, not the cause of them."[219]

Reflecting on how politics precede the use of a certain artefact, political theorist Langdon Winner mentions the infamous case of New York's Southern State Parkway bridges. These bridges, conceived by Robert Moses in the 1920s, were too low for a bus to pass. Plain bad design? Not really. Moses deliberately limited the access of disadvantaged citizens, mostly people of colour, who generally used buses to get into town.[220] This is an unusually blatant case of design wickedness (narratives of design power frequently take the form of a cautionary tale). Winner himself admits that it sounds almost conspiratorial. But from the perspective of power, it can be considered an exception more than a rule, the exception having to do not with racism and classism, which were and are both common, but instead with the coincidence of authority and execution, Robert Moses' *Herrschaft*. In fact, Winner highlights the influence that "the power broker" had over governors and presidents. How likely is it a for a designer to have full jurisdiction to, paraphrasing Winner again, embody their intention in physical form?

The symbol of the ouroboros, a serpent eating its own tail, aptly represents the relationship between design and people, since humans design things, but then those things design them back. "Design designs," as Tony Fry puts it. Design doesn't only shape use, but also meaning:

---

219 Glenn Adamson. "The Communist Designer, the Fascist Furniture Dealer, and the Politics of Design." *The Nation*, February 20, 2021. https://www.thenation.com/article/culture/enzo-mari-ikea-design/.

220 Langdon Winner. "Do Artifacts Have Politics?" *Daedalus* 109, no. 1 (1980): 121–36. For a more intricate account of Robert Moses' activity, see Thomas J. Campanella. "The True Measure of Robert Moses (and His Racist Bridges)." *Bloomberg*, July 9, 2017. https://www.bloomberg.com/news/articles/2017-07-09/robert-moses-and-his-racist-parkway-explained.

it transforms the way people make sense of the world, designers included.[221] However, this circularity might suggest that people are as active in the design of their environment as they are designed by it. Indeed, the environment's capacity to 'design' us is more vigorous than ours to design it. This is because we are born into a pre-designed normality, and not into a void:

> Complicating matters is the fact that we are firmly lodged in this loop before we have even developed any awareness of it, if we ever do. Just as we have no memory of how we acquired language and began to use and be shaped by it, we have no memory of how we began to use and be shaped by design.[222]

COGS AND NEEDLES

Dutch philosopher Koert van Mensvoort proposes an evolutionary reading of the development of a common product, the Gillette razor. His provocative account is radically 'object-oriented:'

> Obviously many designers and engineers have been involved in the creation of my razors over the years. No doubt these are all decent and friendly people – with good incomes too – but what more are these creators of the individual models than little cogs in the perpetuating Gillette Company? Calling them engineers and designers is arguably too much credit for the work they do, as they merely sketch the next razor model, of which one can already predict the 'innovative' new properties [...] It's not like they are in a position to think deeply on the meaning and origins of shaving, in order to

---

221 Fry quote in Willis, *op. cit.*, p. 86.
222 JP Harnett. "Ontological Design Has Become Influential in Design Academia – But What Is It?" *Eye on Design*, June 14, 2021. https://eyeondesign.aiga.org/ontological-design-is-popular-in-design-academia-but-what-is-it/.

CHAPTER 4

Design Thinking! comic. The strip humorously reflects on
the designer's perceived authority.

138

> reinvent this ancient ritual. Like bees in a beehive their work is determined by the logic of the larger structure.[223]

As we have seen, it's not the first time that a designer is compared to a pollinating insect: Karl Marx deemed imagination the fundamental difference between the architect and the bee, the human and the animal.[224] Van Mensvoort reverses the axiom, showing that this faculty cannot be fully exercised within a highly crystallised or interrelated industry. In a perverse twist, the commodity is here the powerful agent shaping the work of designers. The thing makes us more than us making the thing, not only in a physical sense, with the assembly line determining the gestures of the worker, but also intellectually, with market forces setting objectives and constraints to be grappled with. The picture is bleak, probably too bleak. And yet, many designers feel trapped in such an "iron cage," to use Max Weber's notorious expression.

MoMA design curator Paola Antonelli is more optimistic. In a recent interview she states that:

> Design has a lot of power that is still untapped and unexplored. There are many different types of designers. They all have influence on our behavior. Some have fundamental, earth-shattering influence, like the designers behind apps and electronic appliances and the interfaces we use all the time. Facebook, Instagram, Twitter. That's design of the system but also the interface. Other designers might have less effect, but they all act under different pressure points under the great acupuncture system of human life.[225]

---

223 Koert van Mensvoort and Hendrik-Jan Grievink. *Next Nature: Nature Changes Along with Us*. Barcelona: Actar, 2015.
224 See chapter 2.
225 Paola Antonelli. "MoMA curator: '[Humanity] will become extinct. We need to design an elegant ending.'" Interview by Suzanne LaBarre. *Fast Company*, January 8, 2019. https://www.fastcompany.com/90280777/moma-curator-we-will-become-extinct-we-need-to-design-an-elegant-ending.

CHAPTER 4

While acknowledging the sheer variety of existing designers (whose number, especially in the digital sector, is growing),[226] Antonelli adopts a poetic image that conflates them, with the risk of mitigating the immense power differential that designers can have. Furthermore, the acupunctural analogy doesn't say much about the specific power that design holds and the peculiar way in which such power is exercised.

TOO LOW IN THE POWER STRUCTURE

The case of "earth-shattering influence" of apps and digital devices deserves further scrutiny. Interdependence, complexity and hierarchy limit the designer's effort to impress their personal or professional agenda on the artefacts. Like a cobweb, the structures of production, distribution and consumption form a tense and yet mobile mesh of interrelations. This means that a radical intervention is unlikely, and even more unlikely is the possibility that the designer alone or in a team would take such action. The power of design is before everyone's eyes: design has indeed changed the face of our planet, our way of conceiving it and the way we exist within it. Design is indeed "one of the most powerful forces in our lives," as Alice Rawsthorn argues.[227] But the fact that design is powerful doesn't necessarily imply that designers are.

This seems to be true both for the everyday designer, be they a smalltown solo practitioner or a corporate employee, and the design maestro. In 2004, Enzo Mari published a paid advertisement in the architectural magazine Domus.

---

226   See Forrester. "The $162 Billion Design Industry Won't Stop Growing." *Forbes*, March 25, 2021. https://www.forbes.com/sites/forrester/2021/03/25/the-162-billion-design-industry-wont-stop-growing/.

227   Rawsthorn quoted in Steven Heller. "'Design Is One of the Most Powerful Forces in Our Lives.'" *The Atlantic*, March 13, 2014. https://www.theatlantic.com/entertainment/archive/2014/03/design-is-one-of-the-most-powerful-forces-in-our-lives/284388/. The British critic's statement is unconsciously but fittingly reminiscent of the opening line of Haug's 1971 book on commodity aesthetics: "Commodity aesthetics is one of the most powerful forces in capitalist society." Wolfgang Fritz Haug. *Critique of Commodity Aesthetics: Appearance, Sexuality, and Advertising in Capitalist Society*. Cambridge, UK: Polity Press, 1986, p. 10.

It read: "Highly experienced and qualified designer / seeks desperately / not only for himself / YOUNG ENTREPRENEUR." He did so to highlight the fact that in his line of work the one that truly allows things to happen is the entrepreneur.[228]

On more than one occasion, Don Norman raised doubts about Victor Papanek's oft-quoted claim that "There are professions more harmful than industrial design, but only a very few of them." According to Norman, the motto is "well-intended but wrong: [Papanek] gives too much credit to designers who are generally too low in the power structure to matter." He adds: "Designers then (and today) are servants of their masters: Their client or employers. Design is a tool of industry, and because industry does not pay for externalities, they think nothing of destroying the environment in mining for maters (*sic*), in manufacturing, and in disposal of poisonous stuff."[229] Norman is echoed by John Maeda, design-star who popularised the idea of a *design-led* company. In 2019 he made a sobering declaration: "In reality, design is not that important." Here's his reasoning: "We know that tech people are in charge of the world: They can approve pull requests and they push the code out and right or wrong happens." Designers, far from being the centre of the design process, are ancillary to it. Would it be good, then, to change this state of affairs? Not according to Maeda, who thinks companies led by designers might achieve resonance among a design-savvy crowd, but their technical structure might be brittle, leading eventually to failure.[230] Massimo Vignelli, interviewed together

[228] Enzo Mari. "Inserzione a Pagamento." *Domus*, April 2004. It is worth pointing out that Mari still had a pretty romantic idea of the impact of design. From the ad: "A design entails a passionate alliance between two persons: a soldier of utopia (the designer) and a tiger from the real world (the entrepreneur). It is always the tiger, if he wishes, who can allow at least a fragment of utopia to be attained. Today tigers seem to be extinct." Here, Mari didn't consider the idea that the tiger of the real world, the entrepreneur, might be caged in economic imperatives.

[229] Don Norman. Emails to the PhD-Design Mailing List, August 9, 2020 and March 18, 2021.

[230] Katharine Schwab. "John Maeda: 'In Reality, Design Is Not That Important.'" *Fast*

CHAPTER 4

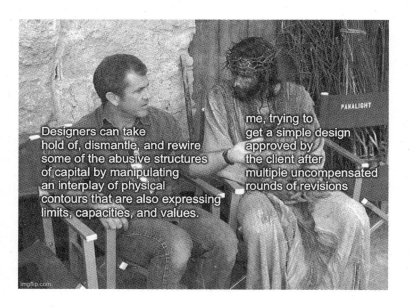

@ethicaldesign69 (2021). The meme is a sarcastic response to
a claim by Keller Easterling, represented on the left.

with his wife Lella by Barbara Radice, adds a tint of moralism to this socially determinist view – right after having bragged about their Rolls-Royce:

> [Transforming society] was always our utopia, the dream of Unimark, the reason we went to America. Until we realized that instead design cannot transform society but that it is society that determines design. There is nothing to be done. Every society has the design it deserves.[231]

So, what is the real chance of designers injecting their intentions into the design and therefore the world? First, Winner reminds us that the leeway for changing an artefact is greater when its typology is introduced for the first time: after that phase its malleability decreases and the artefact becomes stabilised. But not every designer can be a pioneer. Most will work with consolidated types of product, such as the razor. Second, the actual position of the designer in the hierarchy of an organisation matters: generally too low, according to Norman. And one can assume that the larger the structure, the more difficult it is to rise to the top.

THE HUMAN FACTOR

These accounts of design power, devoid of any trace of agency or free will, might sound depressingly deterministic. Design historian John Heskett offers an alternative point of view:

> Whether executed well or badly (on whatever basis this is judged) designs are not determined by technological processes, social structures, or economic systems, or any other objective source. They result from the decisions and choices of human beings. While the influence of context and circumstance may be considerable, the

---

Company, March 15, 2019. https://www.fastcompany.com/90320120/john-maeda-in-reality-design-is-not-that-important.

231 Massimo Vignelli and Lella Vignelli. "Emigranti di lusso." Interview by Barbara Radice. *Modo*, March 1981, p. 21. Thanks to Michele Galluzzo for this source.

> human factor is present in decisions taken at all levels of design practice. With choice comes responsibility. Choice implies alternatives in how ends can be achieved, for what purposes, and for whose advantage. It means design is not only about initial decisions or concepts by designers, but also about how these are implemented and by what means we can evaluate their effect and benefit.[232]

Heskett emphasises the multitude of choices that are made throughout the design process. These choices, as we have seen, are only partially made by designers. The "human factor" in these decisions is the very reason we should not consider this decision-making process a linear, logical one, but one that is affected by temperament, irrationality and chance. Out of the Brownian motion of all the particles involved (those who make choices) on the micro scale, a direction emerges on the macro scale. Some decisions, however, are more *decisive* than others. "Taken by whom?," Maldonado asks. He wonders about "the requirements needed to turn Design into Revolution; what power structures, existing or to come, must delegate to designers the responsibility for radically changing all the technical structures of the human environment, in a planetary-scale operation."[233] Anthony Masure, head of research at the Geneva University of Art and Design, has an answer:

> I'm not a pessimist, but I think designers have little power. I think a policy maker, for example, has a lot more impact on society. The question is why we have come to this. I think it's a problem, it's also the designers' fault. Most have relinquished power to decision-makers. Designers rarely place themselves in these decision-making

---

232 John Heskett. *Design: A Very Short Introduction*. Oxford: Oxford University Press, 2005, pp. 5-6.
233 Maldonado, *La speranza progettuale, op. cit.*, p. 58.

> positions… In France, for example, we will find relatively few designers who create businesses. We will obviously find designers in companies, but few who carry projects from scratch, who initiate or who join as partners and not as executors.[234]

Masure tends to idealise the policy maker as the figure whose decisions matter the most. This is not uncommon. Here, we can obliquely recognise the synthetic urge to determine lower processes, designing being one among them. How can designers be authentic decision-makers? One option is to become entrepreneurs, that is, to hold the decision-making reins of a project in its entirety. In the '70s Victor Papanek used the case of designers as entrepreneurs as evidence to demystify the "myth of the designer's lack of control:" the bad products that they create while controlling every aspect of the design, production and marketing, were a proof, albeit negative, of design agency.[235] Both the designer as entrepreneur and the designer as policy maker betray an isolationist attitude: a technocratic image of decision-making that hides, once again, its chaotic, conflictual and plural dimension – its politics. Obviously, there is no such thing as full control. The sum of all decisions made by managers, engineers, clients, competitors, etc. provides only a fragile and provisional synthesis. Thus, synthesis is not so much the 'product' that the designer can offer but the emergent quality of a series of political forces clashing. Free will exists, but since it is plural, it leads to indeterminate results.

POSTPARTUM

In 1993, Adam Richardson recognised not only the designers' lack of control, but also their unwillingness to admit it. He noticed an identity crisis in industrial designers

---

[234] Anthony Masure. Interview by Karl Pineau, August 2019. https://livre-ethique-numerique.designersethiques.org/content/interviews/interview-anthony_masure.html.

[235] Papanek, *op. cit.*, p. 232-3.

CHAPTER 4

Tweet by Billy Fleming (2021).

Screenshot of the website of the What Design Can Do initiative.

due to the fact that they "do not do what they generally say they do. That is, they have much less control over the process of product development than one might be led to believe by the common rhetoric. In addition, how users and cultures respond to the products which designers help create is not well understood." Richardson saw two specific limits in the way design impact is conceptualised. First, the designer's ability to shape the outcome of the design process, namely, the artefact. Second, the ability of an artefact to transforms culture *directly*, and in the way originally intended by the designer. Richardson's second point stands on semiotic grounds: inspired by Roland Barthes, he argued that every user would interpret the product differently, and shared culture would weigh on this interpretation far more than the designer's intention: "The culture-product interaction is a postpartum activity, so to speak, one that takes place after actual production." Referring to two distinct Barthesian "deaths" of the designer, Richardson showed how the designer's understanding of control is illusory:

> The issue here is that of control, or rather the illusion of having it when in fact it is in the hands of others. In the case of the first death, designers work as though they have control over the product once it enters the use-place. Although, as we have seen, this is not so. With the second death, designers are primarily passive spectators when it comes to initially deciding the function of products, and conveniently submerge this fact by stating, "I designed that."[236]

The first illusion, that of controlling meaning and interpretation is particularly present in the field of graphic design, where, for the most part, it is very difficult – if not impossible – to decipher the cultures that digest the

---

236 Adam Richardson. "The Death of the Designer." *Design Issues* 9, no. 2 (1993): 34. https://doi.org/10.2307/1511672, p. 41.

signs. As a result, cultural purposes acquire priority over cultural results. The quality of a project tends to align dangerously with its (good) intentions. This leads to a 'moralism of things,' exemplified by the irrelevance of poster competitions with social aims. Rather than 'educating the public,' these competitions seem to serve another function: to sanction the cultural and moral distance that separates designers and users.

Especially since the '90s, a novel idea of the role of design has gained momentum: the idea that design can be not just about objects or services hitting the market, but about projects acting as rhetorical devices, artefacts or scenarios meant to prove a point or mobilise conflicting worldviews. Such design outputs should make people think about and discuss relevant issues, perhaps even making them change their point of view. These products (be they speculative devices or fiction films) don't belong to the everyday life of the users but are divorced from it: they act like a commentary. This is what Bruce and Stephanie Tharp broadly call "discursive design."[237] The general framework they propose is more about the intention than the outcome of a design endeavour. Design critic Francisco Laranjo sheds lights on their emphasis on intentionality over result. Discussing Speculative Design, he highlights some key aspects of design equally applicable to the field of graphic, product and interaction design as "generation of discussion as an end in itself, reducing 'debate' to being mentioned in a press-release, a newspaper, a design blog."[238]

Such media insularity is a symptom of an excessively humanistic turn. Here, the textual production of

---

237   Bruce Tharp and Stephanie Tharp. "The 4 Fields of Industrial Design." *Core77*, January 5, 2009. https://www.core77.com/posts/12232/The-4-Fields-of-Industrial-Design-No-not-furniture-trans-consumer-electronics-n-toys-by-Bruce-M-Tharp-and-Stephanie-M-Tharp. See also Anthony Dunne and Fiona Raby. *Dunne & Raby*, 2009. http://dunneandraby.co.uk/content/bydandr/36/0. I shall return to these currents in chapter 6 and 7 to offer a theory of their popularity.

238   Francisco Laranjo. "We Don't Need Speculative Design Education, Just Better Design Education." *SpeculativeEdu*, November 17, 2020. https://speculativeedu.eu/interview-francisco-laranjo/.

speculative design is larger and more important than its artefactual counterpart, raising the suspicion that the artefact is not even necessary to the alleged generation of debate. For Daniel van der Velden, it is the very idea of debate that, in the age of platforms, vacillates:

> The structure that emerges out of the fusion of these technologies and platforms with each other and the world makes the idea of having a 'debate' seem quaintly inadequate, especially since most words lag behind the normlessness that is this structure's *de facto* governing force. In devouring the real by indexation, taxonomy, and optimization, technology platforms pre-own our critiques of them, meaning that our subjectivity and 'debates' are fully pre-included, pre-implied in their own dynamics and models.[239]

FLIPPING THE TABLE

In the last decade, designers who work with and for companies, especially in the UX field, have clamoured for a 'seat at the table.' They demand access to what they consider the true locus of decision-making. And yet, the idea of the seat at the table can be seen as a theory of power in itself, not dissimilar from that proposed by Carl Schmitt. According to the German jurist, power always relies on experts: a king is, to a certain extent, dependent on his counsellors.[240] Here, power coincide with *access to the locus of power*.

Clearly, asking for a seat implies its current absence. Design's preoccupation with decision-making can be read as a manifestation of its relative powerlessness: the one who has power doesn't ask for it. Not everyone agrees, though. According to Evan Osherow, designers are in the process of obtaining that coveted office chair:

---

239 Daniel van der Velden. "Lyrical Design." In de Vet, *op. cit.*, p. 58.
240 Carl Schmitt. *Dialogo sul potere*. Milano: Adelphi, 2012.

> We now have chief product officers. The McKinsey Design Index is a commonly known metric showing the business value of design. And the demand for UX designers is expected to continually grow.[241]

In other words, design is a factor of company growth, designers have pompous titles (and incomes) and the demand for them is expanding. This perspective is shared by Kate Aronowitz (Google Ventures): "We're making key strategic decisions and helping to shape the direction of companies. We got here because we proved design can solve big problems in a way that others cannot."[242] Daniel Burka questions these equivalences with rare frankness:

> Let's be honest. At some companies in 2020, designers make a lot of money, have important-sounding titles, and get invited to the leadership table. But even at huge companies with famous design teams, design loses many key battles when it comes to creating good user experiences. We have achieved $300,000 salaries but we have little of the power. What's the point in driving a BMW if we can't make good products for our users?[243]

It would seem that the designer's authority is recognised and remunerated as long as it aligns with the goals of the company. Put otherwise, the high bonuses and perks, more than a manifestation of design power, are a proof of the acquiescence or even complicity of designers with the cause of the company.

But what if power within an organisation doesn't

---

241 Evan Osherow. "Designers, Stop Asking for a 'Seat at the Table.'" *UX Collective* (blog), March 7, 2020. https://uxdesign.cc/designers-stop-asking-for-a-seat-at-the-table-4ab933d7037f.

242 Aronowitz quoted in Katharine Schwab. "Take The Survey: Do Designers Have A Seat At The Table?" *Fast Company*, April 25, 2018. https://www.fastcompany.com/90169455/take-the-survey-do-designers-have-a-seat-at-the-table.

243 Daniel Burka. "Mission Accomplished? The Hard Work of Design Is Still Ahead of Us." *Thinking Design* (blog), July 9, 2020. https://medium.com/thinking-design/mission-accomplished-the-hard-work-of-design-is-still-ahead-of-us-a4e47e5a0c8c.

coincide with the authority and prestige it gives? What if having power doesn't mean just having the possibility to take part in the conversations that lead to decision-making, but to *oppose* a decision altogether? An understanding of power as such is intrinsically conflictual, agonistic, if not antagonistic. Is power always confrontational? Is true power the power to veto? In a Twitter conversation, user @maetl quipped:

> In design leadership conversations for years, there was a thing about 'design needing a seat at the table' in orgs and governance – in hindsight this was all wrong, and the conversation should have been about flipping the table.[244]

TAKE HOLD, DISMANTLE, REWIRE

Claiming design's power through intricate formulations, some academics end up causing a sense of detachment among practitioners. Symptomatic of this approach is the latest book by urbanist Keller Easterling, entitled *Medium Design*. Here, the designing activity is extended to encompass activism, spatial organisation and politics. A quote from an article summarising the book's argument provoked a small social media stir:

> Designers can take hold of, dismantle, and rewire some of the abusive structures of capital by manipulating an interplay of physical contours that are also expressing limits, capacities, and values.[245]

Twitter meme account @ethicaldesign69,[246] who can be considered the most inventive public voice of design disillusion, matched the quote with "me trying to get a simple design approved by the client after multiple

---

244 https://twitter.com/maetl/status/1432190569854345216.
245 Keller Easterling. "On Political Temperament." *The Double Negative*, January 18, 2021. http://www.thedoublenegative.co.uk/2021/01/on-political-temperament-keller-easterling/.
246 At the time @neurotic_arsehole.

uncompensated rounds of revisions" in a gruesome template derived from the backstage of Mel Gibson's *The Passion of the Christ*. The meme went relatively viral.

Despite its abstruseness, Easterling's statement makes sense. Abusive capitalist structures can be curbed and mutated. Designers are indeed able to intervene. The issue here is not one of veracity but one of rhetoric: the grand statement that – if you're honest to yourself – can only make you feel pretty small. The register of the quote doesn't match the register of everyday life, except if your everyday life is mostly made of design conferences. The meme derives its strength from the distance that separates expectations from reality.

Another meme inverts Keller Easterling's point. Here, we see the Suez Canal blocked by a colossal container ship (representing Capital), while a small excavator (design) has been sent to unstuck it. The allegory could have served as an illustration for Kevin Rogan's review of Easterling's book: "The medium designer does not exist and never will exist; capital executes the plan and the designer must dance along as they always have." The medium designer is, according to Rogan, a theoretical fiction, one used to empower the author rather than the architectural field.[247]

Who's right? It seems that ideas about design's power are more a matter of attitude than analysis – a matter of optimism. Antonio Gramsci famously said: "I'm a pessimist because of intelligence, but an optimist because of will." Here, we have a peculiar reversal: infusing intelligence with optimism, as academics and practitioners often do, unwittingly spurs a pessimism of the will.

THE DESIGN AND THE PLAN

At this point, it is useful to make a distinction. According to Indian-American anthropologist Arjun Appadurai, the

---

247 Kevin Rogan. "Keller Easterling's Medium Design Ignores the Role of Power in Design." *The Architect's Newspaper*, February 22, 2021. https://www.archpaper.com/2021/02/keller-easterling-medium-design-review/.

categories of design and planning share many similarities: they're both "as old as humanity," they both are linked to a "universal inclination to utopias," they both relate to "the fear of disaster and dislocation." But they also differ – design is rooted in the explosion of industry and the growth of markets, while planning is linked to the goals and ambitions of the state. This is how Appadurai understands the separation between planning and design:

> Planning is more explicitly concerned with sustainability – both social and environmental – than design, and so it has a regulatory relationship to design, just as design has a regulatory relationship to fashion.[248]

Admittedly, it is not easy to make an essential distinction between designing and planning. It is tempting to assign a social value to the plan and a technical value to the design, but that would be a mistake, since any social decision is a technical one and "technology is society made durable."[249] Instead, we could simply posit a hierarchical relationship: the plan rules over the design. In such case, we need to add a political component, more evident in planning than in design. Our current masterplan is not even run by a human entity, but dictated by the highly dynamic machinic assemblage we call capitalism.[250] In this scenario, we can think of designing and planning in terms of strategy and tactics. The plan is not the cumulative result of various

---

[248] Arjun Appadurai. *The Future as Cultural Fact: Essays on the Global Condition.* London: Verso, 2013, p. 266.

[249] Bruno Latour. "Technology Is Society Made Durable." *The Sociological Review* 38, no. 1 (May 1, 1990): 103–31. https://doi.org/10.1111/j.1467-954X.1990.tb03350.x.

[250] "In collecting goods and people from around the world, capitalism itself has the characteristic of an assemblage. However, it seems to me that capitalism also has characteristics of a machine, a contraption limited to the sum of its parts. This machine is not a total institution, which we spend our life inside; instead it translates across living arrangements, turning worlds into assets. But not just any translation can be accepted into capitalism. The gathering it sponsors is not open-ended. An army of technicians and managers stand by to remove offending parts – and they have the power of courts and guns. This does not mean that the machine has a static form." Anna Lowenhaupt Tsing. *The Mushroom at the End of the World: On the Possibility of Life in Capitalist Ruins.* Princeton, NJ: Princeton University Press, 2021, p. 133.

designs, but the force able to select certain designs by excluding others. The plan consists of an impersonal strategy, while design is a personal tactic. According to Michel de Certeau, tactics are deployed by those who do not possess a full view of the strategic field.[251] In the case of design, it is not the view that is lacking, but the means to engage with the perceived field. This is the tragic state of design: seeing the field but not being able to modify it.

A relational understanding of design power can now be provided: designers might exert a certain influence over the *design* but they generally have little or no control over the *plan*. As the plan governs the design by structuring its field of action,[252] the plan is intrinsically unchangeable by the design; what is more: the design is a product and a function of the plan. Whereas design is a pawn, the plan is the chessboard. The plan, as Appadurai puts it, "limits the infinitude" of the design.[253] In order to change the plan, design cannot remain design. It has to enter the chaotic realm of agonism and antagonism. That of the plan is an "uneasy space" where action evolves into political action, be that in the form of activism, protest, revolt, etc. In other words, design needs to transubstantiate into a counter-plan, which will in turn generate new designs.

The designer who plots a counterplan is, while doing so, not a designer: they may be a citizen, a politician, a terrorist, an activist, a lobbyist, etc., namely, a political actor. They become a designer again when deploying the plan through design. Trying to get hold of the plan means

---

251 Langdon Winner mentions two types of choice when it comes to work with new technology. The first is a binary one: should it be developed in the first place? Yes or no. The second has to do with the way in which such technology should be developed. The former is normally out of the designers' scope, while the latter is within their purview: designers aren't asked *if* something should be done or not, they are asked *how* such a thing should be done. The first question is a matter of the plan, which can be in the hands of authorities like the firm or the state; the second relates to the design, which can be, to a certain extent, in the hands of the designer, unless the designer doesn't actively operate to obstruct the plan. Winner, *op. cit.*, p. 127.
252 Here, I'm borrowing Michel Foucault's notion of governmentality. For a basic introduction, see https://en.wikipedia.org/wiki/Governmentality.
253 Appadurai, *op. cit.*, p. 265.

setting aside one's profession. Maldonado was interested in how to change the world without changing one's job.[254] The relationship between the plan and the design suggests that to do so one needs to transcend the profession, as the profession is governed by the plan.

DAMNED IF YOU DO, DAMNED IF YOU DON'T

Designers rarely exert power as a direct form of command (the instructions they formulate as blueprints, prototypes, etc. are always prone to negotiation and to the final say of the client), so they often speak of their power indirectly, by means of its implication. The keyword is "responsibility." In fact, the most memorable aphoristic legacy from Spiderman's uncle, namely, that "with great power comes great responsibility," is frequently heard during public design events. Here, responsibility implies power. So, a rhetoric of responsibility can be understood as a form of 'power signalling,' or even "hero bait."[255] In the '70s, German philosopher Wolfgang Fritz Haug attributed an "exaggerated illusion of use-value" to commodities,[256] but the same can be said of the design field as a whole. Consider designer Mike Monteiro's *Ruined by Design*. Monteiro opens his book on design ethics with the following statement:

> Design is a craft with responsibility. The responsibility to help create a better world for all. Design is also a craft with a lot of blood on its hands. Every cigarette ad is on us. Every gun is on us. Every ballot that a voter cannot understand is on us.[257]

---

[254] Maldonado, *La speranza progettuale, op. cit.*, p. 124.
[255] "Even though the books that they promote are likely more nuanced, the claims have been reduced to a power promise, divorced from any limits or doubts. Let's call them hero bait – invitations to play the role of a saviour, carefully crafted for a designer who feels stuck at their desk doing non-meaningful work." Gijs de Boer. "Between Fox Traps and Hero Bait." *Design Drafts*, no. 1 (2023).
[256] Haug, *op. cit.*, p. 36.
[257] Mike Monteiro. *Ruined by Design: How Designers Destroyed the World, and What We Can Do to Fix It*. San Francisco, CA: Mule Design, 2019.

FLIPPING THE TABLE

Critical Graphic Design (2015).

Who actually is this "us?" That's not very clear, since the author, following Jared Spools, argues that "[a]nyone who influences what the design becomes is the designer."[258] Such a generalisation avoids the fundamental question of the *specific* power that design has and justifies the examples of good and evil the author gives in the book: almost none of them involve designers *stricto sensu*.[259] Thus, his appeal to an ethical conduct becomes a generic one, one that masks hierarchies and relations of authority. It could even be read as a way to please the readership by granting them a potency that they (individually, as designers) don't have. In fact, the solution provided by Monteiro, when the company for which the designer works is crooked beyond repair, is to quit.

This is a not unusual example of self-aggrandisement by over-responsibilisation, an idealised narrative that sees design more as an individual moral framework than a practical philosophy. The logic is akin to that of ethical consumption, where the centrality of individual ethics compensates for design's subordination. Undoubtedly, the designer affects the world with their work and their choices, but this generally happens in unspectacular ways which wouldn't be worthy of the Spiderverse. Indeed, most designers concur that the quality of their work depends solely on the extent to which the client allows it.[260]

While studying schizophrenia, Gregory Bateson and his colleagues developed the concept of the double bind. This takes place when a figure of authority makes an injunction on the subject while implicitly expressing a secondary demand that contradicts the primary one: "damned if you do, damned if you don't."[261] In our case, the pri-

---

258 https://twitter.com/jmspool/status/836955987860914176.
259 Among the cases of virtue: a doctor halting the distribution of a painkiller with tremendous side effects; among those of wrongdoing, an engineer's complicity in the 2015 Volkswagen emissions scandal.
260 From *Graphic Designers Surveyed*, to the question "Is it true that your work is only as good as your client will let it be?" 62% of the respondents agreed, *op. cit.*, p. 288.
261 Gregory Bateson, Don D. Jackson, Jay Haley, and John Weakland. "Toward a

mary injunction is to design ethically, while the secondary one is dependent on daily requirements of the job that leave no room for any kind of ethical consideration. The result "leaves the subject torn both ways, so that whichever demand they try to meet, the other demand cannot be met. 'I must do it, but I can't do it' is a typical description of the double-bind experience."[262] On the one hand, designers are told that their work has a profound, terrible impact on society; on the other hand, society utilises them as "mere executors of strategic decisions made well before they were employed."[263] To understand design disillusion in this context, we can implement Expectation confirmation theory (ECT): our satisfaction with a product or a service is not absolute, but relative to what we expect from it: a product is good when it positively exceeds our expectations.[264] So, if our expectation as designers is to save the world, we get disappointed when all we are asked to do is make the logo bigger.

Chermayeff & Geismar – who have done branding for oil companies, banks and pharmaceutical companies – explain their view on corporate identity design as follows:

> When we create a great logo for an environmental organization, we do not see ourselves as saving the planet. In the same way, we cannot take responsibility for the 'evil' actions of corporations we brand.[265]

While this might sound like a dismissal of complicity, it could also be read as a sober understanding of design

---

Theory of Schizophrenia." *Behavioral Science* 1, no. 4 (1956): 251–64. https://doi.org/10.1002/bs.3830010402.
262 https://en.wikipedia.org/wiki/Double_bind.
263 Gerritzen and Lovink, *Made in China...*, *op. cit.*, p. 57.
264 See Richard L. Oliver. "Effect of Expectation and Disconfirmation on Postexposure Product Evaluations: An Alternative Interpretation." *Journal of Applied Psychology* 62, no. 4 (1977): 480–86. https://doi.org/10.1037/0021-9010.62.4.480.
265 Aaron Kenedi. "Marks Men: An Interview With Ivan Chermayeff, Tom Geismar, and Sagi Haviv of Chermayeff & Geism." *Print*, September 14, 2011. https://www.printmag.com/designer-interviews/marks-men-an-interview-with-ivan-chermayeff-tom-geismar-and-sagi-haviv-of-chermayeff-geismar/.

power. Is a studio that hasn't worked for any problematic organisations irreproachable? Or did they simply never receive an unethical brief? Does a rhetorical display of virtue conceal powerlessness and detachment? When there is no chance to 'sin,' the issue of responsibility can become an indirect form of self-congratulation.

One of the main issues of responsibility is that it is hard to pinpoint. Philosopher Vilém Flusser understood this well:

> The division of labor has as a result the impossibility to assign responsibility to any one of the people involved in the process. If a robot kills, who shall be held responsible: the designer of the robot, of the knife [held by the robot], or the man who has calculated the robot program? It is not possible to ascribe ethical responsibility to some error in design, in programming, or in production. And what about assigning the ethical responsibility to the industry that produced the robot, or the whole industrial complex, or finally the whole system of which that complex is part and parcel?

While he pointed out the complexity of conceiving a design ethics, he believed in its necessity: "unless some kind of ethics in industrial design be elaborated, total ethical irresponsibility will follow."[266]

DESIGN ETHICS? NO THANKS!

In a talk given at IxDA Budapest in 2020, Berlin-based designer Cade Diehm questions the design ethics frameworks that consider the ills of a technology as the direct result of decisions made by a designer or a design team. Designers who adopt such frameworks insist on a responsibility to assess their own motivations over what they choose to build.[267] The limit of this approach derives,

---

[266] Vilém Flusser. "Ethics in Industrial Design?," March 20, 1991. Transcript of a talk given at the Eindhoven symposium.
[267] https://vimeo.com/483988793.

according to Diehm, from its reliance on dubious notions of consent and inclusion. Emphasising the former means involving users in decision making, but informed consent, even when powered by a seamless user interface, "crumbles at scale:" there are simply too many intertwined systems with their own legal and technical complexities (such as terms of service and privacy settings) to take into account. Similarly, the notion of inclusion in a certain kind of technology doesn't take into consideration the actual political power to opt out of it.

Diehm gives the example of biometric data gathering. While the inclusive perspective focused on issues of representations (namely, the racial bias of facial recognition systems), the 2019 Hong Kong protests showed its failure: the only possible way for the protesters to avoid surveillance was a Luddite one: tear down the poles equipped with sensors and cameras. It appears, then, that agency and power are more concrete when expressed negatively: power, here, is the power to prevent, the agency of *not* doing something.

For Diehm, design ethics is a form of reductionism "that allows designers to escape the scrutiny of their work." It's a simplistic answer given to Flusser's complex questions. Not unlike Guy Julier's idea of design as a laxative,[268] Diehm sees technology as an "accelerant" which makes societal problems metastasise through quick fixes that, counterintuitively, *impede* change. Therefore, he invites us to reject the seductive image of design ethics, as it masks the ongoing trajectories that designers follow, consciously or not.[269]

---

268 Julier, *op. cit.*, p. 174.
269 Similarly, Susanne Bødker and Morten Kyng find the excessive focus on ethics within the field of Participatory Design troublesome. They write: "We find the issues of how researchers should behave, ethical issues, important. At the same time, we find it problematic that politics has been reduced to how researchers should behave and act fairly when involving users in projects. We would argue that politics is more than fairness and ethics, and we hypothesize that the tendency to avoid profound conflicts also makes it difficult for current PD to engage in some of the more controversial areas where researchers could really help people by taking side with them." See "Participatory Design That Matters –

CHAPTER 4

BAD BOYS

In a time when modernity manifests its tragic shortcomings, designers' emphasis on responsibility and ethics is increasingly linked to design's culpability. Designers have exhumed the *confiteor:* "mea culpa," they utter. The international organisation What Design Can Do, known for its social design initiatives, exemplifies this attitude. "I've been a bad designer" is the motto of its No Waste Challenge. Here, a group of renowned designers and design theorists from around the globe confess that they have contributed to waste and pollution, like naughty kids apologising for their mischief.[270] Under the influence of capitalism, design has adopted a "new spirit" that enables it to capitalise on the criticism it receives: design actively assimilates accountability and converts it into a form of self-reflective sentimentality associated with a sense of responsibility.

There is a parallel with the world of tech. A counter-narrative, popularly dubbed *techlash*, is emerging around digital platforms. It stands in opposition to the messianic narrative of Big Tech amplified by the media throughout the '10s. Here, mistakes are acknowledged. Careers are built out of an anti-tech evangelism and boosted by public acts of atonement. The irony is that these negative evangelists are often the very same people at the top of the professional elite ladder, now repentant. If it's true that, as Beatriz Colomina and Mark Wigley point out, design has always been a pedagogic and moralising project, it now acquires the double role of the judge and the culprit.[271] A strange disassociation takes place, where design is simultaneously the good force and the evil one. This circularity is perfectly exemplified by a statement in an Arte documentary entitled, *ça va sans dire*, The Power of Design:

Facing the Big Issues." *ACM Transactions on Computer-Human Interaction* 25, no. 1 (February 13, 2018): 4:1-4:31. https://doi.org/10.1145/3152421, p. 9.
[270] https://www.whatdesigncando.com/stories/havent-we-all-been-bad-designers/.
[271] Colomina and Wigley, *op. cit.*, p. 77.

Many designers today agree: that design is partly to blame for our current problems, and that the solutions to these problems should come from design.[272]

POWER USERS

The amplification of potency granted by technics complicates the question of power. As Carl Schmitt points out, power exceeds the one who holds it, whoever they may be. Power is an autonomous force – a Leviathan. What most people refer to when they speak of the power of design, is actually the power of technics, which has grown immensely since the beginning of modernity and is largely independent from the will of the people who make use of it. Because of the division of labour, the humblest of designers cannot help but contributing, at least indirectly, to 'earth-shattering' endeavours. This is why we shouldn't confuse the autonomous, leviathanic power of technics within modernity (in Spinozian terms, *potentia*) with the indirect power held by the designer (*potestas*) which has to do with proximity to the locus of direct power.[273]

This chapter began with a military analogy: an army of commodities, shaped by the designer, that enter the market and drastically change the life of consumers. What if, when it comes to design power, it is still that way? Everyday designers are, after all, themselves consumers: reflex cameras, ergonomic mice, Pantone mugs, etc. Most of these items – in particular the Apple devices – provide both the tools of trade and a mythology of good design (which, as we have seen, is now in decline). What if the designers' multitude is defined more by their lifestyle-oriented equipment than the actual work they do with it? The MacBook can then be seen as the Ford T of the everyday designer: a product with a massive concrete and imaginative presence

---

[272] Reinhild Dettmer-Finke (director). "The Power of Design." *Arte*, 2021.
[273] Gilles Deleuze. *Spinoza: Practical Philosophy*. City Lights Books, 1988, p. 97.

CHAPTER 4

Poster by Valerio Nicoletti (2023) that shows the pyramid of power in design.

spreading the gospel of impact and creativity. From this point of view, design culture appears highly shaped by the dynamics of prosumerism (production as consumption). A depressing suspicion arises: for all the talk about design's role in society, the big-scale impact on the world left by designers as a demographic cohort might lie less in the design work they do than in the consumer choices they make; the laptop they buy counting more than the poster they design with it.

So, power becomes merely a brand idea. However, an idea that is frighteningly similar to the professional narrative of the power of design. Is design culture itself a product to sell? In an issue of *C Mag* on graphic design, curators Chris Lee and Ali S. Qadeer notice that one of the main ways in which design relates to power is by obfuscating its relationships.[274] We can argue that the general framework of professional discourse contributes to this obfuscation, concealing the power relationships in which designers themselves are enmeshed. In certain cases, then, quitting not only the job, but the profession, becomes the only viable solution. This would show that when designers have no power *as designers*, they might do as workers and perhaps citizens.

---

274 Chris Lee and Ali S. Qadeer. "Editorial." *C Mag*, 2019, p. 10.

Part II. Reality

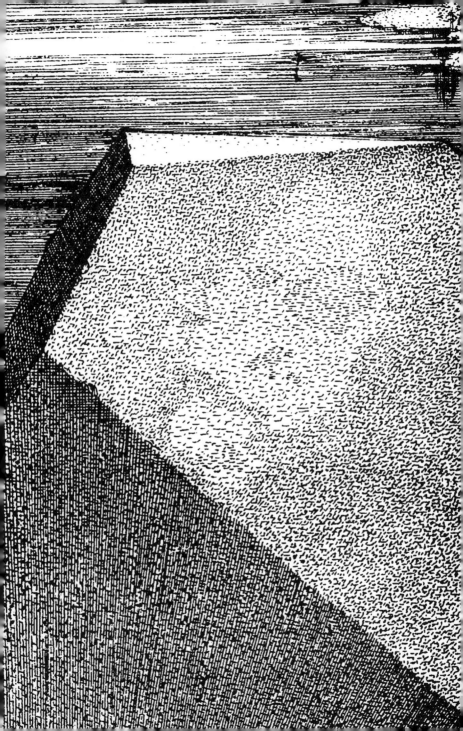

Chapter 5.

Form Follows Format:
On Semi-Automation and Cultural Professionalism

"I see graphic design as something that began in the 1920s and died in 2008. It doesn't exist anymore. And the reason it doesn't exist is because it's completely infiltrated everything."
– Michael Rock, 2021[275]

"Wouldn't it be better if websites just made themselves?"
– The Grid, 2014[276]

"What if – hear me out – WE are the Design Tools"
– @ktsuskin, 2019[277]

You are on the subway. Look at all these people staring at their phones. What are they doing? This woman is chatting, that guy is mindlessly playing Candy Crush, and then there are these kids crafting visual content for social media like Instagram, Twitter, TikTok. Using pretty powerful editing apps, they're creating compositions, correcting colours, tweaking typography, adding stickers and animations. In other words, they are *designing*. And not in a vague, generic sense: they are performing the very same activity as that of a graphic designer, that is, manipulating symbols and pushing pixels around – using just their thumbs.

Sure, "design is a job,"[278] but one could convincingly argue that today the bulk of the designing is performed by casual users – who don't even call it 'design'! The increasingly common availability of digital tools has been crucial in this respect: not only did it create a more subtle awareness of

---

275 Rock quoted in Jarrett Fuller. "Design Criticism Is Everywhere – Why Are We Still Looking For It?" *Eye on Design*, August 19, 2020. https://eyeondesign.aiga.org/design-criticism-is-everywhere-why-are-we-still-looking-for-it/.
276 https://www.youtube.com/watch?v=OXA4-5x31Vo. See also https://www.pagecloud.com/blog/what-happened-to-the-grid.
277 https://twitter.com/ktsuskin/status/1159851862201442304.
278 As the title of a Mike Monteiro book. *Design Is a Job*. New York: A Book Apart, 2012.

design culture in the layperson, but it also altered the perception of the designers' status and, in turn, their relationship to visual culture as a whole. When, in the late '80s, the desktop publishing revolution took place, the designers' reaction was mainly a defensive one against the new barbarians, that is, clueless non-professionals that were quickly catching up. "One of the great fears attached to the advent of the Macintosh and desktop publishing – explains Michael Rock – is that it has initiated others into our secret language; demystified our code of fonts, rags, picas, and leading."[279] This secret language was being converted into a function crystallised in software: (graphic) design had become semi-automated. With this shift, designers' authoritativeness was partially eroded: the semi-automated designer also became a semi-professional one. Speaking about programmers, Ellen Ullman brutally describes the effects of professional demystification: "If regular people, called 'users,' can understand the task accomplished by your program, you will be paid less and held in lower esteem."[280]

A minority of designers, however, were able to escape this fate by gaining the role of cultural producers who highlight and interpret visual culture, and in particular the emerging technical vernacular. Among them, prominent designers such as April Greiman, Zuzana Licko and Rudy VanderLans took up the role of "interpreter and mediator of the social meaning of technology"[281] and helped popularise the aesthetics of the new digital means of production among professionals. The Macintosh brought with it an apparent liberation from the material constraints of layout resulting in a Derridean ethos of non-linearity and deconstruction. The effect was often confusing and sometimes consciously uninviting. A "cult of the ugly" was

---

279   Michael Rock. "On Unprofessionalism." *2x4* (blog), August 5, 1994. https://2x4.org/ideas/1994/on-unprofessionalism/.
280   Ellen Ullman. *Life in Code: A Personal History of Technology*. New York: Picador, 2018, p. 8.
281   Emily McVarish. *Inflection Point*. Berkeley, CA: Emigre, 2017, p. 8.

Sponsored Instagram post for the Adobe Spark app.

formed, as design historian Steven Heller called it.[282] It was time to break the grid, let go of rules, defy tradition. Licko and VanderLans dedicated the 11th issue of their magazine *Emigre* to the relationship between graphic designers and the Macintosh. Analysing the issue, Emily McVarish argues that Emigre's vision of authorship didn't "stake its claim in self-defense against amateur incursions into graphic design's professional territory."[283] In fact, there was no need to do so: amateurs didn't threaten professionals because they were there to be *interpreted*.

Things didn't stop there. From the early 2000s to the present day, various practitioners, inspired by the internet, began adopting the presets, templates and defaults inscribed in desktop publishing and web browsers. Their intervention was minimal. By removing themselves from the typographical equation, designers would show that non-design was itself design, one that was taking place before anyone's actions and had its own aesthetic autonomy. Designer and writer Rob Giampietro dubbed this phenomenon "Default System Design:"

> Default Systems are machines for design creation, and they represent design publicly as an "automatic" art form, offering a release from the breathless pace at which design now runs, as clients ask for more, quicker, now. Default Systems are a number of trends present in current graphic design that exploit computer presets in an industry-wide fashion. They are a quasi-simplistic rule-set, often cribbing elements from the International Style in a kind of glossy pastiche, a cult of sameness driven by the laziness and comfort of the technology that enabled Emigre's rise, the Macintosh.[284]

---

282 Steven Heller. "Cult of the Ugly." *Eye Magazine*, 1993. https://www.eyemagazine.com/feature/article/cult-of-the-ugly.
283 McVarish, *op. cit.*, p. 16.
284 Rob Giampietro and Rudy VanderLans. "Default Systems in Graphic Design." *Emigre*,

FORM FOLLOWS FORMAT

Artwork for *The Life of Pablo* album by Kanye West. Here's how *The Verge* described it: "Designed (typed?) by the Belgian artist Peter De Potter, the post-modern cover features The Life of Pablo in all caps and a small family photo in the bottom corner."

Designers working with Default Systems would deliberately use 'neutral' fonts like Helvetica or default ones like Arial and Times New Roman. Or they would keep the default treatment of web hyperlinks. Or exaggerate ridge borders with CSS. Or indulge in the use of WordArt effects. To the untrained eye, their work is often indistinguishable from that of amateurs. More recently, they would make use of what Silvia Sfligiotti calls *auto-tune typography*, an approach that "transforms words into undifferentiated blocks that can be placed on a page without worrying too much [and] turns visual design into an automatic, a-critical activity."[285] In the context of the internet, terms like 'brutalism' are employed and sometimes nostalgia plays a role. Finally, appearing is a quirky, poetic web design avantgarde that sees HTML tags more as a semiotic text than a merely practical set of rules.[286]

For the defaultists, "form follows format," as designer Hendrik-Jan Grievink put it.[287] That's how template culture comes about, where every new project actually derives from a long sequence of previous projects. When I open Word or InDesign, I run into a template since the page, only apparently blank, already contains a series of design choices registered in advance, such as the margins' width. Why waste time on design decisions when one can celebrate the aprioristic purity of the template? Perhaps, this is the most authentic embodiment of the passion for systems that permeates the modernist ideology. British designer Daniel Eatock epitomised this trend with his generic *Utilitarian Poster* that could be used for any type of event. Resembling a bureaucratic form, it includes boxes for the event's title, description, date, etc. In the 1952 dystopian novel *Player Piano*, Kurt Vonnegut depicts an almost

---

2003. https://linedandunlined.com/archive/default-systems-in-graphic-design/.
[285] Silvia Sfligiotti. "This Is Auto-Tune Typography." *Medium* (blog), August 19, 2020. https://silviasfligiotti.medium.com/this-is-auto-tune-typography-3953e74cc2ac.
[286] See https://brutalistwebsites.com/ and https://html.energy/.
[287] Hendrik-Jan Grievink. "Template Culture." *Mediamatic*, 2009. http://www.mediamatic.net/en/page/116348/template-culture.

Hacking	Defaults
Hacking a Nintendo cartridge to make images	Using MS Paint to make images
	12 point Times New Roman
Net.Art 1.0	???
Anxiety	Banality
"The Man is taking away our privacy... that's lame!"	"We willingly give up our own privacy (i.e. endlessly talking about ourselves on our Myspace profiles)... why?"
Empowering The People by subverting The Man's power	Being and critiquing The People by using the tools made by The Man
Rock & Roll attitude	Exuberant humility
Jodi's blogs	Tom Moody's blog
Sophisticated breaking of technology	Semi-naive, regular use of technology

Guthrie Lonergan (2007).

wholly automated society where it is sufficient to record the movements of a worker on a disk to ensure that the machine will endlessly repeat them with complete accuracy. As in Vonnegut's novel, Eatock has 'recorded' his design choices and, from the point of view of mere production, made himself obsolete.

MIDAS TOUCH

According to Giampietro, both '90s Ugly Design and 2000s Defaultism were rooted in the personal computer:

> Default Systems design claims, "This is how the computer works with minimal intervention." It also claims, "By keeping the designer from intervening, this design language is made available to all." So Default Systems look new, but they arise from the social concerns of the old.[288]

While most designers would immediately alter the setting to reinstate their personality into the work, the postmodernists would push them to their extreme. Defaultists, instead, would treat them as *objet trouvé*, as something that acquires value insofar as it is picked up by a charismatic figure – the designer. Both the maximalist approach of Ugly Design and the minimalist one of Defaultism spoke enthusiastically of the broad availability of a digitally-informed design language. "We are the primitives of a new technological era," the *Emigre* duo proclaimed. However, they ignored that such language was in the process of being made available to all *in the first place*. It was starting to populate the common imaginary ('photoshop' being not just a software, but a verb), regardless of the designer's role and intention. Both Ugly Design and Defaultism attempted to impress their mark on the design language of software. The expectation was one of control and recuperation but, in the meantime, graphic design was becoming an autonomous *Kulturtechnik*, a daily practice

---

288 Giampietro and VanderLans, *op. cit.*

that doesn't need the mediation of experts, akin to taking pictures with a mobile phone.[289]

Giampietro argued that the value of both postmodernists and defaultists's artefacts lays in a "critique of the conditions of their own making."[290] While doing so, though, they also foregrounded a position of cultural arbitrage held by the designer. "Ugliness is smart," opined Heller.[291] Their aesthetics of the technical is at the same time a form of subsumption: art and design elevate technology by injecting it with meaning. This interpretative web forms an invisible threshold around tools and objects. Both the 'template apologist' and the 'layout grammatologist' are cultural professionals. They possess a sort of Midas touch: through their interpretative work, they're capable of turning the mundane into culture. In this way, the cultural professional gains the legitimacy to operate 'unprofessionally,' that is, to venture into the sphere of the ordinary and make something extraordinary with it. The cultural professional is, therefore, a special kind of *amateur*, one who is paid for their *amour*. They're equidistant from the stiff flannel-suited *cadre* and the unpaid dabbler. That's a coveted position to be in, as design historian Chiara Alessi suggests: "designers today are proving to be agents more of the cultural industry than the manufacturing one."[292]

THE GRID

Whereas the Cult of the Ugly was about breaking the grid, and Default Systems are about exposing it, digital platforms have managed to bring the grid (understood here as a set of rules, formats, templates, presets) to a level

---

289 The concept was suggested to me by German artist Sebastian Schmieg, whom I thank.
290 Giampietro and VanderLans, *op. cit.*
291 Heller, *op. cit.*
292 Chiara Alessi. *Design senza designer*. Bari: Laterza, 2016, p. 98. Designers are not alone in their desire to be cultural professionals. Such desire is widespread and commodified under the mandate of being creative, which is propagandised, for instance, by Apple (MacBook *Pro*).

CHAPTER 5

⟨ Ad World (27-29th Oct 2021 / Online)

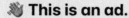 **This is an ad.**

Created by a copywriter & creative strategist*

Plus data from our previous ads.

We expect this ad to generate a flood of sales.

If it doesn't, we will...
Revise it.
Edit it.
Optimise it until it does.

We learned this creative process at Ad World.

Come and learn 100s of advertising lessons.
Meet with 70,000 industry experts next month.
Oct 27-29th

See you there!

*No designer required for this ad

Ad for Ad World event (2021). Made with the Apple's default Notes app, it insists on the lack of any need for a designer.

of omnipresence and, thus, invisibility. Once platforms start mediating content dissemination, the type of content itself, be it modernist, postmodernist or defaultist, becomes irrelevant. According to Daniel van der Velden, "design has externalized its grid function (an element that used to 'stand for' its social ambitions and responsibilities) to the platform while it has itself become that platform's liquid contents."[293] The platform's grid is not just a set of visual proportions but a dynamic structure for organising information, a *medium*. One that generates the very tools that are meant to fill it: photo and video editors, cropping utilities, sorting algorithms, etc.

The defaultist and postmodernist 'authorial capture' of the grid (by means of breaking or highlighting it) was a response to the abstraction of the designer's role, now turned into a process. Today, some twenty years later, not a day goes by without someone wondering if the designer will be made obsolete by artificial intelligence.[294] According to an ultra-cited and now classic 2013 study, 47% of the jobs performed in the US are put at risk by computerisation.[295] The study includes a ranking of about 700 professions ordered by probability of automation in ascending order. Graphic design occupies the 161st place. Not so bad.

Giampietro argued that "[t]o view a computer through its default settings is to view it as it's been programmed to view itself, even to give it a kind of authority."[296] This

---

293   Van der Velden, "Lyrical Design," *op. cit.*, p. 61.
294   See, for instance, Rob Peart. "Automation Threatens to Make Graphic Designers Obsolete." *Eye on Design*, October 25, 2016. https://eyeondesign.aiga.org/automation-threatens-to-make-graphic-designers-obsolete/; Jon Gold. "Taking The Robots To Design School." *Jon Gold* (blog), May 25, 2016. https://web.archive.org/web/20160525193649/http://www.jon.gold/2016/05/robot-design-school/; Tone Bratteteig and Guri Verne. "Does AI Make PD Obsolete? Exploring Challenges from Artificial Intelligence to Participatory Design." In Proceedings of the 15th Participatory Design Conference - Volume 2, 1–5. PDC '18. New York, NY, USA: Association for Computing Machinery, 2018. https://doi.org/10.1145/3210604.3210646.
295   Carl Benedikt Frey and Michael A. Osborne. "The Future of Employment: How Susceptible Are Jobs to Computerisation?" *Technological Forecasting and Social Change* 114, no. C (2017): 254–80.
296   Giampietro and VanderLans, *op. cit.*

CHAPTER 5

authoritative personification of the machine is the narrative that is driving today's frenzy about artificial intelligence applied to design. While the designer becomes a process, artificial intelligence is turned into a person. A case in point is The Grid, an AI-powered system to automatically design websites, announced in 2014 and never actually launched. The Grid had its own personified AI, a bot called Molly, portrayed as someone that is "quirky, but will never ghost you, never charge more, never miss a deadline, never cower to your demands for a bigger logo."[297] After raising a huge amount of money with crowdfunding, The Grid went silent. Currently, their website still promises the release of a third version after the demise of version 2, while a ticker tape reads "AI was the easy part."

Scholars point out that "artificial intelligence is a topic that is perceived between great euphoria and pure dystopia, and on the technical level between surprising functionality and frustrating technical failure."[298] This is not only true for the field of graphic design. Tools like IKEA Place, LiveHome3D or Planner 5D facilitate the work of interior design and are deliberately targeted at amateurs ("Use Planner 5D for your interior house design needs without any professional skills").[299] Most systems boast about their artificial intelligence capabilities, like Leaperr, "an Artificial Intelligence (AI) system that does the job of an interior designer."[300]

The lesson to be learned from The Grid and similar AI tools is not just that full automation, in the field of design as in many others, is difficult and perhaps unattainable, but that it nonetheless reinforces social expectations and

297   Ritupriya Basu. "Algorithms Are a Designer's New BFF – Here's Proof." *Eye on Design*, December 19, 2019. https://eyeondesign.aiga.org/algorithms-are-a-designers-new-bff-heres-proof/.
298   Klaus Neuburg, Sven Quadflieg and Simon Nestler. "Will Artificial Intelligence Make Designers Obsolete?" Berlin, 2020.
299   https://planner5d.com.
300   Harshajit Sarmah. "5 AI-Powered Home And Interior Designing Tools." *Analytics India Magazine*, July 26, 2019. https://analyticsindiamag.com/5-ai-powered-home-and-interior-designing-tools/.

desires. People want to believe that designers, like any other gatekeeper, are replaceable by a docile machine, as this has partly already happened with the personal computer. But, whereas the desktop publishing revolution offered static presets, AI makes them dynamic, updating them on the basis of new collected information – an ever-evolving defaultism.

The Duchampian gesture of 'signing' the system by letting it run without intervention is now paralleled by the designer's ambition to occupy the control room of AI in order to "set parameters and constraints, determine behaviour of automated systems," as Microsoft puts it.[301] The designer aims at becoming a systematist, because it is at the level of systems that synthesis can really happen.[302] Below, things are not so interesting: "what may be a delightfully stimulating plaything for the systems designer, may be the basis for a dehumanised work environment for the user."[303] If defaultists make themselves invisible by means of their lack of intervention, system designers would become invisible by defining the system's variables.

SEMI-AUTOMATION

That of controlling systems is clearly a target that can be met by a minority of designers. Generally, the discussion on AI replacement considers the designer class as a single, homogeneous entity. It might sound obvious, but this is not the case: for one system designer, there is already an army of designers affected by restricted uses of automation or caught in processes of semi-automation. As Ruben Pater explains,

> [...] graphic design is becoming increasingly automated itself. Internet banners and interface

---

301 Jasmine Oh. "Yes, AI Will Replace Designers." *Microsoft Design* (blog), August 22, 2019. https://medium.com/microsoft-design/yes-ai-will-replace-designers-9d90c6e34502.
302 See chapter 3.
303 Mike Cooley. *Architect or Bee? The Human Price of Technology.* Nottingham: Spokesman, 2016, p. 40.

CHAPTER 5

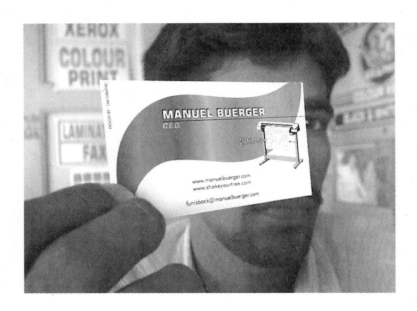

Business card for Manuel Bürger made by OM Graphic, a copy
shop in Mumbai, using Corel Draw 9.0 (2008).

FORM FOLLOWS FORMAT

Logo
Service
24/7

Unused draft for a made-to-measure Variable Logo Service by Vera van de Seyp and Charlotte Rohde (2022). Here, van de Seyp, a researcher at MIT, and Rohde, a professor of typography at the Bauhaus Universität Weimar, mimic the graphic style of car repair shops.

designs are already 'assembled' automatically based on different spaces and user data. A/B testing can update and optimize font styles, colours, and images. If your data profile says you are conservative, perhaps the system chooses the Trajan typeface. In this scenario many graphic design jobs will likely become obsolete within two decades.[304]

Fiverr.com is the biggest online marketplace for freelance services. Many among them revolve around graphic design. These gigs show that there is a fine line between automation and manual labour: some of the tasks performed by these remote designers can hardly be called creative: slide organising, vector tracing, detailed photo retouching… all assignments that show the vast gap, still extant, between fully automated processes and purely manual ones. Everyday designers of this kind temporarily reside within this gap. We want full automation but we predominantly deal with forms of semi-automation, and in some cases even "fauxtomation."[305] While AI-based text-to-image engines, chatbots and logo generators are given huge media attention, hordes of designers are still busy with tedious conversion tasks. Technological expectations clash with the harsh reality of routine work. On Upwork, another marketplace for freelancers, the description of a 'tasker' catches my attention: Belinda J., $25 per hour, claims to be a self-taught graphic designer, since all her previous jobs included tasks where she created graphics. The generalisation of graphic design offers the opportunity to create a gig out of its yet-to-be-automated processes.

Cases like Belinda's might seem distant from the reality

---

304 Pater, *op. cit.*, p. 215.
305 The term was coined by writer and film-maker Astra Taylor. It refers to activities that falsely appear fully automated but are, in fact, manually performed by humans. See "The Automation Charade." *Logic*, August 1, 2018. https://logicmag.io/failure/the-automation-charade/.

of the European or American hyper-scholarised designer, but, as Pater points out, it might not be like that for long:
> Sooner or later, designers too will be challenged by the same forces of global competition that laid off industrial workers. With the rise of algorhythmically produced design, and online job platforms for design services such as Fiverr and a growing designer class, the question is not if design will remain a viable profession in post-industrial societies under capitalism, but for how long.[306]

Not all of this is new. Already in 2006, Daniel van der Velden warned us that the competitive advantage of the European knowledge economy "will quickly become a thing of the past, if holding a mouse proves cheaper in Beijing than in the west of Holland."[307]

Some time ago, Fiverr introduced an online logo generator, based on pre-designed components automatically assembled on the basis of a set of parameters chosen by the user. Once those are entered, an animation appears while the data is being crunched: a flat-style designer working at their table. Here, the figure of the designer is an allegory of the design activity, a sort of skeuomorphism of work, akin to the floppy disk as the icon of saving. The designer as a person is used to illustrate a machinic design process. What brings together Defaultism and semi-automated remote work is that the designer role becomes a function governed by a set of instructions executable by either a human or a machine. And this might be true not just for the remote outsourced workers, but for entire fields like UX design:
> In 2023, being a 'designer' has been reduced to assembling prefab visual components and templated structures. Many of us have recognized early the similarities between using

[306] Pater, *op. cit.*, p. 250.
[307] Daniel van der Velden. "Research and Destroy." *Metropolis M*, 2006. http://indexgrafik.fr/daniel-van-der-velden-metahaven-research-and-destroy/.

design systems in product design, and putting Lego pieces together to 'create' something that resembles a good product.[308]

In his essay, Giampietro was presciently speaking of systems, well before the actual widespread adoption of specific digital tools to apply and replicate parts of a company's interactive corporate identity, with frameworks such as Twitter Bootstrap and Google's Material Design. Giampietro understood that design systems are where management meets automation. Here, the design rules – the defaults – are written in code. The Lego analogy suggests that a default can be thought of as a decision crystallised in software and, therefore, design systems can be conceived as a form of automated decision making, a Taylorism of UX design. After all, "[t]he factory floor prefers interchangeable, replaceable parts."[309] Some examples of this kind of automation are more explicit: from logo generators that simply mix combinatorially pre-existing designs to more advanced ones that employ artificial intelligence. Neither should we forget reusable assets, which are becoming easier to employ within cloud-native software like Figma and Sketch. Something similar is happening in the field of illustration as well, where we have witnessed the rise of the so-called 'flat style.'[310] With its almost childlike simplicity, it is technically prone to semi-automated replication and assemblage.[311] Very popular on Big Tech platforms, this style has been accused of infantilising the user. Here, a

---

308 Corneliux. "Everyone Used to Be a Designer." *UX Planet*, February 13, 2023. https://uxplanet.org/everyone-used-to-be-a-designer-530aa762e415.

309 Garrett, *op. cit*.

310 Also called Corporate Memphis, Alegria art, big tech art, etc. See https://en.wikipedia.org/wiki/Corporate_Memphis and https://knowyourmeme.com/memes/subcultures/corporate-art-style.

311 In fact, there are websites (such as stubborn.fun) that allow a user to combine elements and generate flat style illustrations. See also Rachel Hawley. "Don't Worry, These Gangly-Armed Cartoons Are Here to Protect You From Big Tech." *Eye on Design*, August 21, 2019. https://eyeondesign.aiga.org/dont-worry-these-gangley-armed-cartoons-are-here-to-protect-you-from-big-tech/.

technical operation turns into a reflection of its cultural effects.

Despite all the hype around automation, there is and there will always be a surplus of manual work to be performed, which appears in many different places: from the design studio that needs to adjust the files for print or deployment, to the continuous training of AI models (what scholars Mary L. Gray and Siddharth Suri call "the paradox of automation's last mile"[312]), to the outsourcing of book typesetting to India, as it is still cheaper and quicker than using automated systems. On the one hand, technology makes things easier for designers, relieving them from the burden of dull tasks so they can devote themselves to their creative endeavour. On the other hand, however, technology redefines those very categories by shifting the threshold between creativity and dullness.[313] The extent of this process can be broad: certain operations that are at the core of some designers' practice, can be reduced to automated functions. At this point, designers can either cling to a fully but vaguely conceptual image of their role ('it's the idea that matters'), or hope for a higher meta-position, from which to govern those functions. Actually, though, the position is not occupied by the designer, but by the engineer. Pater briefly explains how this is happening in the field of online advertising, which "is no longer dictated by art directors, but by people with a PhD in mathematics and data science who spend all day thinking how to make people click on ads."[314] If engineers are the ones structuring the system, how do designers make ends meet? In a satirical vision of 2025, Francisco Laranjo offers two options:

> Designers earned a living in two ways: 1) operating their design bots to fulfil a design service;

---

[312] Mary L. Gray and Siddharth Suri. *Ghost Work: How to Stop Silicon Valley from Building a New Global Underclass*. Boston: Houghton Mifflin Harcourt, 2019, pp. 38-63.

[313] "The process by which these two dialectical opposites [creative and non-creative work] are united by the designer to produce a new whole is complex, and as yet an ill-defined and little-researched area." Cooley, *op. cit.*, p. 38.

[314] Pater, *op. cit.*, p. 213.

2) feeding the centralised design bot network by informing the system about the rationale behind their decisions.[315]

Designers, apart from the few that have a say in the process of shaping systems, become either enlightened user-contributors of pseudo-intelligent automated systems, as in both defaultism and postmodernism, or they occupy a position that is missing from Laranjo's speculation – that of the in-house or outsourced clerk who executes tasks yet to be automated. In 2006, Ellen Lupton joked about how designers feared "that secretaries equipped with Times Roman and Microsoft Word would obliterate the design profession,"[316] but we shouldn't forget that for the majority of designers the job is largely clerical.

CHASING TECH

Given the risk of replacement, the tedium of repetitive tasks and the potential, albeit niche, designer's role as a systematist, technology appears at once as something to fear and something to master. But that's not all. Technology is also something to *chase*. Since the advent of personal computers, designers have found themselves 'catching up' with new tools, systems, devices and media. And the current excitement around AI reveals that by technology we mean, generally, *new* digital technology, and that we are somehow enchanted by it. Historian David Edgerton:

> In invoking 'technology,' the designer is blinding herself to the materiality of her world, her tools, her ambitions to transform the material [...] Invoking the concept of 'technology' in design, focused on the disembodied digital meaning of the term, far from putting 'technology' into design, removes most of it, leaving

---

[315] Francisco Laranjo. "Ghosts of Designbots yet to Come." *Eye Magazine*, December 21, 2016. https://www.eyemagazine.com/blog/post/ghosts-of-designbots-yet-to-come.

[316] Ellen Lupton. *D.I.Y. Design It Yourself*. New York: Princeton Architectural Press, 2006, p. 19.

behind only digital simulacra. In other words, rather than bringing in the material to design, or rethinking it, the concept of 'technology' can be a way of getting rid of it. There is a radical difference between a maker culture focused on digital devices and one concerned with physical workshops stuffed with many tools for working many materials.[317]

Edgerton's account is slightly over-dualistic: digital technology doesn't need to be disembodied, or better, it never is. But it is true that often the 'technology' that designers try to catch up with is a digital simulacrum. The design field, thanks to its porous boundaries, expands to include emergent technologies, but the medium's novelty is its only message. Various design schools and studios, for instance, felt the urge to equip themselves with virtual reality setups (an interest recently revived by Mark Zuckerberg's metaverse propaganda). Students and staff now 'experiment' with VR, but their work often acts like an ornament for the technology itself. They try to engage with the medium, but the medium prevails. As in the platform's conceptual grid, the work of designers becomes mere content.

LEARN TO CODE

Many designers and design theorists have tried to chase technological development by acquiring (or inviting others to acquire) the literacy needed to interact with computers on their own terms. This is how 'learn to code' became a sweeping injunction.[318] People debated (and still do) whether this practice should be within the designer's

---

317 David Edgerton, Hugo Palmarola, and Pedro Álvarez Caselli. "Some Problems with the Concept of 'Technology' in Design: Interview with David Edgerton." *Diseña*, no. 18 (January 29, 2021): 2–8. https://doi.org/10.7764/disena.18.Interview.2, pp. 3-4.

318 Designers weren't alone in developing this pressure. See Silvio Lorusso. "Learn to Code vs. Code to Learn: Creative Coding Beyond the Economic Imperative." In *Graphic Design in the Post-Digital Age*, edited by Demian Conrad, Rob van Leijsen, and David Héritier. Eindhoven: Onomatopee, 2021. https://silviolorusso.com/publication/learn-to-code-vs-code-to-learn/.

CHAPTER 5

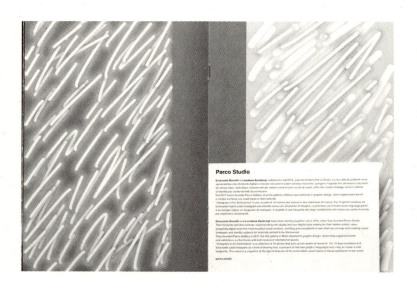

Instagram in un sedicesimo by Parco Studio, published by Corraini. "For 15 days Loredana and Emanuele used Instagram as a kind of drawing tool, a process to find new graphic languages and a way to create a print magazine. The result is a snapshot of the typical features of the most widely used means of visual expression in the world."

FORM FOLLOWS FORMAT

Mark Zuckerberg at the World Mobile Congress of Barcelona in 2016. The people in the audience wearing virtual reality headset look like extras promoting this technology.

domain. For some notable practitioners, such as John Maeda, the answer is a hard yes.[319] Other positions are more down to earth: sure, coding skills are a 'nice to have,' a skill that facilitates dialogue with developers, but in practice, the place of graphic, UI and even UX designers is the wireframe, the mockup, the clickable prototype designed in Illustrator or (goosebumps) Photoshop; and more recently in Figma, Sketch or Invision, with the occasional venture into CSS or SASS territory.

Coding, however, is not just one among many '21st century skills.' Coding is a battleground for authoritativeness and professional prestige, in a context where entire professions, such as graphic design, are perceived as something that it would be good to automate once and for all. If we consider the replacement of a cover image on Facebook or the adoption of a new template for our blog a design endeavour, graphic design suddenly acquires the same professional and cultural value of sending an email. So why not turn such a menial job into a button to press?

The battle is also clouded by the blurred meaning of code – are we talking of concocting a tiny Processing sketch or building a full Node.js application? In any case, code generally means a higher salary and a vantage point in a world that, as programmer and venture capitalist Marc Andreessen assured, is being eaten by software.[320] Coding emerges as a professional panacea for the long tail of everyday designers who are reasonably sensitive to the rhetoric of skill obsolescence and employability. It comes as no surprise, then, that US and UK students consider coding the third most useful skill to acquire (after networking and "idea generation").[321]

---

[319] https://www.youtube.com/watch?v=JGGAitirfRY. See also Liz Stinson. "John Maeda: If You Want to Survive in Design, You Better Learn to Code." *Wired*, March 2017. https://www.wired.com/2017/03/john-maeda-want-survive-design-better-learn-code/.

[320] Marc Andreessen. "Why Software Is Eating the World." *Andreessen Horowitz* (blog), August 20, 2011. https://a16z.com/2011/08/20/why-software-is-eating-the-world/.

[321] Roberts et al., *op. cit.*, pp. 166-7.

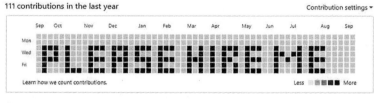

Sentence composed by populating the contribution chart of Github, the most popular hosting service for software development.

CHAPTER 5

Not only does code promise to upgrade individual practices, but also the activities of design's museum-educational complex. The result: a phantasmagoria of screens and interactive installations in exhibitions and final shows, often paired with the inadequacy to restructure cultural programs around computational ideas and approaches.[322] The edge afforded by coding, however, won't last long: while programmers and computer scientists possess an acknowledged and relatively arcane expertise with a correspondingly high salary, coding is increasingly perceived as semi-skilled labour. The programmer belongs to a profession, the coder to a workforce.

MANAGERIAL CAPTURE

In an episode of *Età dell'oro*, an Italian web series on the hardships of a group of creative workers from Milan, we see an art director instructing a graphic designer by perpetually repeating "two points to the left, no no, two points to the right." Here we see how graphic design can become micromanagement, turning the designer into a Kafkaesque, voice-controlled mouse. The scene seems like an aberration of the design practice, but might in fact be its essence. Design historian J. Dakota Brown retraces the evolution of the 'managerial capture' of typographers' trade knowledge and labour, from the theorisation of W. A. Dwiggins, who coined the term 'graphic design,' to Walter Paepke, who founded the International Design Conference in Aspen to convince people that design shouldn't be a mere appendix of production but a branch of management. In this sense, the whole history of design *stricto sensu* can be understood as a progressive disconnection of the brain from the hand, itself part of the larger phenomenon of the division of labour. The last act of Brown's historical pièce brings us to the present. Here, a bitterly

---

[322] Some exceptions exist. Among them, the School for Poetic Computation in the US and Hackers and Designers in the Netherlands.

ironical reversal takes place: graphic designers, who were among the agents of printers' deskilling, are now themselves the victims of the deskilling caused by digital democratisation.[323]

According to Mieke Gerritzen and Geert Lovink, "after the democratization of the design discipline, the leading designer will become a software developer,"[324] but that ain't exactly easy, both technically and professionally, as it involves the risk of perverting one's acquired aptitude. Luckily, there is another way out of an unrewarding democratisation and it's called 'design thinking.' Albeit in decline,[325] design thinking is still the most successful managerial expression of design. At best, it's a methodology designed to fuel the innovative capacities of organisations; at worst, it's a form of self-help for organisations facilitated by designers.[326]

Either way, with its five easy pillars (Empathise, Define, Ideate, Prototype, and Test) design thinking is, unlike high-level programming, rather accessible. In fact, it aspires to become a democratic organisational instrument. One of its main proponents, Tim Brown, co-chair at the consulting firm IDEO, argued that "[design] has become too important to be left to designers."[327] This might be one of the few aims that design has actually achieved. In fact, as Beatriz Colomina and Mark Wigley

---

[323] J. Dakota Brown. *Typography, Automation, and the Division of Labor: A Brief History*. Chicago, IL: Other Forms, 2019.

[324] Gerritzen and Lovink, *Everyone Is a Designer in the Age of Social Media, op. cit.*, p. 96.

[325] Several articles deeply critical of design thinking have been published over the last few years. Among them, Rebecca Ackermann. "Design Thinking Was Supposed to Fix the World. Where Did It Go Wrong?" *MIT Technology Review*, February 9, 2023. https://www.technologyreview.com/2023/02/09/1067821/design-thinking-retrospective-what-went-wrong/. Vinsel, *op. cit.*

[326] Self-help for organisations goes hand in hand with individual self-help: "In the Stanford d. school we attempt to bring students through a series of experiences that change their self-image so that they think of themselves as being more creative. We call this boosting their *creative confidence*." The emphasis is mine. Bernard Roth. *The Achievement Habit: Stop Wishing, Start Doing, and Take Command of Your Life*. New York, NY: Harper Business, 2015.

[327] Tim Brown. *Change by Design: How Design Thinking Transforms Organizations and Inspires Innovation*. New York, NY: Harper Business, 2009, p. 8.

note, "design has gone viral [...] 'Design thinking' has become a dominant business model affecting everything from politics to education, personal relationships, research, communication, and philanthropy [...] Design has become dangerously successful."[328] New card sets of 'methods' and guides have popped up everywhere,[329] functioning not only as pedagogical tools that are easy to disseminate, but also as a form of guerilla promotion of a few design consulting firms.[330]

Design thinking is managing innovation, but what constitutes innovation, exactly? Design thinking helped designers realise that outputs were less important than the process, leading to what Anja Groten defined "workshopisation," that is, an intensification of design's performative dimension, its fetish for collaboration[331] and, subsequently, "a general disappointment in what workshops are actually capable of."[332] Similarly, Guy Julier speaks of a virtualist tendency in the field:

> [design's] emphasis on process and collaboration, its customer experience mapping or its frequent use of workshops, hackathons and jams makes it appear to contribute to a kind of virtualism where things are made real but not actual.[333]

Here, design gets close to the world of contemporary art, which is, according to Boris Groys, "basically art production

---

[328] Colomina and Wigley, *op. cit.*, p. 46.
[329] Among them, IDEO's *Field Guide to Human-Centered Design*, "[a] step-by-step guide that will get you solving problems like a designer." https://www.designkit.org/resources/1.html.
[330] See Julier, *op. cit.*, p. 25. Another term that describes a similar phenomenon is UX Theatre, which "happens when designers are asked to *pretend* to do the work of design and aren't actually *permitted* to do the work of design." Tanya Snook. "UX Design Has a Dirty Secret." *Fast Company*, October 18, 2021. https://www.fastcompany.com/90686473/ux-design-has-a-dirty-secret.
[331] Anja Groten. "Towards a Critical Collaborative Practice." In de Vet, *op. cit.*, p. 40.
[332] Anja Groten. "The Workshop and Cultural Production." *Open!*, June 1, 2019. https://www.onlineopen.org/the-workshop-and-cultural-production.
[333] Julier, *op. cit.*, p. 157.

without a product."[334] Similarly, Paul Rodgers & Craig Bremner have argued that "design is largely a process of the management of its own spin, and management is the only product of the mature neo-liberal service economies."[335]

CULTURAL PROFESSIONALISM

One stratagem adopted by designers to reaffirm their expertise is to ridicule the lack of 'design common sense' of the amateur, who is guilty, for instance, of having aligned the text to the right, rendering it hard to read. The monopoly of common sense, however, has an expiration date: as the commandment that forbids the use of Comic Sans for something that is not comical became commonplace, so have the few precepts that are sufficient to create a decent poster. And if these, together with fashionable tricks, are then incorporated into commonly used software and templates – as happened for example with the Trend Generator by Trend List[336] – the monopoly might expire soon. Indeed, it might have expired already. We could be in the process of realising that, instead of being a set of rigorous structuring principles, graphic design might just be one composite style among many within the ocean of visual culture, an 'aesthetic' – call it *graphicdesigncore*.

When attacking non-professionals, graphic designers generally appeal to the notion of *quality*. They argue that the client should be 'educated' to recognise it. Perhaps, it is still possible to tie the concept of quality to some specialised activities like type design or the design of way-finding systems. One could argue about quality with some degree of objectivity in the case of large-scale projects, such as the identity of big museums or companies. However, quality acts first and foremost as a device for

---

334   Boris Groys. "Under the Gaze of Theory." *E-Flux*, May 2012. https://www.e-flux.com/journal/35/68389/under-the-gaze-of-theory/.
335   Rodgers and Bremner, *The Design of Nothing, op. cit.*, p. 553.
336   https://apprecs.com/ios/767377188/trend-generator.

CHAPTER 5

Adjusting colors...

Screenshot from Fiverr.com. Animation showing their
automated logo generator process. Manual labour is here
depicted "skeuomorphically".

198

professional legitimation, and this function, of course, can't be expressed too openly, as "every profession is a conspiracy against the laity."[337] Profession, then, has the double meaning of competence and declaration of a belief, namely, the belief in the expert. Such belief, however, seems to be fading due to a crisis of legitimisation that involves the whole "professional-managerial class."[338] The phenomenon is not new: as early as the '70s intellectuals like Luhmann and Habermas were debating the *Legitimationsprobleme*. The laity were becoming aware of the conspiracy.

According to Ruben Pater, "the [design] profession is a form of protection and exclusion, limiting the access to knowledge, the access to the means of production, and the influence over discourse."[339] Several critiques of professionalism, like this one, or even calls for deprofessionalisation, legitimately denounce how the design profession has disproportionately excluded marginalised groups. But, as already pointed out, a professional can be seen as someone who claims "extraordinary knowledge in matters of human importance," getting in return "extraordinary rights and privileges."[340] If the rights and privileges granted by a profession are extraordinary, it must mean that a profession is necessarily exclusive: it is an elite. But what kind? A useful distinction is that between "core elite" and "general elite." The designer is usually general elite because they mostly execute the directives of the core elite. Furthermore, this general elite resembles an army with increasingly approximate skills. Less a small clan than a swarm.[341] The anti-professional critique neglects the mechanisms of

---

337 George Bernard Shaw quoted in Rittel, *op. cit.*, p. 155.
338 Alex Press. "On the Origins of the Professional-Managerial Class: An Interview with Barbara Ehrenreich." *Dissent Magazine*, October 22, 2019. https://www.dissentmagazine.org/online_articles/on-the-origins-of-the-professional-managerial-class-an-interview-with-barbara-ehrenreich.
339 Pater, *op. cit.*, p. 334.
340 Schön, *op. cit.*, p. 4.
341 For a detailed overview of the analytical tools to categorise elites and professional cohorts, see Ventura, *Radical Choc, op. cit.*, pp. 55-63.

CHAPTER 5

deprofessionalisation that affect the design field *in the first place*. This is a problem, because higher education – which is where these calls generally originate – is bound to generate resentment and anger if it cannot guarantee its student body, which invests time and money in its institutions, the social and economic benefits of the profession. In this scenario, calling for a complete deprofessionalisation of design in the name of inclusivity is mere populism.

How can we solve design's *Legitimationsprobleme*? The magic words are culture and intelligence, as well as research and knowledge, which together form the ability to discern good from bad, to draw distinctions of both aesthetic and moral value. According to the Canadian designer Bruce Mau, who co-authored a massive book with Dutch architect-theorist Rem Koolhaas, "the only way to build real equity is to add value: to wrap intelligence and culture around the product. The apparent product, the object attached to the transaction, is not the actual product at all. The real product has become culture and intelligence."[342] In turn, the designer takes up the role of someone who produces culture intelligently. As the following excerpt shows, the invite for designers to become cultural producers was explicit:

> The true investment is the investment in design itself, as a discipline that conducts research and generates knowledge – knowledge that makes it possible to seriously participate in discussions that are not about design. Let this be knowledge that no one has asked for, in which the designer is without the handhold of an assignment, a framework of conditions, his deference, without anyone to pat him on the shoulder or upbraid him. Let the designer take on the debate with the institutions, the brand names or the political parties, without it all being about getting the

[342] Mau quoted in Foster, *op. cit.*, p. 23.

FORM FOLLOWS FORMAT

Goya's *Saturn Devouring His Son* redrawn by Twitter user @clayhor using the Corporate Memphis illustration style (2020).

> job or having the job fail. Let designers do some serious reading and writing of their own. Let designers offer the surplus value, the uselessness and the authorship of their profession to the world, to politics, to society.[343]

This proposed role reminds us that, less enthusiastically put by Norman Potter, of designers as cultural generators: "obsessive characters who work in back rooms and produce ideas, often more useful to other designers than the public."[344]

DIGITAL VERNACULAR AND THE REVENGE OF THE AUTHOR

This emphasis on knowledge and culture often coincides with a partial renunciation of the not so safe grounds of technical expertise, as well as a renunciation of the 'technical' at large. By this I don't mean that designers stop using any technical equipment or technique, but that these retreat into invisibility, while the focus of the work becomes more humanistic – rather than a tool to act in the world, technics itself becomes the object of a humanistic perspective. At this point, a clarification of what, in this context, I mean by 'technical' is needed. Here, the technical character of a practice is relative to the extent of its adoption. For instance, the alphabet can be rightly considered a communication technology, but you wouldn't call a writer a 'communication technician.' This is to say that the explicit *technicity* of successful technologies lasts for a limited period, after which it fades into the background. A counterexample: today, unlike in the late eighties, the act of double clicking to open a computer folder is not seen as a technical act unless you are human-computer interaction engineer. When the technicity of a practice becomes implicit, such a practice becomes a cultural one – it has

---

343   Van der Velden, "Research and Destroy", *op. cit.*
344   Potter, *op. cit.*, p. 12.

become a 'text' in Barthesian terms, to read and interpret. This is how the author avenges their death at the hands of technological democratisation.

In the '80s, art director Tibor Kalman and his design company M&CO began glorifying 'low,' vernacular visual cultures, following the analogue move of Robert Venturi, Denise Scott Brown and Steven Izenour in the field of architecture. It was time to learn. Not only from Las Vegas, but also from the roadside sign or the diner's menu. "Design without designers" became the motto, conceived by Kalman himself for an invitation to an event he organised. Who's motto, though? Of a group of hyper-professionalised graphic designers, of course. "We're interested in vernacular graphics – Kalman stated – because it's the purest and most honest and most direct form of communication. We will unabashedly steal from vernacular work."[345] But, if vernacular design is so pure and honest, why do we need professional graphic designers stealing from it? Because this gives the designer a new role, that is, to infuse the everyday with meaning and an ethos. What about the role of the vernacular, then? "[R]ather than being in opposition to modernism, [it] can be seen as a means of imprinting a sense of place onto modernity."[346] Given the diffusion of networked computers, vernacular recuperation of 'the Other' increasingly blends with digital default. In 2008 German graphic designer Manuel Bürger visited a copy shop in Mumbai to commission the design of his own business card, giving total freedom to the owner. Unsurprisingly, the card included several signifiers of graphic design's technicity such as a rainbow gradient and the clipart of a plotter machine.[347]

---

[345] Kalman quoted in Rick Poynor. *No More Rules: Graphic Design and Postmodernism*. London: Laurence King, 2003, p. 81.
[346] Beegan and Atkinson, *op. cit.*, p. 311.
[347] See https://manuelbuerger.com/business-card. Today, we might turn up our noses at such a project, but we need to consider the fast pace at which our cultural sensibility evolved over the last decades. At the time, for instance, the notion of cultural appropriation wasn't common knowledge, as it is now.

CHAPTER 5

Utilitarian Poster by Daniel Eatock (1998). "A generic form/template silkscreened on newsprint paper, methodically guides the user through the steps of creating their own advertisement, and includes blanks in which to insert relevant information, such as titles of events, images, persons to contact, etc."

There are many present-day instances of the cultural recuperation of digital vernacular. A common one is the established design studio that uses the Comic Sans font in their social media posts and job announcements to signal a certain easy-going attitude. Here, Comics Sans does not appear so much as a manifestation of the bad taste of digital vernacular, but as an iconic residue of technological democratisation. Similarly, the infamous "graphic design is my passion" meme is less a mockery of amateurs than an embodiment of the materiality of design software, with its default fonts, standard visual effects and clipart libraries. How can a professional use what is generally deemed a non-professional font? Here's a little test for you: if you use Comic Sans and you can still be taken seriously, it means that you operate in a cultural sphere.

Cultural professionals, such as postmodernist and defaultist graphic designers, often take part in accelerating the mutation of technical into cultural. Their focus might be on practices that, until then, didn't feel the need to manifest self-awareness and didn't have any incentive to explicate their own theory and philosophy. Before being recuperated, the vernacular is always 'technical', as its culture *resides* in its technique, it's *Kulturtechnik*. After recuperation, the vernacular has become 'cultural' in a narrative, interpretive or moral sense: the technique is now the content of a story or a parable. Vernacular recuperation is, therefore, the production of narratives around techniques. Ultimately, there are two approaches towards the vernacular: ironic detachment and dignifying attachment, often confusedly combined (while Kalman spoke highly of the authenticity of vernacular design, critic Rick Poynor asked: "Was there not also an unspoken assumption in such borrowings, as visual ideas were transported from low culture (everyday designing) to high culture (professional design), that high was inherently superior?"[348]). They

---

348 Poynor, *No More Rules, op. cit.*, p. 84.

both, however, signal a distance. The ability to create and maintain such a distance is the distinctive trait of the cultural professional. What about autochthonous pride, then? As the shepherd doesn't call his sheep 'nature', in this case we cannot speak of vernacular, since there is no distance between the subject and the object.

Filipino designer Clara Balaguer and Dutch curator Nathalie Hartjes offer a temporal definition of the vernacular, that is, "[w]hat is truly of its time, often concocted through bucking propriety – for example, African-American vernacular English slang that thumbs its nose at canonical English. What is newest and thus not yet institutionalised/cannibalised. What has not yet been distilled and bottled into the formal. When a language formalises, this is when it can begin to alienate people." That being said, cannibalisation is not a destiny for Balaguer, who believes in the ability to "write about the vernacular *in* the vernacular": "[t]o understand how far you could go with that kind of popular working tool is to deeply listen to the literacy of the body popular. If you can understand where they're coming from, maybe you can learn to speak a similar language, opening a space of negotiation."[349]

GUILT AND LOSS

In the end, the most potent critiques offered by designers using Default Systems seem to be linked to guilt and loss. Default Systems, and the formats that they include, comment not just on the mechanics of systems but on systemic thinking in general, and on the new life of man in the networked Global Village. The computer has changed design, but it has also changed our process of thinking and making. Formats and systems govern everything from our weaponry

---

[349] Rhys Atkinson and Clara Balaguer. "Learning from the Vernacular." *Futuress*, June 16, 2021. https://futuress.org/stories/learning-from-the-vernacular/.

systems to our guidelines for citizenship.[350]
Guilt, fear, loss, ambition. Our relationship with technology is not just an operational one, but it's linked to a whole spectrum of sentiments: designers worry and get excited, they mourn the demise of a technique, and they celebrate the birth of new know-hows. The territory is murky and not without risks, such as that of deskilling, that is, the relative contraction and devaluation of specific skills. Here, the case of graphic design is emblematic: outside design circles, the graphic designer is considered a sort of technician who possesses a certain adroitness with desktop publishing applications. This perception determines the social value of the designer as a professional figure, and to some extent also their compensation. As happened with the service sector as a whole, some skills – some trades, even! – have been incorporated into general-purpose software. The Adobe suite has objectified some of the design know-how, it has turned practical knowledge into fixed capital. In the face of deskilling, how can design react? By replacing a specific competence – technical, if you will – that is no longer valuable, with an extended cultural competence. We can think of it as a process of *softskilling*. Paraphrasing design theorist Tomás Maldonado, the designer is increasingly intellectual and decreasingly technical. Unfortunately, however, the humanistic approach doesn't seem very lucrative: who will buy the narrative products of the cultural professional? I will try to answer this question in the last two chapters.

---

[350] Giampietro and VanderLans, *op. cit.*

Chapter 6.

Kritikaoke: On Ornamental Politics and Identity as a Skill

"Formerly, like Kant and Hume, [artists] signed their letters 'Your most humble and obedient servant,' and undermined the foundations of throne and altar. Today they address heads of government by their first names, yet in every artistic activity they are subject to their illiterate masters."
– Max Horkheimer and Theodor W. Adorno, 1944[351]

"All that which today declares itself marginal, irrational, a revolt, anti-art, anti-design, etc. [...] all this obeys, willy-nilly, the same economics of the sign."
– Jean Baudrillard, 1972[352]

"My biography is more interesting than my art"
– *foundationClass collective at Documenta 15, 2022

CHARISMA

In 2017, I found myself in Berlin attending Re:Publica, an international conference on innovation meets politics meets branding meets tech. On the main stage, just after the vocal intervention of Russian chess master and activist Garry Kasparov, it was the turn of Dr Nelly Ben Hayoun, experience designer and "manufacturer of the impossible." Ben Hayoun is unanimously described, by the likes of Hans Ulrich Obrist and Michael Bierut, as a force of nature, "an inexhaustible source of renewable energy."[353] While the sheer scale of her design experiences for clients like NASA, MoMA or Airbnb implies the work of a team ("we work," "we believe"), Nelly Ben Hayoun Studios is clearly framed around a charismatic leader. Their productions are truly impressive, often including two dozen lines

---

[351] Max Horkheimer and Theodor W. Adorno. *Dialectic of Enlightenment*. London: Verso, 1997, p. 105.

[352] Jean Baudrillard. "Design and the Environment: Or, The Inflationary Curve of Political Economy." In *The Universitas Project, op. cit.,* p. 60.

[353] Aimee Mclaughlin. "Nelly Ben Hayoun on Her Theory of Total Bombardment." *Creative Review*, June 27, 2018. https://www.creativereview.co.uk/nelly-ben-hayoun-on-her-theory-of-total-bombardment/.

CHAPTER 6

of credits. Faced with such a vast and energetic orchestration of talent, any practitioner blanches.

Nelly Ben Hayoun was there, in prime time, to present the University of the Underground, a new postgraduate course made up of "dreamers of the day" with the goal of forming the "very hard working" critical thinkers and radical designers that our world is so much in need of these days. A school for the "the Willy Wonkas of modern times, the contemporary Joy Divisions, JG Ballards, Marie Curies and Rauschenbergs, action researchers and designers, mythologists and makers of new worlds!"[354] On stage, the French experience designer lived up to the endorsements: her performance was cheerfully chaotic, with a giggling audience and multiple plot twists (speaking of charismatic leadership, at a certain point there were *three* Nellys on stage).

The University of the Underground, hosted in Amsterdam by the prestigious Sandberg Instituut but established in London as well, is just one among the many experiments, large and small, in alternative education and pedagogy.[355] So, what makes the UUG a particularly fascinating case study? Besides its laudable commitment to tuition-free education and the ambitious plan to run its MA for 100 years, the bombastic branding, positioning and charismatic leadership of the University of the Underground – winking at grass-roots movements and do-it-yourself experiences but at the same time emphasising free will and personality – represents a good opportunity to reflect on the meaning of counterculture today and evaluate its role. How is it that institutions, both emergent and well-established, can neutralise, regurgitate and then even administer countercultural expressions?

---

[354] http://nellyben.com/projects/experiences/the-university-of-the-underground/.
[355] Among them, within the field of design, the Scuola Open Source in the south of Italy, the Parallel School and the nomadic Relearn sessions. Zooming in the Netherlands, Hackers and Designers and Open Set.

MYTHMAKERS, CREATIVE SOLDIERS, FUTURE PRESIDENTS

Within the UUG, chaos is considered "a method of public engagement." Rooted in Anthony Dunne and Fiona Raby's Critical Design, influenced by theatrical practices and inspired by Roland Barthes' idea of the mythologist, the school trains "creative soldiers" to infiltrate institutions in order to "engineer change" with the hope that – who knows – some of them might become presidents one day. "Manufacturing countercultures" and providing a "positive inspiration and disturbance" is the way to go. The set of references informing the culture of the school is maximalist and eclectic: punk, Artaud's theatre of cruelty, "pirate utopias,"[356] The Smiths, and so on. The school presents itself a bit like a teenage bedroom: a ludic space organised in such a way as to signal a sense of belonging to certain groups, to suggest different breeds of *coolness*.

Signalling plays a crucial role here. Describing the International Space Orchestra project, Ben Hayoun elucidates her understanding of counterculture, somehow derived from Pierre Bourdieu's model of the different forms of capital.[357] In a sense, it seems as though the University of the Underground has incorporated Bourdieu's analysis *a bit too well*. Its branding combines a critical/disruptive lexicon with an array of progressive cultural icons, a very diverse dream team of advisers, and a street aesthetics reminiscent of punk zines involving stencils, xerography and markers. This straightforward mobilisation of cultural capital both in its embodied and objectified state speaks of the current institutional landscape

---

[356] See https://en.wikipedia.org/wiki/Pirate_utopia.

[357] Pierre Bourdieu. "The Forms of Capital." In *Handbook of Theory and Research for the Sociology of Education*, edited by J. Richardson, 241–58. New York: Greenwood, 1986. https://www.marxists.org/reference/subject/philosophy/works/fr/bourdieu-forms-capital.htm.

CHAPTER 6

Example of a faux-picket at Re:Publica 2017. Photo by Dennis Knake/Lemonbeat GmbH.

– which is not afraid of 'agitators' anymore, instead it welcomes them – and pitches the school to mildly progressive media outlets and their audience. These are the new "rules for radicals."[358]

Clearly, mobilising various forms of capital is both unavoidable and necessary. Yet, it seems that the UUG, like many other instances of 'radical change' in design, simply replicates traditional dynamics of accumulation, obfuscating them under the veil of "criticool" jargon.[359] Working with institutions? Boring... We "infiltrate" them. Designers? No thanks, Please call us "creative soldiers." A semblance of antagonism is the perfect accessory to the casual look of prestige. Paradoxically, the manifestation of a pseudo-antagonist social and cultural capital becomes a means of acquiring more of it in a pacified, institutionalised form, disguising direct and indirect economic conversions that happen elsewhere. 'Anti' is the precondition of 'into', and later its corollary.

Bourdieu himself recognised counterculture as an attempt to constitute a market with its own rules:

> Thus, what is nowadays called the 'counter-culture' may well be the product of the endeavour of new-style autodidacts to free themselves from the constraints of the scholastic market (to which the less confident old-style autodidacts continue to submit, although it condemns their products in advance. They strive to do so by producing another market, with its own consecrating agencies, that is, like the high-society or intellectual markets, capable of challenging the pretension of the educational system to impose the principles of evaluation of competences and manners which reign in the scholastic market,

---

358 See Saul D. Alinsky. *Rules for Radicals: A Practical Primer for Realistic Radicals*. New York: Vintage Books, 1989.
359 Francisco Laranjo. "Critical Everything." *Modes of Criticism*, August 4, 2015. https://modesofcriticism.org/critical-everything/.

or at least its most 'scholastic' sectors, on a perfectly unified market in cultural goods.[360]

What he didn't anticipate, however, is that the institutional market would be able to digest the countercultural one. Culture and social relationships become respectively cultural and social capital when they are used to compete, consciously or not, against other agents. Compete for what? Platforms of expression, attention, funding. And these are rarely redirected to those who reject the 'disruptive' role models institutionally tailored to the docile high-end creative professional. Shouldn't the goal of counterculture be to reveal the hidden automatisms behind the acquisition, mobilisation and conversion of, not only economic, but also social and cultural capital?

IRONIC ATTACHMENT

During the Re:Publica presentation, one candidate's application was showcased to convey the vibe of the school. His application consisted in a videoclip of himself playing an '80s song featuring several clichés of contemporary design discourse ("I want to change the world," "I'm process-led, concept-driven"). Ironically, his gig conveyed the idea that radical expression as an institutionalised practice is the new default. The performance was a parodic *mise-en-scène* of disposition, inspired by a common part in a common play, that of the creative mind addressing an organisation. The irony is in the juxtaposition of the solemn and enthusiastic ambition of changing the world to a dry inflection and a frivolous tune for entertainment and mindless consumption – enthusiastic engagement as muzak. Was the applicant trolling? Maybe. One thing is certain, though: on a meta-level of irony, what was a dig at enthusiastic commitment was then unironically used to actually commit.

---

[360] Pierre Bourdieu. *Distinction: A Social Critique of the Judgement of Taste.* Cambridge, MA: Harvard University Press, 1984, p. 96.

The Indiani metropolitani, a post-hippie and art-oriented subcultural youth group which was part of the Italian '77 movement, used irony as a disorienting strategy for public protest, yelling slogans like "We demand to work harder and earn less!" Inspired by both *Grundrisse* and Dadaism, they were fascinated by the ambiguous nature of irony:

> What interests us is the sense of bitterness that irony leaves us with, its flattening action. Irony opens spaces, it unhinges, it reveals what cannot be hidden anymore [...]. Irony lacks flesh and blood, it is only partially a practice of liberation, as partial as is violence and its organization. Finally, irony is a frustrating "language that marks the space between our desires and the difficulty of their realization."[361]

Irony, then, was a way to inhabit the gap between expectations and reality. But our society is post-ironic, for it has learned to neutralise irony's subversive power by simply incorporating it. A global online marketplace can shamelessly launch a campaign that promotes unhealthy workaholism,[362] while H&M can successfully bring to market UNEMPLOYED hoodies.[363] As David Foster Wallace pointed out, irony, especially in its postmodern breed, moved away from its antagonistic origins to evolve into a mere advertising technique that, while pleasing the audience, acts as a protective shield against criticisms, because how can you ironically criticise something that is already ironic about itself?[364]

---

[361] Patrick Cuninghame. "'A Laughter That Will Bury You All': Irony as Protest and Language as Struggle in the Italian 1977 Movement." *Libcom*, January 5, 2012. https://libcom.org/article/laughter-will-bury-you-all-irony-protest-and-language-struggle-italian-1977-movement.

[362] See Silvio Lorusso. "We, the Doers: Fiverr's Entrepreneurial Populism and a 3-Day Workweek." *Entreprecariat* (blog), March 20, 2017. https://networkcultures.org/entreprecariat/we-the-doers/.

[363] Brian O'Flynn. "Class Struggle: When Did 'Unemployed' Become a T-Shirt Slogan?" *The Guardian*, May 3, 2018, sec. Fashion. https://www.theguardian.com/fashion/2018/may/03/class-struggle-working-class-unemployed-become-t-shirt-slogans.

[364] David Foster Wallace. "E Unibus Pluram: Television and U.S. Fiction." *Review of Contemporary Fiction* 13, no. 2 (1993). http://jsomers.net/DFW_TV.pdf.

Paraphrasing DFW, the applicant's videoclip manages simultaneously to make fun of itself, the design world, and the ones who are meant to evaluate his attitude, pleased by the fact that they *get the joke*. However, I'd like to offer another interpretation of the ironic stance of the videoclip, one that has to do with detachment. Commonly, irony functions as a means of coping with a feeling of powerlessness and irrelevance. When switched on, the 'ironic detachment' mode allows us to distance ourselves from collective and individual miseries. In exchange, we pay the toll of disengagement. What is the song, if not a disengaged take on impotent engagement?

TERRIBLE SITUATIONS, GREAT OPPORTUNITIES

During the Re:Publica talk, the notion of "performance of politics" caught my attention. The term indicated a technique to incite public engagement (this was before the expression 'performative activism' became derogatory). Tweaking it a bit, the notion can be used to identify one constitutive aspect of design's ambiguous value system. Design has long learned to abhor its commercial, utilitarian, wasteful and dehumanising nature. Key figures like Victor Papanek and Ken Garland vocally criticised the sheer amount of time and energy that designers spend on polishing the cogs of the capitalist machine. More recently, the aforementioned Anthony Dunne and Fiona Raby advocated a design that makes us think instead of making us buy (a questionable opposition, to be frank).[365] Designers have learned to jot down manifestos – and so have advertising agencies.[366] Of course, the UUG has

---

365 Anthony Dunne and Fiona Raby. "A/B." *Dunne & Raby*, 2009. https://dunneandraby.co.uk/content/projects/476/0.
366 See http://www.manifestoproject.it/ and Tara-Nicholle Nelson. "What Transformational Brands Do: Manifesto Marketing." *Ad Age*, April 25, 2017. https://adage.com/article/agency-viewpoint/transformational-brands-manifesto-marketing/308572. In 1978, Rem Koolhaas asked "how to write a manifesto in an age disgusted with them?" In 2023, the question becomes "how to write a

EMOTIONAL LABOR INVOICE

Marginalized Folks, Inc.

TO: Potential Ally
Privileged Folks, Ltd

SERVICE PROVIDER	SPECIALIZATION	DUE DATE
Marginalized Person You Know	Existing in Oppression	DUE ON RECEIPT

DESCRIPTION	#	UNIT PRICE	LINE TOTAL
Helped you understand your racism/sexism/transphobia/ableism/etc.		$ 100.00	
Endured your microaggression(s)		$ 200.00	
Taught you about microaggressions & structural oppression		$ 300.00	
Explained something about oppression you could've Googled		$ 125.00	
Clarified that you are not entitled to my time		$ 250.00	
Clarified that you are not entitled to my pain		$ 350.00	
Softened my reaction to spare your feelings		$ 500.00	
Made you feel like a "good" ally		$ 600.00	
Listened to "not all…." and similar derailments/fragility		$ 750.00	
Smiled when you apologized for not speaking up in the meeting		$ 1,000.00	
		Subtotal	
		Marginalization Tax Adjustment	$ 1,500.00
		Amount Due:	

© Anastasia Collins
This work is licensed under a Creative Commons Attribution-NonCommercial-ShareAlike 4.0 International License.

Emotional Labour Invoice by Anastasia Collins.

CHAPTER 6

its own.[367] In the meantime, plenty of labels like Social Design, Critical Design, Speculative Design, etc. have followed one another and continue to do so. Each of these iterations has contributed to an increasingly urgent but also abstract focus on the big issues of our time. This focus is not just the mirror image of design hubris, but also a symbolic return of investment in the currency of confidence, for those who have spent years becoming designers.

The saga of design heroes fighting against gargantuan societal problems has been successfully packaged in events like What Design Can Do, a Dutch platform created to "demonstrate the power of design; to show that it can do more than make things pretty. To call on designers to stand up, take responsibility and consider the beneficial contribution that designers can make to society."[368] Every year a new challenge is launched, such as the "refugee challenge" or the "climate change challenge," so that a multidimensional geopolitical issue becomes, as the *Volkskrant* newspaper reported, a Dragon Den-like competition. Here, design positions itself as the "ultimate problem-solving discipline," superior to governments or NGOs.[369] Global tragedies become design opportunities. I mean, literally. Bruce Mau, author of the *Incomplete Manifesto for Growth*, reportedly stated that "a terrible situation is a great opportunity to use design thinking."[370] The same design thinking that can be sold to companies and corporations. The wet dream of a universal design language comes true in the paradigm of design thinking-as-consultancy.

Undoubtedly, individual designers are genuinely concerned with specific issues, whether small or large, and

---

manifesto in an age enthralled by them?"
367   https://universityoftheunderground.org/design-experiences-manifesto.
368   https://www.whatdesigncando.com/.
369   Ruben Pater. "Treating the Refugee Crisis as a Design Problem Is Problematic." *Dezeen*, April 21, 2016. https://www.dezeen.com/2016/04/21/ruben-pater-opinion-what-design-can-do-refugee-crisis-problematic-design/.
370   Bas van Lier. "If Things Are Bad, That's Good." *What Design Can Do*, March 28, 2017. https://www.whatdesigncando.com/stories/things-bad-thats-good/.

sympathise with or belong to particular social groups, but design as a field tends to target general problems concerning a category, a user group, a set of personas. Design is humanitarian, in the sense that it is not concerned with *some* human beings, but with Humanity. This is, at least partially, a form of professional propaganda aimed at policy makers to let them pour money into the creative industries machine, financing the next social design event or prize. An ecumenic notion of societal impact is appealing. Political and social engagement is thus performed, at least in some measure, to please the policy-making big Other. In doing so, design constructs an imperfect but highly artificial image of the world in order to offer a solutionist happy ending, which, as in many Messianic cults, is constantly postponed. Who will "interrupt the cycle of capitalism?" Designers, of course.[371]

Inevitably, this type of magical thinking influences education insomuch as students, explicitly or not, are encouraged to wield 'conspicuous morality' and use it to satisfy their ambition – they become *moral climbers*.[372] Progressiveness, together with social and political engagement, becomes a form of positional consumption and, as such, it is an added value to the project and to the designer. This sets the context of evaluation by teachers, funding bodies and stakeholders alike. Thus, the design museum-educational complex offers a dispositional *Grundkurs* where one is urged to feign a more or less standardised expression of critical and socially concerned thinking within safe and somehow predefined ethical boundaries. A sort of humblebrag of good intentions that doesn't hurt or upset anybody. Against this backdrop, the notion of performance of politics is less a form of deep engagement than a garnish

---

[371] Diana Budds. "9 Ideas Shaping The Future Of Design, According To Ideo, Microsoft, Autodesk, MIT, And More." *Fast Company*, September 12, 2017. https://www.fastcompany.com/90139617/9-ideas-shaping-the-future-of-design-according-to-ideo-microsoft-autodesk-mit-and-more.

[372] I owe this expression to Italian writer Guido Vitiello.

to apply to one's own projects and practice. The consequences, according to the anonymous admins of Instagram architectural meme account @dank.lloyd.wright, are dire: "The problem is that traditional power relations and patterns of extraction carry on as usual under a veneer of progressive language. The awareness of that disconnect doesn't lead to systemic change, but instead to feelings of disaffection and powerlessness."[373]

ORNAMENTAL POLITICS

> Anyone dealing with the Creative Industries Funds may notice that projects with a strong *social* undertone have been given preference in the last few years. Not only 'multifacetedness,' but politics itself becomes a survival strategy for designers – a necessary branding and important checkbox on our portfolios.[374]

Designers like Anastasia Kubrak, quoted above, realise that a way to facilitate their success in the cultural arena is to "design your struggle."[375] Being 'political' is a plus. However, the idea of politics that informs this attitude is reductive: it is more about what the work *says* than what it *does*. The statement, the manifesto, the invective is more positively scrutinised than the inner logic of a project or the social relations that it produces. Politics functions as a badge rather than a process, with the further risk of turning it into a fetish, a formal requirement, a norm. Politics acquires a decorative value, it becomes *ornamental politics*: the radical slogan, the activist posture, the glorious declaration are adopted as decorations of purely autonomous practices, that is, cut off from the murky waters

---

[373] James Brillon. "Instagram Account Dank.Lloyd.Wright Aims to 'Amplify Narratives That Are Excluded from Architecture's Official Consensus.'" *Dezeen*, August 30, 2022. https://www.dezeen.com/2022/08/30/instagram-dank-lloyd-wright-interview/.

[374] Anastasia Kubrak. "Under Unwritten Terms & Conditions." In de Vet, *op. cit.*, pp. 166-7.

[375] Gerritzen and Lovink, *Everyone is a Designer in the Age of Social Media, op. cit.*, p. 103.

of micro and macro politics.[376] Often, but not always, the political is reduced to the equivalent of a Che Guevara pin on a Fjällräven Kånken backpack.[377] Certain symbolic forms in these cultural arenas confirm this, such as the 'faux-picket,' that is, a bunch of picket signs, with innocuous or even meaningless slogans that function as temporary installations in festivals and conferences.[378] Are we facing a good-willed, institutionalised aestheticisation of politics? Or is this a fetishism of rebellion where expression matters more than design, and in which practitioners are urged to love the 'revolt' more than the world to which it might give rise?[379] Let's listen once again to Walter Benjamin, who "demanded that artists must not merely adopt political 'content,' but must revolutionize the means through which their work is produced and distributed."[380]

In 1998, Mr. Keedy wrote in *Emigre*: "Today's young designers don't worry about selling out, or having to work for 'the man,' a conceit almost no one can afford anymore. Now everyone wants to be 'the man.' What is left of an avant-garde in graphic design isn't about resistance, cultural critique, or experimenting with meaning. Now the avant-garde only consists of technological mastery: who is using the coolest bit of code or getting the most out of

---

376 This is not to say that ornaments cannot be political. The problem, here, is with the reduction of politics to ornament. In short: "yes to political ornaments, no to ornamental politics." I thank Sofia Gonçalves for provoking this reflection.

377 See Schessa Garbutt. "Black Lives Matter Is Not a Design Challenge." *Design Toast* (blog), July 14, 2020. https://medium.com/design-toast/black-lives-matter-is-not-a-design-challenge-f6e452ff7821.

378 One faux-picket took place at the very Re:Publica event discussed above. Another one took place during the 2019 edition of Dutch Design Week. That said, even highly meaningful political statements can be made ornamental. This is the case, for instance, of a giant painting of a pedestrian section in downtown Washington, D.C. that reads "Black Lives Matter" in full caps. According to philosopher Olúfẹ́mi Táíwò, this is an example of "the elites' tactic of performing symbolic identity politics to pacify protestors without enacting material reforms." *Elite Capture: How the Powerful Took Over Identity Politics (and Everything Else)*. Chicago, IL: Haymarket Books, 2022.

379 Cf. See Maldonado, La speranza progettuale, *op. cit.*, p. 99.

380 Ellen Lupton. "Designer as Producer." In *Graphic Design: Now in Production*, edited by Ellen Lupton and Andrew Blauvelt. New York, 2012.

CHAPTER 6

Meme by @ethicaldesign69 which mobilises the tension
between the critical and the aesthetic disposition (2023).

their HTML this week."[381] In the museum-educational complex, quite the opposite is true: explicit cultural critique comes at the expense of "mastery," which is deemed as narrow-mindedness. The antidote? A broad understanding of politics in which a work that makes its politics explicit shouldn't be deemed superior to a 'formal' work which implicitly enacts its politics.

Manifestations of ornamental politics, virtue signalling, political performativity, etc. are generally interpreted through the lens of sincerity. If you take a political position for your own economic benefit, you're 'selling out' or you've been co-opted. This lens is not analytically useful: political purity (which is different from coherence) is a feature of martyrs. More interesting than looking at the veracity of the virtue that is signalled is to interpret the mechanisms of such signalling. If politics is an important checkbox on a designer's portfolio, it means that it is analogous to a skill. Therefore, a political position or, more precisely, the *manifestation of being politically positioned* in what is considered an acceptable or even correct way, becomes a form of competence. Within this line of thought, Raffaele Alberto Ventura concludes that political correctness "is not an innate merit but no less than an acquired skill."[382]

CRITICAL DISPOSITION

The aesthetic disposition was, according to Pierre Bourdieu, the traditional instrument of distinction between the masses and the elites. In 2018, Nicholas Holm argued that the aesthetic disposition was being replaced by a critical disposition. This is how the latter works:

> Like the aesthetic disposition, this new critical disposition is founded upon a distinct set of

---

[381] Mr. Keedy. "Graphic Design in the Postmodern Era." *Emigre*, 1998. https://www.emigre.com/Essays/Magazine/GraphicDesigninthePostmodernEra.

[382] Raffaele Alberto Ventura. "La cattiva notizia è che la cancel culture esiste eccome." *Wired Italia*, May 10, 2021. https://www.wired.it/play/cultura/2021/05/10/cancel-culture-esiste-debunker-politicamente-corretto/.

rules for both interpreting and judging culture. However, whereas the aesthetic disposition attends to form and expression, the critical disposition encounters texts in terms of their politics: their entanglement in wider structures of power [...] In such a world view, what is thought to divide elites from the common people is no longer high culture, but a critical orientation towards the world that frequently manifests in terms of cultural interpretation.[383]

Mentioning magazines, blogs, podcasts such as *Buzzfeed*, *NPR*, and the *New Yorker*, Holm demonstrates that the critical disposition, which is often presented as a source of pride within design culture, is in fact a general phenomenon. Of course, the emergence of the critical disposition has a detrimental effect on the aesthetic one, hence formalist readings of an artefact are cast as naive. Within design culture, the aesthetic disposition derives from the notion of function (even when it opposes it!). If we consider functionalism as "appearance of use-value," we understand that it is nothing but a peculiar type of aesthetic judgement. However, when the critical disposition becomes pervasive, the designer obsessed with *gute Form* starts occupying a lower position in the cultural arena, hence all the attempts to catch up with the ever-growing inventory of critical-political concepts.

Designers display a critical disposition by expressing their ambition to raise awareness on a certain issue or problem. This impulse surely derives from the pedagogical role that designers aspire to occupy in society, but it's also linked to the larger scope of liberalism. According to artist Brad Troemel, "raising awareness is ultimately the process of making people aware that you are aware of

---

[383] Nicholas Holm. "Critical Capital: Cultural Studies, the Critical Disposition and Critical Reading as Elite Practice." *Cultural Studies* 34, no. 1 (January 2, 2020): 143–66. https://doi.org/10.1080/09502386.2018.1549265, pp. 10-7.

the conversation that needs to be had."[384] The issues one raises awareness of are always 'urgent'. By emphasising the urgency of the issues they raise awareness of, individuals also proclaim their own cultural significance. This becomes clear in social media campaigns. Similarly, Catherine Liu states that "[l]iberal members of the credentialed classes love to use the word *empower* when they talk about 'people,' but the use of that verb objectifies the recipients of their help while implying that the people have no access to power without them."[385] Thus, the empowering act creates a distinction, at least symbolic, between the powerful and the powerless. It's important to consider the economic aspect of raising awareness, as it is not expensive in terms of means. Issuing a statement requires less time and energy than building a product, hence the privileged position of graphic designers as critical actors. According to Glenn Adamson, "Graphic design in particular lends itself to gestures of protest, from punk album covers to handmade banners. But architecture and product design, where the big money is, have always been service businesses."[386]

ACTIVIST OR AUTHOR?

It's not uncommon for designers to present their work as a form of activism. To what extent is this fair to conventional activists who semi-anonymously take part in movements? Ann Thorpe, who proposed a set of criteria to identify what constitutes design activism, indicates that the practices of Critical Design are characterised by a certain detachment: "Critical design examples often skirt the twin issues of making specific claims for change and of clearly identifying how the change benefits a wronged or excluded group. Instead they show design's efforts to

---

384 https://www.patreon.com/posts/left-cant-meme-77324335.
385 Catherine Liu. *Virtue Hoarders: The Case Against the Professional Managerial Class*. Minneapolis, MN: University of Minnesota Press, 2021, p. 1.
386 Adamson, *op. cit.*

change or challenge cultural discourse."[387] Here we see, once again, that the arena of the self-anointed activist designer is the culture industry, more than society as a whole. In some educational contexts this orientation is explicit, such as the curriculum on auto-ethnography in design developed by Louise Schouwenberg, who considers design "a practice of cultural critique."[388] In an Instagram post, later deleted, design critic Alice Rawsthorn enthusiastically states that "[t]here are many examples of great design activism: from the simple physical gesture of raising and clenching a fist [...] to the colour-coded strategy [...] adopted by British suffragettes in the early 1900s." Design panism is here deployed according to a clear cultural strategy: by qualifying any form of activism as *design* activism, the cultural professional can write, curate and speak about anything.

From this perspective, politics and activism can be seen as a subset of a broader authorial approach, which has been long formulated and defended by designers in order to maintain, or more precisely gain, "critical autonomy."[389] Designer and writer Michael Rock recognises that for the designer-as-author there is no fundamental difference between any kind of self-directed work:

> The general authorship rhetoric seems to include any work by a designer that is self-motivated, from artist books to political activism. But artist books easily fall within the realm and

---

[387] Her criteria to consider design as activism: "It publicly reveals or frames a problem or challenging issue; it makes a contentious claim for change (it calls for change) based on that problem or issue; it works on behalf of a neglected, excluded or disadvantaged group; it disrupts routine practices, or systems of authority, which gives it the characteristic of being unconventional or unorthodox – outside traditional channels of change." Ann Thorpe. "Defining Design as Activism." In *Journal of Architectural Education*, 2011, p. 6.

[388] Schouwenberg quoted in Jarrett Fuller. "The Auto-Ethnographic Turn in Design." *Design and Culture*, April 27, 2022, 1–3. https://doi.org/10.1080/17547075.2022.20611 38. This turn is, of course, connected to autonomy. Schouwenberg continues: "We stressed the importance of designers formulating their own agendas and ideals and of basing theses on personal interests and artistic talents."

[389] More on this in the next chapter.

descriptive power of art criticism. Activist work may be neatly explicated using allusions to propaganda, graphic design, public relations and advertising.[390]

This lack of a 'client' is somewhat perplexing when it comes to activism, which is generally a communal activity in which a group has some specific needs and demands. In Thorpe's words: "Finally, most scholars of social movements note that activism is effective only as part of a broader movement or campaign."[391] However, for the critical designer-as-author, politics is the *content* of the work, more than the driving force of a horizontally negotiated praxis. We end up, again, in the domain of interpretation, where society is read as a text. What the critical designer, the radical designer, the activist designer, the designer as researcher, the speculative designer have in common is that they all manipulate their own content. Thorpe's conclusion is dispiriting: "In activist terms designers mainly talk to themselves."[392]

The example of Italian Anti-Design from the '60s and '70s helps shed light on the systemic reasons that lead designers to adopt a design practice consisting in activism as a form of cultural critique. Curator Emilio Ambasz described the approach of the 'anti-designers' as follows:

> Torn by the dilemma of having been trained as creators of objects, and yet being incapable of controlling either the significance or the ultimate uses of these objects, they find themselves unable to reconcile the conflicts between their social concerns and their professional practices. They have thus developed a rhetorical mode to cope with these contradictions.[393]

---

390 Michael Rock. "Designer as Author." *2x4* (blog), August 5, 1996. https://2x4.org/ideas/1996/designer-as-author/.
391 Thorpe, *op. cit.*, p. 6.
392 *Ibidem*, p. 14.
393 Ambasz quoted in Wizinsky, *op. cit.*, p. 177.

It is important to recognise that, as Matt Malpass points out, much of the anti-design activism happened during an economic downturn plagued by a high level of unemployment. Radical designers resorted to critical practices because of their lack of opportunities to operate as service providers: "these designers couldn't find work."[394]

THE IDENTITY TRAP

A particular case of political positioning within design has to do with politicising one's identity, understood here as the belonging to an oppressed or minoritarian group. It is not uncommon today to find practitioners who "identify as a mother," or use in their bios labels such as "queer designer," "black designer" or "liberatory designer." Whereas in the past one would find identification in the profession (for example, one's uncle or aunt would be characterised as 'the architect' or 'the doctor'), today we witness the professionalisation of identity. Clearly, the professional bio is one of the many means to manifest pride and a sense of affinity, especially in the face of the systemic exclusion that professional environments have enacted throughout history. That said, this development should be read against a broader shift in the role that identity plays in the labour market.

Some designers argue that their identity is inextricable from their practice. For instance, Dantley Davis, vice-president of digital product design at Nike, speaks of his racial identity as a sort of superpower: "I couldn't imagine my design practice without race; it helped me advance in so many ways. With it I see around corners that my peers can't see."[395] However, one of the risks concerning the professionalisation of identity has to do with the expectation that a person's work *must be* concerned with their identity,

---

[394] Malpass quoted in Wizinsky, *op. cit.*, pp. 174-5.
[395] Davis quoted in Anne H. Berry, Kareem Collie, Penina Acayo Laker, Lesley-Ann Noel, Jennifer Rittner, and Kelly Walters, eds. *The Black Experience in Design: Identity, Expression & Reflection*. New York: Allworth Press, 2022, p. 68.

if such identity suffers or has suffered oppression, while hegemonic subjectivities are granted flexibility and autonomy of identity production. In 2016, E. Jane wrote a manifesto, entitled Nope, where they declared:
> I am not an identity artist just because I am a Black artist with multiple selves. [...] I am not grappling with notions of identity and representation in my art. [...] I am not asking who I am.[396]

More recently, Mohammed Al-Hawajri, argued that, for artists like him born in refugee camps in the Gaza Strip, making non-political art is *itself* a political gesture, since "a political reading is always projected unto their work, regardless of whether they intended it or not. That is how 'the other' sees them: as politicized bodies from a politically charged area."[397]

A recent meme format reminds us that a job, a hobby or even a pathology "is not a personality." In many cultural contexts we see the commingling of identity and personality. The political performance of identity can be a tool to claim recognition, equal opportunities, etc. – it is a form of strategic essentialism. At the same time, however, the prominence of personality can be seen as the ultimate outcome of the postmodern phenomenon of 'sampling' the self, that is, constructing an authentic self from bit and pieces of different cultural expressions, like music genres, artistic styles, and more recently the various -cores. Here, the root of the authenticity of that self lies in its very constructedness, one that reflects the micro-targeting of advertisers.[398] Already in the late '70s, social critic Chris-

---

396 https://e-janestudio.tumblr.com/post/132335744305/i-am-not-an-identity-artist-just-because-i-am-a.
397 https://thequestionoffunding.com/Documenta-Fifteen.
398 Some parallels can be found in the contemporary crafting of nonbinary identity. "Today, 'gender identity' references a core selfhood that requires no expression, no embodiment, and no commonality — in the case of some of the microidentities spreading on the internet — with genders as they are lived by others in the world. In this sense, contemporary gender identity is the apotheosis of the liberal Western fantasy of self-determining 'autological' selfhood, a regulatory ideal that gains meaning only in opposition to the 'genealogical' selfhood, overdetermined by social bonds, ascribed to racialized and indigenous peoples.

topher Lasch pointed out that personality had a role to play in the labour market: "In our time, the elimination of skills not only from manual work but from white-collar jobs as well has created conditions in which labour power takes the form of personality rather than strength or intelligence. Men and women alike have to project an attractive image and to become simultaneously role players and connoisseurs of their own performance."[399]

"Everything you make has you-ness – and part of what you will do at design school is develop this you-ness as you develop skills as a designer."[400] This is how US educator Mitch Goldstein speaks of a designer's personality and its role in their job. Goldstein might be more right than he thinks: the self – what he calls "you-ness" – doesn't just develop alongside professional skills: *the very self has become a skill*. And those who suspect that the self-as-skill is a reductive idea of individuality might find solace in the words of Horkheimer and Adorno: "only because individuals are none but mere intersections of universal tendencies is it possible to reabsorb them smoothly into the universal."[401]

CONDEMNED TO INDIVIDUALISATION

In 2011, Rob Giampietro noticed an emphasis on biography and a heightened self-awareness in design schools. He didn't consider this biographical focus as the result of a narcissistic leniency, but as one of the main burdens of the modern subject. As sociologist Ulrich Beck maintained, "people are condemned to individualization."[402] Being

> [...] It is therefore difficult to imagine an identity more provincially Western and less decolonial than contemporary nonbinary identity." Kadji Amin. "We Are All Nonbinary." *Representations* 158, no. 1 (May 1, 2022): 106–19. https://doi.org/10.1525/rep.2022.158.11.106, p. 116.

399 Christopher Lasch. *The Culture of Narcissism: American Life in an Age of Diminishing Expectations*. New York, NY: W. W. Norton & Company, 1991, p. 92.
400 Mitch Goldstein. *How to Be a Design Student (and How to Teach Them)*. New York: Princeton Architectural Press, 2023.
401 Horkheimer and Adorno, *op. cit.*, p. 125.
402 Rob Giampietro. "School Days." In *Graphic Design: Now in Production*, edited by

proudly international, some schools value and encourage biographical expression as an interface to cultural difference, a badge of honour given their multicultural ethos. However, a biography perceived as uncommon – in geographical, class or bodily terms – can be exoticised and therefore 'othered' once again. Here, the unfamiliar biography is made valuable ('one's roots') not for its intrinsic value as the story of a unique life, but because of its scarcity. A work that mobilises an unfamiliar life story is framed as a cultural statement, while one that is rooted in a relatively ordinary biography might be deemed mere egotistic indulgence. Not everyone's 'becoming who they are' is validated in the same way. Either way, schools are in trouble because they struggle to discern the biographical from the personal, what relates to one's place in society from what is a feature of individual character, what is debatable from what should be unquestionable.

A keyword that points to such tensions is *position*. In the Netherlands, for instance, a frequent question asked in high-level design schools is "how do you position yourself?" The question is, of course, of a maieutic kind: it is meant to help students situate themselves within the issue they are investigating. The question works as an injunction because it forces the student to produce a self-image. The position can be the one of designer as mediator, as problem-solver, as activist, etc. Or more broadly as male, as Western, as able-bodied. Positional complexities are now at the heart of the design field's identity crisis. As schools rarely have the conceptual tools to address such complexities, this identity crisis (that, as we have seen, is somewhat intrinsic to the design field and now just feels more apparent) is shared with, if not off-loaded on, the student-practitioner.

What's the institutional responsibility here? How can schools facilitate the generative crisis of the field without

Ellen Lupton and Andrew Blauvelt. New York, 2012. https://linedandunlined.com/archive/school-days/.

turning it into the identity crisis of individual students? Positional maieutics is a valid and useful means, but the dilemmas and wicked problems that it engenders should not be merely outsourced. Furthermore, schools shouldn't use those dilemmas either as formal or informal evaluation criteria. It is a risk for an educational organisation to engage with biography, especially in a time when individuality is forced upon individuals. Not every facet of biography should be scrutinised. And the ones that deserve attention, shouldn't be personalised. To manage this complexity, schools should become able to navigate intimacy, privacy and confidentiality. Most of all, they should avoid flattening a life story into a project-practice surface for evaluation or promotional purposes.

THE BUREAUCRACY OF IDENTITARIAN SKILLS

According to Fred Moten & Stefano Harney, "critical education only attempts to perfect professional education."[403] This statement distantly echoes Benjamin Bratton, who believes that "Institutional Critique is actually the last vestige of faith in the authority of art institutions."[404] As we have seen, there is a strong connection between a critical or political position, especially when rooted in one's identity, and the dynamics of professionalisation. That said, are there forms of profitability of the professionalised identity other than individual positioning? Created by Anastasia Collins, the Emotional Labour Invoice is a conversation piece that highlights the cost of all the invisible work which is traditionally carried out by marginalised folks ("endured your microaggression(s)," "made you feel a 'good' ally," and so on). The fictional invoice, which can be read as a simple and yet powerful example

---

403 Stefano Harney and Fred Moten. *The Undercommons: Fugitive Planning & Black Study*. Wivenhoe: Minor Compositions, 2013, p. 32.
404 Benjamin Bratton. *Revenge of the Real: Politics for a Post-Pandemic World*. London: Verso, 2022, p. 10.

of speculative design, has a strong polemical value. But it can also be taken as an opportunity to reflect on the institutional monetisation of identitarian competence. Professionalised identity can be capitalised through its formalisation, that is, its bureaucratisation. Several universities now offer courses to obtain "diversity and inclusion" certificates.[405] This will soon be a requirement for a new managerial class profoundly embedded in institutions, who will produce their own frameworks and criteria to evaluate internationalisation, diversity and inclusion. We already see emerging a combination of design thinking methods with identity content, such as the Positionality Worksheet by design scholar Lesley-Ann Noel, a tool for self-reflection meant to help designers understand how features of their identity such as gender, level of education, class, etc. influence their practices.[406] While tools such as this represent an accessible way to introduce intersectional notions, they can easily become managerial tools in line with the reductionist achievements of design thinking, and therefore an enclosure of expertise. Furthermore, it cannot be denied that positionality itself is a pretty crude reflexive instrument, to the extent that it can be misleading. This is because it presents itself as multidimensional, but is in fact flat. While mapping their positionality, subjects do not acknowledge their *very act of positioning*, that is, in essence, a negotiation between their identity and the categories of an identitarian bureaucracy. In this way, positionality hides the acquisition of symbolic

---

[405] Cornell, for instance. The program's fee is $3699.00. See https://ecornell.cornell.edu/certificates/leadership-and-strategic-management/diversity-equity-and-inclusion/.

[406] Noel adds: "I've gotten positive and negative feedback in response to the wheel, and I have tried to take that in consideration when I facilitate positionality reflection activities. Some information that I provide when facilitating workshops: a) positionality conversations and reflections can be uncomfortable, b) the 12 elements of identity are suggestions and a starting point, there may be other reflection points needed in different contexts, c) there are tools to reflect on positionality. I created this one thinking of design practice, and at the time lived in California, so perhaps was thinking more internationally about designers in tech." Personal exchange via email.

CHAPTER 6

Positionality Worksheet
12 things about me that help me see the water that I swim in!

The Positionality Worksheet by Lesley-Ann Noel (2019).

capital and the affiliations it weaves in the very moment it is performed. As a result, several interviewees of the Design Threads report "seem dissatisfied with mainstream attempts at inclusivity, specifically those in corporate contexts. Take for example: diverse representations without material inclusion/benefit, image-driven DEI efforts and other initiatives that end up resulting in tokenism instead of change in organizational structures."[407]

It's also worth noticing that a certain mode of exercising inclusivity *seamlessly* lends itself to managerial and bureaucratic approaches, to a sort of office politeness, even in settings, such as clubs, that one would expect to be adversarial or at least ambiguous. Attending a series of talks on club culture at the Circolo del Design in Turin, Valerio Mattioli, notices that,

> from safe spaces, clubs became sterile environments where to enact codes of behaviour as irreproachable as regulated by a kind of perfect woke etiquette – all agreeable in theory, yet all sort of polluted by a certain academically-flavoured pedantry. "Healthy" behaviours and "non-toxic" attitudes were being performed rather than internalised into a larger system of codes in the making. Words such as risk, conflict, desire, transformation were strictly banned, sacrificed in the name of an idyllic and sweetened pacification.[408]

STREET CRED

In educational institutions, the explicit attention to diversity and inclusion has another profitable function, that is,

---

407 See https://www.designthreads.report/.
408 Valerio Mattioli. "RIP Club Culture (finalmente)." *Not*, June 15, 2021. https://not.neroeditions.com/rip-club-culture-finalmente/. Before gasping at the use of the term 'woke' by an Italian writer who might not be fully synchronised with the nuances of a terminology in relentless evolution, I would invite the reader to finish the chapter.

to attract foreign students.[409] Commenting on the decision of the Willem De Kooning Academy of Rotterdam, a school that boasts an inclusive curriculum, to forcibly remove a pro-Palestine banner, Alina Lupu, a Romanian writer and artist, wrote:

> I guess it's safe to say, in the case where statements have gone missing or advocate neutrality after teaching decolonial theory, that your institution isn't woke, it's just instrumentalizing you for street cred. It's taking your hopes, your dreams, your aspirations, your country of origin as a marker for international reach, tolerance, and openness. And this used to be fine up until recently, up until spines started growing left and right within the art field. This used to be a symbiotic relationship. I scratch your back, you scratch mine. I give you my support, you give me yours [...] You take my image, you bend it and fold it and turn me into a worthy product. [...] In spite of the students asking on an open online stage, there was no instant materializing of general institutional accountability. But when faced with the sincerity of the demand, the institution laid itself bare as what it is, a neoliberal instrument which can be used to further one's career but isn't a real community, with ties that bind, but merely a casual, temporary, colorful, accumulation of individualities.[410]

Lebanese designer and researcher Imad Gebrayel notices that the deployment of performative criticality can be particularly appealing to those who are in need of an exit strategy: "A design program is sometimes a way out, an

---

409   In one of the schools where I used to teach, for example, the number of international students rose from 25% to 65% in the last five years.

410   Alina Lupu. "The Palestinian Conflict Rippling Across Dutch Art Educational Institutions." *The Office of Alina Lupu* (blog), 2022. https://theofficeofalinalupu.com/printed-matter/the-palestinian-conflict-rippling-across-dutch-art-educational-institutions/.

unclaimed, unlabeled, unofficial asylum-seeking process for individuals struggling with different forms of oppression, wanting an exit-route that isn't necessarily terminal."[411] These cases show something that will become more and more obvious in the future: the fact that the equilibrium of an institution can be disrupted not only by action, but also by inaction. It is becoming increasingly costly for self-proclaimed progressive institutions *not* to express solidarity for a marginalised group. This is why a pragmatic form of activism is one that makes the costs of 'doing the wrong thing' visible. Some people consider call-out culture a form of blackmail, but an economic understanding of institutional power shows that call-out culture is strategically rational, because such power is unevenly distributed.

At this point, we can draw a full circle of inclusivity. First, an intrinsically bureaucratic approach to identity is tested in autonomous spaces such as clubs. Then, it is used to attract students in institutions partly run by a section of the managerial class who sets the criteria for sanctioning this approach. Finally, the students themselves acquire familiarity with such knowledge to imbue their investment in education with meaning. As Brad Troemel puts it, "becoming bilingual in the language of inclusivity gives purpose to college degrees people paid much for."[412] Now, they are the bureaucrats – and they're looking for work. Holm invites us to have a realistic image of cultural environments: "No matter how much we might wish it to be otherwise, education – including that which we impart ourselves as teachers of cultural studies – is not simply a means to develop socially, politically and culturally productive awareness, but also a means of distinguishing sanctioned from unsanctioned forms of knowledge [...]". The use of specific terminologies, modes of inclusion and

---

[411] Imad Gebrayel. "The Design Exit: Don't Look Behind!" In *Unununimimimdededesign*, edited by Joannette van der Veer. Eindhoven: Onomatopee, 2022.

[412] https://www.patreon.com/posts/left-cant-meme-77324335.

approaches of strategic essentialism are turned into sanctioned forms of knowledge possessed by a selected cohort.

That said, not always is the sanctioning of 'correct' knowledge explicitly formalised. Speaking of her classes, theorist and educator bell hooks mentions the "gasp" that students made when one of them admitted they didn't know a prominent feminist author, something deemed "unthinkable and reprehensible."[413] The act of sanctioning happens tacitly, through gasps and perplexed facial expressions. It manifests, for instance, through the cringey feeling provoked by the non-native English speaker who misuses an outdated critical term.

KRITIKAOKE

Mattioli lamented the academic flavour of inclusive etiquette, suggesting that theory and critique, typical features of academia, aren't just methods of knowing and understanding, but tactical assets to position one's argument and oneself. As J. Dakota Brown explains, designers have been increasingly resorting to theory since the heydays of postmodernism:

> Postmodernists sought out intellectual justification for these new forms and methods, and they increasingly found it in "theory:" specifically, in contemporaneous writing on the postmodern condition and in the "cultural" and "linguistic" turns in the humanities. By the late 1980s, the critique of modernist principles had intensified under the flag of "deconstruction."[414]

In a context where praxis is not a necessary feature of a design practice, designers appear increasingly *condemned* to theory: what's left to them, to avoid succumbing to a submissive technical role is to indulge in sociology, anthropology, political theory... that is, to appear convincing by

---

413 bell hooks. *Teaching to Transgress: Education as the Practice of Freedom.* New York: Routledge, 1994, p. 113.
414 Brown, "American Graphic Design in the 1990s..", *op. cit.*

producing an allure of professionalism linked to their humanistic formation. Many project descriptions nowadays seem like AI-generated regurgitations of philosophy because designers (and artists alike) are busy practising what Italian essayist Tommaso Labranca used to called "kritikaoke."[415] Critical Design is probably the best known form of kritikaoke. Toke Riis Ebbesen neatly summarises its limits:

> Conceived basically as "useless," the value of critical design "ultimately lies in its ability to valuate: articulate, refuse, critique, spark, turn, transgress, formulate, transform etc" (Rosenbak, 5.15). However, circulating mainly in "art galleries, conference halls and academic publications" (Blythe, Yauner & Rodgers, 2015), useless critical design artefacts have been criticized for never entering everyday life (Bardzell & Bardzell, 2013). It has been argued that most critical design instead "reflect the fears, anxieties, desires, imaginaries, and ultimately, politics of an intellectual, liberal progressive white middle class" (Ansari & Hunt, 2015, 4). Removed from practical use, critical design may then become another echo chamber for designers, where they can safely repeat the slogans of design modernism without changing the world.[416]

The features of Critical Design's style of expression are very close to what Alix Rule & David Levine call International Art English:

> IAE has a distinctive lexicon: *aporia, radically, space, proposition, biopolitical, tension, transversal, autonomy*. An artist's work inevitably interrogates, questions, encodes, transforms, subverts, imbricates, displaces – though often it doesn't do these things so much as it serves to,

---

415 Labranca, *op. cit.*, p. 48.
416 Toke Riis Ebbesen. "Why Critical Design Is Useless: Criteria." Sursock Museum, Beirut, Lebanon, 2017.

> functions to, or seems to (or might seem to) do these things. IAE rebukes English for its lack of nouns: *Visual* becomes *visuality, global* becomes *globality, potential* becomes *potentiality, experience* becomes... *experiencability*.[417]

In this context, capitalism, as it is most broadly understood, has become the favourite scapegoat of the design cultural sphere. But the ritualistic vilification of capitalism is part and parcel of capitalism – that's its romantic mirror image. Baudrillard in 1972:

> Design is based from the start on the same rational abstraction as the economic system. There is no doubt that this rationality is virtually absurd, but it is so, in both cases, for the same reason. Their apparent contradiction is nothing but the logical outcome of their deep complicity. Designers complain that they are misunderstood and that their ideal is disfigured by the system! All puritans are hypocrites.[418]

At this point, we can briefly list the features of kritikaoke: a critical disposition functioning as a tool of distinction; the deployment of ornamental politics; an abstract notion of public that is to be made aware; the adoption of a critical-theoretical jargon – vaguely anticapitalist – adjacent to International Art English; a performance of identity as a professional skill that fits the criteria of an identitarian bureaucracy. What type of design does kritikaoke produce? To answer, we can resurrect Michael Rock's 2003 scrutiny of Dutch Design, which is probably the type of design that does kritikaoke best: "convoluted, challenging, intelligent, difficult, self-reflexive, coy, clever, often staggeringly beautiful [...]"[419]

---

[417] Alix Rule and David Levine. "International Art English." *Triple Canopy*, 2013. https://canopycanopycanopy.com/contents/international_art_english.

[418] Baudrillard, *op. cit.*, p. 59.

[419] Michael Rock. "Mad Dutch Disease." *2x4*, August 9, 2003. https://2x4.org/ideas/2003/mad-dutch-disease/.

KRITIKAOKE

An Artist Who Cannot Speak English Is No Artist by Mladen Stilinović (1992). Collection of Van Abbemuseum, Eindhoven. Today, one could imagine an International Art English update.

CHAPTER 6

CLASH OF
COUNTERCULTURES

To conclude, let us return to the University of the Underground. At a first glance, its most revolutionary aspect is the fact that it is tuition-free, a noble pursuit, given the rise of student expenses and the subsequent extortion known as student debt. The UUG's tuition fees are supposedly funded in part by philanthropic contributions and donations (80%) and in part by state funding (20%). Originally, the contributions from the government amounted to 50%. Generally, obtaining financial support entails a compromise regarding the way in which a project is presented to the funding bodies. Individual artists asking for grants are required to adopt the *néolangue* of the creative industries, and to detail their "competitive advantage." Antagonistic purity is rarely a good investment.

The UUG's conspicuous countercultural stance, however, clashed with a more traditional expression of counterculture: a group of students from the Sandberg Instituut penned an open letter to criticise (fiercely but politely) their own institution.[420] Their core concerns revolved primarily around the issue of corporately funded education: yes, the programs are tuition-free, but 80% of private and individual contributions opened the door to "direct privatisation." Other concerns included the lack of transparency regarding roles in the school and the smearing, so to speak, of the 'critical reputation' of the hosting institution. Finally, they rejected the UUG's countercultural branding, maintaining that it was improperly reminiscent of activist endeavours. Perhaps as a result of the open letter, much of the original countercultural jargon disappeared from the UUG website, as well as the characterisation of private contributions as philanthropy.

The concerns about countercultural branding and

420   *Medium*. "UUGH! Or: Issues Regarding University of the Underground," September 22, 2017. https://medium.com/@uugh/issues-regarding-the-university-of-the-underground-and-the-sandberg-instituut-fe58dbbf889b.

Sandberg's critical purity may be a cause of doubt: what does it mean nowadays to be an immaculately critical institution? Would that be effective anyway? If even Pepsi can adopt protest imagery, why wouldn't the UUG do the same? And yet, between the lines of the dispute between school management and students (and apparently some Sandberg teachers as well) we get a glimpse of what counterculture might be and perhaps has always been: a permanent distrust of opaque administration, especially when it presents itself as progressive; a constant tension against the ossification of certain power relationships, both implicit and explicit, against new elitist formations, especially when they pretend to speak for the masses. Maybe, then, counterculture is just crippling institutional self-doubt.

Chapter 7.

The School as Real World: On Aspirations and Compromise

"The starting point for organizing the program content of education or political action must be the present, existential, concrete situation, reflecting the aspirations of the people."
– Paulo Freire, 1968[421]

"In a period of 'diploma inflation' the disparity between the aspirations that the educational system produces and the opportunities it really offers is a structural reality which affects all the members of a school generation, but to a varying extent depending on the rarity of their qualifications and on their social origins."
– Pierre Bourdieu, 1984[422]

How do art and design schools produce their subjects, namely professional designers?[423] What values, criteria and mechanisms are tacitly or explicitly deployed in education? In this final chapter I explore the relationship between the school and the real world, the affinities between old and current waves of student protests, the targets of institutional critique, and the role that cultural capital plays in emerging professional models. Furthermore, I discuss how a broadly humanistic turn of design, which makes the designer an intellectual of technics more than a technical intellectual, is less a spontaneous evolution of the field than the logical outcome of design's unstable position within the technical domain. Finally, I lay out an ethos of compromise against the more commonly adopted one of autonomy, as the latter obscures various forms of dependency.

---

[421] Paulo Freire. *Pedagogy of the Oppressed*. London: Penguin Books, 2017, p. 68.
[422] Bourdieu, *Distinction, op. cit.*, p. 143.
[423] I deliberately use the generic 'art and design school' formula because various institutions dedicated to the cultivation of design disciplines (academy, university, private school, master, summer school, etc.) share the issues I tackle here. The reasons why I insist a bit punctiliously on keeping art and design together will become obvious, I hope, throughout the chapter.

CHAPTER 7

However, shouldn't education, being the inception of a practice, have been discussed at the beginning of this book? The odd placement of this chapter is due to the fact that we need to look at education from the point of view of work. From this perspective, education appears at the same time as the outcome of all the 'expectations' discussed above, and as a reality in itself, which belongs, at least indirectly, to the sphere of work. We can understand work as an activity, a system of relationships and, above all, a *myth*, that is, as a story we tell ourselves and one another.[424] Therefore, offering a realistic perspective of work means painting a picture which is not at all immune to idealisations and rhetorical veneers. One of these idealisations is the notion of 'real world,' that dimension that follows, in theory, the period of study. It is precisely this sequence that needs to be reconsidered.

Generally speaking, a school is conceived as a space protected from the disorienting brutality of the world of work. Traditionally, it was understood as the privileged place of *vita contemplativa*, as opposed to the context of labour, the domain of *vita activa*. There are many reasons why this is not the case, and some of them are specifically linked to the field of design. Years ago, Enzo Mari, a designer who rose to the status of "critical conscience of design," noted that, provided a design degree is considered on a par with a product, it is legitimate to say that the most impressive sector of this field, also in terms of turnover, is the "industry" of design schools. Thus, the structural reasons of the market interact *already at school* with the "hopes, strategies and naivety" of future designers.[425] Here, not only is the culture of design reproduced, but the subjects that will engage with it are generated.

However, there is another reason, more general and more alarming, to consider the school as an organ of the

---

424 See Lorusso, *Entreprecariat, op. cit.*
425 Mari, *25 modi per piantare un chiodo, op. cit.*, pp. 122-3.

real world. In times of crisis, it provides less and less protection from the typical concerns of workers: students are not unfamiliar with steep rents, housing shortages, debts of various kinds, poorly paid jobs or internships that don't pay at all. Moreover, the instability of the labour market changes the meaning of the school experience: in a climate of uncertainty, you don't need to know who Gary Becker is to instinctively adopt the prism of *investment* when it comes to education. In short, the problems of school are hardly distinguishable from the problems of life.

Although less protected than we imagine them to be, art and design schools remain, at best, a space that allows for critical thinking. While in the past, critique of design and through design has been primarily outward-looking (examining, for instance, dominant online platforms, pollution, and the ideologies that guide styles), today we are increasingly witnessing a self-referential critique that originates in institutions and points the finger at them, blaming their values and organisational models. The spectre of institutional critique, which until recently mainly haunted museums and art biennials, now also appears in design schools.

In the Netherlands, Germany and the UK, a network of unofficial Instagram pages has sprung up. These are anonymous accounts linked to the various academies that engage in a daily, all-round institutional critique: bureaucratic absurdities, sexism, bogus meritocracy, precarious contracts... all conveyed through the language of memes, inside jokes at once esoteric and accessible that are devoid of the pedantic seriousness typical of the movements. It is in these pages that, in the darkest months of the pandemic, students and staff felt the fervour of a community, much more than in the unctuous paternalism of official communications.[426]

---

[426] See Silvio Lorusso and @wdka.teachermemes. "'May the Bridges We Burn Light the Way': Five Questions to a Dutch Design School's Meme Page." *Other Worlds*, no. 3 (July 26, 2021). https://buttondown.email/otherworlds/archive/ow-3-may-the-bridges-we-burn-light-the-way-five/. See also Tessel ten Zweege. "Calling Out Dutch

CHAPTER 7

THE SCHOOL AS REAL WORLD

CHAPTER 7

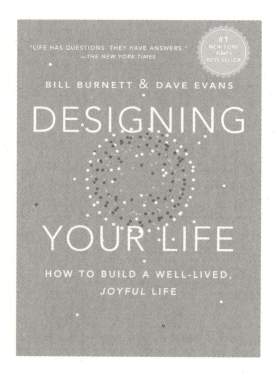

← "University is a garden where unemployed flowers blossom,"
DAMS, Bologna (1977). Photo by Enrico Scuro.

There are many books that mix elements of self-help with design culture. The circle closes: artistic expression becomes a tool for the realisation of one's own life and work project.

THE LOOOOONG '68

This is not the first time that the boundaries between the school and the real world have become so fragile and porous. The student protests of '68 and '77 were born out of a sense of alienation and precariousness, just as they are today. They were colossal events capable of breaking the spell that made the school a natural, and therefore immutable, phenomenon. In the eyes of Giancarlo De Carlo, who analysed the crisis of architecture faculties in Italy, students appeared "accidental and extraneous passengers in an institution that should be made for them and is justified only by their presence."[427] What then can be said about temporary faculty? "Sperm cells feverishly searching for an ovule that will give them a concrete configuration." Having followed the students' debate with keen interest, De Carlo reported in full the communiqués of the students from Turin:

> The current university does not meet the needs posed by society's existing labour demand. Our objective, however, is not simply to adapt to the needs of the demand for work. We believe that the University can and must provide those who attend it [...] with adequate professional preparation and critical tools.[428]

Not much has changed. Students then were aware of the "fate that would be reserved for them once they left the school, clueless in an indecipherable world," just as they are now.[429]

THE SCHOOL AS MARKET

As the communiqué suggests, both students and faculty conceive the school through either a materialist or

---

Art Institutions." *Futuress*, February 26, 2021. https://futuress.org/stories/calling-out-dutch-art-institutions/.
427   De Carlo, *op. cit.*, p. 46.
428   *Ibidem*, p. 54.
429   *Ibidem*, p. 73.

idealist lens. Materialists share a pragmatic focus on future employment, skills, market needs. Idealists, in turn, are divided between pessimists and optimists. Pessimist idealists argue that the school is a place of discipline and repression. They also lament the subjugation of education to the labour market. Schools, according to this point of view, are becoming a factory, only apparently egalitarian, for corporate executives, freelancers, workers or even the unemployed. Optimists see the school as a space for liberation through the exercise of critical thinking and the suspension of familiar preconceptions. On one side the pessimist Ivan Illich, on the other the optimist bell hooks.

Everybody is right, at least partially. How do we then merge their respective positions into a model? Claiming that art and design schools are an integral part of the real world is not enough. Nor is it correct to contrast professional training with the development of critical thinking. For example, are we really sure that a professionalising school cannot be liberating, or that emancipation is not, in some cases, a form of discipline? Pierre Bourdieu offers a useful synthesis of the issue. For the French sociologist, the school is first and foremost a *market* in which cultural capital is formed and exchanged, but above all legitimised and sanctioned.[430] Talking about culture as capital is crucial: it means emphasising that culture – criticality included – can be converted into economic capital, that is, money.

Scholastic capital, that is, the body of knowledge legitimated by the school, is a subset of cultural capital. At each level of education, the learner brings with them a varyingly substantial (sometimes even negative!) inheritance of cultural capital that is evaluated by the educational institution. No one enters school empty-handed. The art and design school is a special case because here, more than elsewhere, the student is encouraged to turn

[430] Bourdieu, *Distinction, op. cit.*, pp. 80-1.

THE SCHOOL AS REAL WORLD

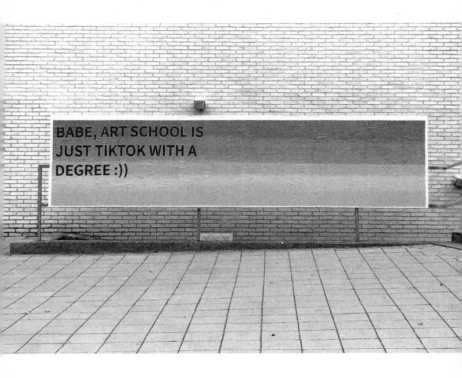

Babe, art school is just tiktok with a degree :)) by Content y Contenido (Ingeborg Kraft Fermin & Lucía Vives), billboard at the Rietveld art school of Amsterdam NL (2021).

CHAPTER 7

László Moholy-Nagy photographed by Lucia Moholy in 1926.
He is wearing a tie and a shirt under a coverall, a perfect
outfit for the 'technical intellectual.'

→ Instagram post by Jack McArdle, Studio AAA (2022). The
mere existence of this kind of propaganda shows that the
expectations criticised here are themselves a reality.

THE SCHOOL AS REAL WORLD

EXPECTATIONS VS REALITY WHEN...

HIRING A DESIGNER

↓

EXPECTATION
Somebody working to make whatever you want on their computer.

↓

REALITY
A passionate creative who has most likely sacrificed years of their life and lots of money learning their craft and ammassing a huge library of fonts, assets and expensive software(s), learning about typography, licensing, pricing, working WITH you on your project.

their own cultural baggage, especially the most personal (interests, passions, hobbies, reading, ethical and political ideals, etc.) into a *practice*. Following Bourdieu, a design practice can be understood as the activity through which culture becomes profit and cultural consumers become cultural producers.

While the 'emancipatory school' reveals itself in the apparently autonomous ambitions of students and teachers, the 'conservative school' hides itself in the mechanism of legitimisation of these same ambitions. It can therefore happen that indignation, an emphatic manifestation of the critical spirit, becomes a legitimate or even prescribed value, as I have observed in some academies. However, this does not eliminate the mechanism of legitimisation *itself*, often tacit and made up of frictions, impediments, micro-censorship, which extend from the school to the labour market. The school will naturalise certain values, while hiding the way in which it legitimises them. One of these values is authenticity.

BECOMING YOURSELF

> Home was the place where I was forced to conform to someone else's image of who and what I should be. School was the place where I could forget that self and, through ideas, reinvent myself. [431]

The school of bell hooks, a black woman who grew up in a segregated, patriarchal environment, is the antithesis of home: a territory of reinvention outside the bastions of tradition.[432] Art and design schools go further and render reinvention a rediscovery. Here, the insistence is often on the authentic self, on what 'you and only you' can do or appreciate. By adopting a rhetoric of

---

431 hooks, *op. cit.*, p. 3.
432 Yet, as we have seen, the separation between home and school is blurred. One always carries to school, intentionally or not, part of the domestic burden. And the school environment may not necessarily be less conformist than the home one.

authenticity, design producers and consumers are promised to 'become who they are.'

This consideration allows us to address the age-old question of the relationship between art and design. Without wishing to resurrect the old distinctions (commissioned versus independent work, rationality versus intuition...), it is useful to consider the relationship between design of the self and design of things. Distinguishing the two is no easy task. After all, isn't design a reflexive practice in which, by designing the world, we redesign ourselves? And isn't art the making of artefacts that are partly independent of the person who creates them?

The things we design designs us back, no doubt, but there is an essential distinction between the design of the self and the design of things. This distinction is made evanescent by the constant praise of glorious designers who pour their personality into the things they conceive. The celebrated design figure is a pale copy of the romantic artist who survives in the promises of the school and the hopes of the students. It is, after all, a question of value. While the design dimension of the art and design school tends to value things and services, its artistic dimension – which is certainly not devoid of design – tends to value the expression of an autonomous and distinct identity. That said, what I'm suggesting here goes further: art and design schools are first and foremost laboratories for self-design, and only secondarily a context where things are designed.

Personal branding, human capital, identity politics: nowadays the design of the self is a project that is consciously (and often polemically) implemented. To what extent is it a liberating practice? In order to answer this question, it is necessary to clarify that self-design is *one of the key facts of modernity*, both an opportunity and a curse for anyone who inhabits an environment that is not entirely traditional. Since there are no predefined trajectories or 'careers,' we cannot refrain from designing

CHAPTER 7

Chris Ashworth (2021).

THE SCHOOL AS REAL WORLD

@wdka.teachermemes (2021).

CHAPTER 7

Me and the boys asking that one professor who worked at Herzog 15 years ago if he knows of any opportunities

@b0ysfirm (2021). An allegorical manifestation of the hysteresis in architecture schools.

ourselves. Life appears to us as a more or less restricted gamut of risks and possibilities.[433] In this sense, the expressive drive that is generally associated with art is nothing but a reflection of the modern inevitability of self-design. No wonder, then, that creativity, a popular synonym of art as individual expression (and perhaps precisely for this reason frowned upon by designers), has acquired such primacy in recent decades.

Self-design carries a risk, though. In its extreme forms it is navel-gazing and pathologically self-reflexive – it's bad literature. By measuring itself obsessively against the ghost of identity, it is perturbed by an essence that does not always manifest. It is not difficult, then, to understand the disappointment of students who go to an art and design school believing they will grapple with a system of ideas, and instead find themselves placed in front of a mirror. The mirror image of the emancipatory school of bell hooks, self-design is an easy pedagogical shortcut, since it delegates the definition of content to students ('what do you hold dear?'). In a time devoid of consensual role models, the question 'who do I want to be?' is substituted by an incessant 'who am I?'. In this way, the school becomes a recruitment centre for subjectivities.

Identity is expressed through difference, via the distinctive device of taste. We should not think of taste as the snobbish prerogative of the *connoisseur*, but rather as a system of preferences (from TV series to political orientations) that actually constitute lifestyles. The art and design school, operating as a marketplace of differences, identifies and legitimises identity components and turns them into distinctive *skills* (like those, for example, of the mad genius) to be spent subsequently in the world of work, presenting some of them as authentic and therefore inalienable. This form of authenticity is, at least in part, a mechanism that

---

[433] It is exactly from this consideration that design theorist Ezio Manzini describes a condition in which "everybody constantly has to design and redesign their existence, whether they wish it or not." Manzini, *op. cit.*, p. 1.

CHAPTER 7

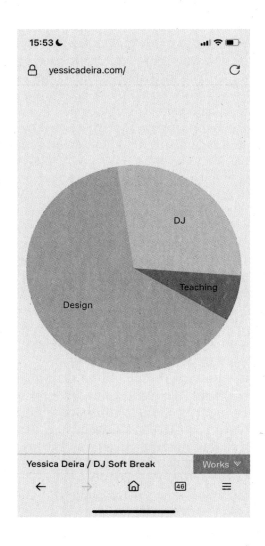

Online portfolio of designer Yessica Deira, designed by Justus Gelberg and Lukas Engelhardt. The pie chart is a playful visualisation of the multi-hyphenate condition.

is hidden from others and even from oneself. Through the self-hypnosis of authenticity, specific personality features can appear *true*. This is how the subject can become who they are. It is therefore possible to be inauthentic and sincere, or insincere and authentic. This mechanism makes it possible to explain, at least partly, the autobiographical turn of schools, already noted years ago by various observers.[434] However, with the encouragement of autobiography comes the omission of the fact that not all biographies are equally expendable, not all identities lend themselves to a favourable symbolic conversion. The mobilisation of identity and subjectivity is, thus, an integral part of the professionalisation effort. Let's look at it in detail.

AMBIGUOUS ASPIRATIONS

Design is, like art, protean: its shape constantly changes. It is no coincidence that much of its specialised literature, rather than clarifying its nature, tries to direct its aims. Schools, as forges of currents and manifestos, actively participate in such an effort. This is of course reflected in the multiplicity of roles that the designer can perform: the charisma of the maestro, the kitsch of the star designer, the nostalgia of the craftsman, the pride of the expert and, increasingly, the struggle of the worker, can all converge within design.[435] One could say, paraphrasing Bourdieu, that since design is a fluid and confusing field, it allows for professional goals that are also fluid and confusing.[436] Its ambiguity gives rise to aspirations that are never fully

---

[434] Among them, Rob Giampietro, who proposed an analogy between design school and creative writing courses. "School Days," *op. cit.*

[435] Italian graphic designer and author Riccardo Falcinelli explains that none of these attitudes is truer than the others: "Everyone will choose for themselves what kind of designer or audience they want to be: they may prefer functionalism or expressive design; they may aspire to strictly informative or postmodern graphic design; they may believe in efficiency or practice performance. The important thing is that you don't mistake these convictions for inescapable truths, but take them for what they are. It's the only way to not end up in the shallows of moralism, like those who believe there is only one right way to do things." *Critica portatile al visual design: da Gutenberg ai social network.* Torino: Einaudi, 2014, p. 301.

[436] Bourdieu, *Distinction*, *op. cit.*, p. 159.

CHAPTER 7

 Skills I thought you needed to be a good designer

 Skills you actually need to be a good designer

@MIKE_SUNDAY

Clout chasing

Chaining together high profile speaking engagements

Hiding the fact you have rich parents

AI expertise

Being antagonistic

Being an influencer

DJing fashion events

Creating content for IG, TikTok, YouTube

A good eye

Optimistic nihilism

Proficiency with a few good tools

Podcasting

Being able to rationalize design decisions

Being popular + social

Taking on projects that have no budget for underground musicians

Showing process

New Work posts

Creating decks with buzzwords to get funding

Being your own media production house

Getting new designer clothing every week

Getting blasted 6 days out of the week

Ripping darts

Big Twitter following

Knowing other influential designers

Mike Sunday (2022). A humorous representation of the importance of cultural and symbolic capital for the development of a design practice.

264

realised nor completely frustrated, an ambiguity that is also useful to those ambitious youngsters who don't want to forgo either the 'real job' or certain hypothetical symbolic benefits.[437] It is tempting to replace the modernist diktat "less is more" with the vague "more or less"...

Design's intrinsic vagueness has, thus, a precise logic: aspirational ambiguity propels its growth. And the aspiring professional shouldn't be concerned with the recognition of their profession, since professionalisation, understood as the promotion of the designer's role by professional associations, seems to be an outdated problem. Aggie Toppins, a US designer and lecturer, recently argued that "the field's most pressing imperative today is no longer professionalisation; it's to make design practice a responsible part of building equitable, sustainable futures." As evidence of the success of professionalising efforts, Toppins reports that "graphic design is now an in-demand college major and it is more visible in popular media."[438] A statement that confirms Mari's thesis of the school as the main design industry.

It is critical to recognise, as Toppins does, that the design profession has historically been a means of excluding women, minorities and oppressed groups. But it's also important to remember that nowadays the professional issue is far from resolved. A study of 30,000 design graduates in the UK (design being the most popular undergraduate degree) showed that only a quarter of them end up working in high-skilled, well-paid jobs in the design field.[439]

MASS ELITISM

When it comes to design work, one cannot help but talk

---

[437] De Martin, *op. cit.*, p. 71.
[438] Aggie Toppins. "We Need Graphic Design Histories That Look Beyond the Profession." *Eye on Design*, June 10, 2021. https://eyeondesign.aiga.org/we-need-graphic-design-histories-that-look-beyond-the-profession/.
[439] Sarah Dawood. "Design Most Popular University Choice – but Graduates Aren't Becoming Designers." *Design Week*, February 15, 2018. https://www.designweek.co.uk/issues/12-18-february-2018/design-popular-university-choice-graduates-arent-ending-designers/.

about technology. Democratisation, automation and disintermediation are keywords that are hard to escape. Ruben Pater sums up the long debate around the advent of desktop publishing in the following way:
> "By making our work so easy to do, we are devaluing our profession," warned design historian Steven Heller. "With everything so democratic, we can lose the elite status that gives us credibility." That hasn't been the case, as Ellen Lupton points out in her book on DIY design, seeing that "the field got bigger rather than smaller."[440]

Now that the word 'elite' has become almost an insult, taking Ellen Lupton's side certainly feels more comfortable. However, the growth of the graphic design sector expected over the next ten years is lower than that of other career paths – 3% against an average of 8%.[441] Moreover – and this matters even more – Heller pointed out a problem of perception that translates into a decline in earnings and especially in symbolic profits. This is a reality that schools cannot take lightly. At a time when a significant portion of the student body does not have the opportunity to convert their substantial educational investment into a position of professional elite, a problem arises, and it is no small one.

For political scientist Jo Freeman, "an elite refers to a small group of people who have power over a larger group of which they are part, usually without direct responsibility to that larger group, and often without their knowledge or consent."[442] This definition, suited to a criminal organisation or a secret sect, doesn't really capture the essence of a profession's elite status. Let's recall, instead, Donald Schön's definition of a professional as someone who "claims extraordinary knowledge in matters of human importance, getting in return extraordinary rights and

---

[440] Pater, *Caps Lock, op. cit.*, p. 329.
[441] See https://www.bls.gov/ooh/arts-and-design/graphic-designers.htm#tab-5.
[442] Freeman quoted in Táíwò, *op. cit.*, p. 22.

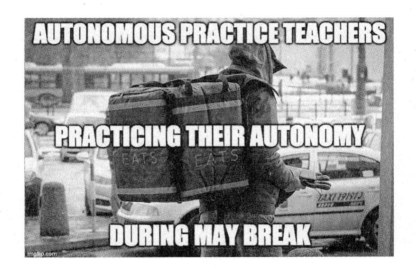

@wdka.teachermemes (2021).

CHAPTER 7

sy allowing visitors to ex
a greater awareness," e   raises awareness for the
step further? Ann d   to protect the pig industr
challenges the idea set of costumes raise awareness of the w

on approach to raising awareness, t: A magazine that raises awareness
e plants themselves. There's a speci
raising awareness,   you raise awareness
        oduces an exaggerated depiction of
boost awareness, ality to create an awareness of the ; wants to raise awareness
                   atre of politics. 3D avatars of leading
                                        addiction. It is intend
                   with porcelain clay o raise awareness
                   her pieces will con
n Hou has create   create awareness   rsonal audio can damage hearing unkn
raise awareness   oothing' is a modular device that increas
                                            the impact of sound, while helping you to

"Awareness." Collage of graduate project descriptions from
Design Academy Eindhoven. Afonso Matos (2022).

268

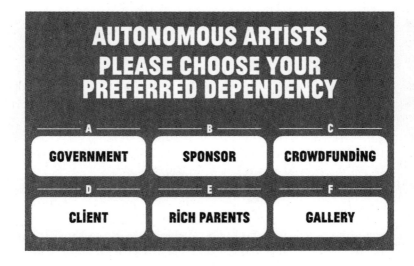

Illustration by Yuri Veerman (2021).

privileges."[443] This definition demonstrates that that of a professional is an inherently exclusive role (but not necessarily *excluding*, as it has been in the past). Here, the phrase 'professional elite' becomes almost tautological.

If designers' knowledge is not considered, at least in part, a form of expertise, they will hardly be recognised as professionals. This is the case of graphic design, a field whose know-how has lost its esoteric aura. The common perception is that, thanks to digital devices and the web, anyone can design a logo or a book. For some, the fact that graphic design is an actual university degree is even a source of amazement. My aim is not to debate whether this perception is right or wrong, but to point out that it does shape the general economic relationships between clients and designers, and thus the status of the designer. The effects are already evident in the wage gap between specialists in UX design, a field still considered esoteric, and those in graphic design, a practice now demystified.[444] The suspicion arises, therefore, that professionalisation is considered an outdated problem by those who have overcome this problem *individually*, that is, those who are considered to all effects professionals, perhaps members of a cultural elite, able to obtain both material and symbolic benefits from it.[445] They antagonise elitism, but while anti-elitism, as a practice, is the very 'emotional atmosphere' of the lower classes, as a discourse, it's the Trojan horse of the elites. As a practice, it is intuitive, matter-of-fact, material, lived; as a discourse, it is formal, theoretical, abstract, distinctive.

ECONOMIC RESPONSIBILITY

In 2022, I wholeheartedly signed Platform BK's open letter entitled "Graduates of art academies deserve more

---

[443] Schön, *op. cit.*, p. 4.
[444] $74,000 of UX Designers vs. $41,000 of graphic designers. Teo Yu Siang. "How to Change Your Career from Graphic Design to UX Design." *Interaction Design Foundation*, September 12, 2020. https://www.interaction-design.org/literature/article/how-to-change-your-career-from-graphic-design-to-ux-design.
[445] Cf. Rock, "On Unprofessionalism", *op. cit.*

THE SCHOOL AS REAL WORLD

QUESTO MANIFESTO VALE I CIRCA 50.000 € CHE I MIEI GENITORI HANNO SPESO PER FARMI LAUREARE AL D.A.M.S CINEMA INVECE DI COMPRARE UN' AUTOMOBILE TEDESCA DI LUSSO

"This poster is worth the approximately €50,000 that my parents spent to get me to graduate from the D.A.M.S Cinema instead of buying a German luxury car." Poster by Giuseppe de Mattia (2021).

agency over their future."[446] Addressing the boards of Dutch art academies, the signatories argued that education should prepare students for "the unruly reality of the cultural sector's job market." The plan included four points: development of post-precarity courses; social engagement and self-organisation; insights into the world after the academy; student involvement in institutional developments. An earlier version of the letter called for "economically responsible art education." The question is: how to define economic responsibility? Up to this point, I have tried to show that an economic perspective does not only entail income and bills, nor mere entrepreneurial spirit, but that there are also inflections of symbolic capital, a gap between public perception and professional *proprioception*.

Within various art and design schools, both faculty and students are beginning to address the problem of the profession by taking the side of an exploited proletariat. Although, as the data show, there are very good reasons for adopting this stance, there is something self-defeating in it: by begrudgingly accepting the neo-worker condition, the legitimate professional aspirations of designers, which are not really working-class aspirations, are concealed. This is the reason why generic calls to unionisation, which re-emerge every five years or so, do not yield the desired results within the design professions. Again, we are in the presence of a double bind: the school educates students as professionals but demands of them a proletarian consciousness. A generic appeal to unionisation runs the risk of betraying design's professional promise,[447] not only by 'creating losers,' but by turning their resentment into material for courses and syllabi.[448]

446   https://www.platformbk.nl/en/graduates-of-art-academies-deserve-more-agency-over-their-future/.
447   See Silvio Lorusso. "No Problem: Design School as Promise." *Entreprecariat* (blog), December 7, 2020. https://networkcultures.org/entreprecariat/no-problem-design/.
448   I am aware of the weight of this remark, and I do not make it lightly, as the authors to whom I refer do not make it lightly either. See, in particular, Bourdieu,

ME, AN INTELLECTUAL

"The thing that pisses me off the most is the degradation of the intellectual role of the designer." This is what a designer friend told me once, as we listened to each other's anguished outpourings replete with VAT numbers, short-term contracts and late payments. In the introductory text of Ellen Lupton's aforementioned book (written together with her MICA students in Baltimore: it is a book born in a school), the historian likens the figure of the designer to the Gramscian "organic intellectual." Considering design "a *social* function, rather than as a profession or an academic discipline," Lupton suggests that

> These organic intellectuals could merge physical and mental labor, building "new modes of thought" out of acts of doing and making. Their skills would be both technical and theoretical.[449]

But what exactly is an intellectual? To this question, Tomás Maldonado, a complex and prolific figure in the field of design, has devoted an entire, wide-ranging volume which spans from Cervantes to Jonathan Swift, from Erasmus to Heidegger.[450] According to Maldonado, intellectuals are born *committed*. They "take a stand" and sign manifestos. Sometimes, however, they have a decorative function within the party they support and by which they are supported. Moreover, the moment they become modern, they cannot help but work on themselves:

> He expresses "the modern identity" as a way of being an intellectual that privileges "radical reflexivity." He is the intellectual "after Montaigne." With Montaigne "the self enters the scene." The intellectual is born who is turned in

---

Distinction, op. cit., p. 143, and Ivan Illich. *Deschooling Society*. London: Calder & Boyars, 1971.

449 Lupton, *op. cit.*, p. 21.
450 Tomás Maldonado. *Che cos'è un intellettuale? Avventure e disavventure di un ruolo*. Milano: Feltrinelli, 2010.

upon himself, but who offers himself to the gaze of others.[451]

The affinity with the prototype of the designer envisioned and promoted by the art and design schools is evident: this is an intellectual who takes a position, critiques and educates, who designs themselves and makes this work their own content to disseminate, their own voice. This type of intellectual meets the criteria of acting, but what about the making typical of designers, that is, their technical dimension?

THE TWO CULTURES

We now understand what an intellectual is. But how does this role relate to the designer? Maldonado offered a compelling definition: the designer is a *technical intellectual*.[452] This way, he attempted to abolish the false dichotomy that opposes humanistic culture to scientific culture. As Giovanni Anceschi explains,

> "Technical intellectual" is an expression that strikes us as an oxymoron, but it is such only according to the banal thinking and schizoid prejudice that continues to believe in the "two cultures."[453]

The attempt to "drive out this very concrete activity from the professionalist and practice-heavy middle-brow" is meritorious, yet things aren't that simple.[454] The difficulty lies in the fact that the distinction between technical and intellectual survives in the general perception of professional roles, and, broadly speaking, the designer is perceived more as a technician than an intellectual.

What kind of technician, though? It is true for many designers what Bourdieu argues about those who occupy

---

451 *Ibidem*, pp. 27-8.
452 Oddly, the word 'designer' never appears in his excursus on the role of the intellectual.
453 Giovanni Anceschi. *Tomás Maldonado intellettuale politecnico*. Milano: Edizioni del Verri, 2020, p. 35.
454 *Ivi*.

THE SCHOOL AS REAL WORLD

"Become who you are." Still from a TV ad for the Italian Accademia del lusso (2020).

the lower ranks of the ruling class. They "are relegated to the position of *technicians*, i.e., executants without economic, political or cultural power."[455] This is evident in the lamentations of the various design sub-sectors, not only in graphic design, which is in decline, but also in those on the rise such as interaction design, which is clamouring for its 'seat at the table.' There is a difference, then, between the technician and the *technologist*, a professional in their own right, recognised synthesis of the two cultures.

How, then, does one explain the intellectualistic, 'monocultural' propensity of contemporary design? Having failed to establish themselves authoritatively in the technical sphere, the designer attempts to occupy the humanistic sphere. This is a sensible move, albeit a largely unconscious one, consisting in the replacement of a technical elite (which is elite no longer) with an intellectual pseudo-elite, which stands as the 'consciousness' of technics. Schools can thus claim a formally autonomous role, which is the exercise of critical thinking and the production of awareness. Here, the focus is more on the why and less on the how, as Tibor Kalman once put it. In their latest book, Mieke Gerritzen and Geert Lovink frame this mainly European phenomenon through a scathing title: *Made in China, Designed in California, Criticized in Europe*.[456] Long gone are the days when "[t]he technical and commercial forms of vocational education became the desired goal through the constant ridiculing of the 'impractical' professor and the 'idealistic' intellectual [...]"[457] Today, the main object of ridicule is instead the 'hard realist.' But "[w]hen such 'derogatory' matters as arts, crafts, and machine technology are regarded as ballast and thrown out from liberal arts education, the student is left in a thin atmosphere of mere verbalism."[458]

---

455 Bourdieu, *Distinction, op. cit.*, p. 316.
456 Gerritzen and Lovink, *Made in China...*, *op. cit.*
457 Moholy-Nagy, *op. cit.*, p. 22.
458 *Ivi*.

THE PROBLEM WITH PROBLEMS

The shift from the technical intellectual to the intellectual *of technics* is most evident in Speculative Design, also called Critical Design.[459] This is the practice of imagining future scenarios in order to rethink – and thus transform – our present. The founding manifesto of the current, undersigned by Anthony Dunne and Fiona Raby in 2009, clarifies a number of principles.[460] Among them is a shift from an affirmative to a critical intention; design is no longer for production but for debate; provocation replaces innovation; and applications make way for implications. The result is a figure all in all similar to the traditional humanist intellectual. Indeed, Speculative Design is also sometimes called *design for debate*.

Every current has its excellences and its mediocrities. I am not interested here in determining the general validity of Speculative Design, but rather in giving reasons for its popularity, especially in pedagogical and academic circles. Notwithstanding some historical precedents acknowledged by speculative designers themselves, the novelty lies in defining and redefining problems through scenarios and prototypes, rather than devoting oneself to solving them. In doing so, Speculative Design solves *the problem of access to problems*. By creating fictions that are linked to reality and yet completely autonomous, it can disconnect from the concretely social dimension of technology, that is, what Galbraith used to call *technostructure*, which includes CEOs, policy-makers and corporate executives.[461] Moreover, on a pedagogical level such a practice lends itself to isolationism: a tenuous link to reality is enough to create a fictional world. A reality that for many designers is moreover second-rate: if problem solving is reduced to mere

---

459   See Dunne and Raby, *Speculative Everything*, op. cit.
460   Dunne and Raby, "A/B", op. cit.
461   John Kenneth Galbraith. *The New Industrial State*. Princeton: Princeton University Press, 2015.

execution, problem *framing* has the allure of cultural production, the traditional task of intellectuals. Hence, the shift from problems to solve to problematic situations to address.

This explains a growing scepticism toward problem solving. Such scepticism is not only about staging the 'wickedness' of complex problems, but also about evading the social obstacle that prevents one from participating in their resolution. This also explains the propensity to investigate colossal problems, since they lend themselves perfectly to the stunned gaze of the critic. By focusing on the highest systems, one can ignore those concrete, smaller systems from which they are excluded or over which they have no power.[462] In the words of Victor Papanek, "[i]t is also in the interest of the Establishment to provide science-fiction routes of escape for the young, lest they become aware of the harshness of that which is real."[463] Deploying images of preferable futures, these science-fiction routes inevitably tend to mobilise notions of ethics and politics. Once again, the question to ask is: how do ethics and politics *function* in the context of the art and design school?

IMPOTENT ETHICS

British historian Alison J. Clarke writes:

> Much present design discourse upholds a polarized model of design hatched in the broadly neo-Marxist 1970s paradigm that buoyed Papanek's vitriolic critique: [...] rehearsing a rhetoric that pits a morally and ethically virtuous design practice (sustainable, socially embedded, community-based, codesigned, etc.) against a model of designers as the handmaidens of a profit-driven corporate culture.[464]

---

462 See chapter 4.
463 Papanek, *op. cit.*, p. 283.
464 Alison J. Clarke. "Design for the Real World: Contesting the Origins of the Social in Design." In *Design Struggles: Intersecting Histories, Pedagogies, and*

This ethical binarism is not unrelated to the inaccessibility of problems. Generations of students and practitioners have passionately read Ken Garland's *First Things First* manifesto, which has been updated and republished several times in recent decades.[465] The original, explicitly anti-consumerist version indirectly lamented the reduction of the designer to a mere executor of a plan whose "trivial pursuits" are decided by others. Garland's consciousness-raising was thus not only ethical but also positional. Referring to the 2000 edition of the manifesto, J. Dakota Brown argues that "like earlier attempts to understand and to contest design's status as an 'institution of power,' the manifesto's critique was quickly rehabilitated into an apolitical affirmation of 'the power of design.'"[466] On closer inspection, then, the ethical afflatus of design, with its rhetoric of excessive responsibility, turns into self-aggrandisement. When designers and theorists proclaim that design has a great deal of responsibility, or even culpability, they are also saying: "we are important, influential, if not decisive." Examples of this excess are found both in canonical texts, such as Papanek's *Design for the Real World*, and in recent works, such as Monteiro's *Ruined by Design*.[467]

Turning the attention to individual ethics (a fundamental component of self-design) is a way to mask one's own subordination. Undoubtedly, designers influence reality through their work and choices, but generally this is done in ways that are far from spectacular and hardly fit the cartoonish myth of a great power deriving from great responsibility. In fact, many designers agree that the success of a project depends largely on the goodwill of the client, understood as trust in the designer's competence.[468]

Perspectives, edited by Claudia Mareis and Nina Paim. Amsterdam: Valiz, 2021, p. 89.
465 Garland, *op. cit.*
466 Brown, *The Power of Design...*, *op. cit.*, p. 2.
467 Monteiro, *op. cit.*
468 62% according to Graphic Designers Surveyed, *op. cit.*, p. 288.

CHAPTER 7

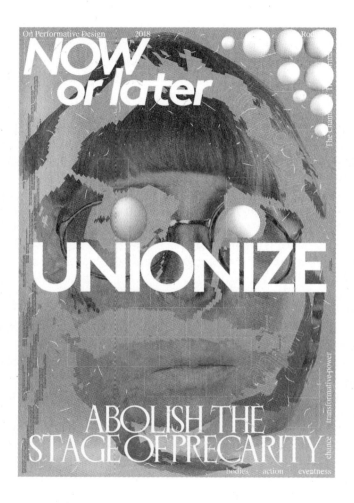

This poster by the duo The Rodina (2018) stages the professional double bind: the workerist slogan clashes with the blown up portrait of a studio member, a more or less conscious manifestation of the performative activity required to create a professional and cultural aura out of one's individuality.

The many variations of the "Old Economy Steve" meme are a perfect instance of hysteresis. The memetic Steve doesn't understand the difficulties of the present because he looks at them through his own, allegedly easier, experience. Ironically, the actual Steve, now in his fifties, is a graphic designer who struggles to find work while dealing with chronic back pain.
Thanks to J. Dakota Brown.

CHAPTER 7

Music and Apocalypse, directed by Max Linz in 2019. The student protest appears here depowered and reduced to an ornamental motif. It also adopts the same generically political language of academia.

The evil entity that seduces, manipulates and deceives consumers, embodied from time to time by the organisation, the client or the designer themselves, is often a straw man. This abstract maleficence is the perfect target of a school that legitimises a distinctive lifestyle – *an attitude*, as Moholy-Nagy describes it. It is an attitude characterised by an affiliation with a kind of moral vanguard.[469] Within its ranks, what professional positioning – which is far from guaranteed – cannot provide, is instead provided by ethical positioning. If it's true that, as Tony Fry argues, design "either serves or subverts the status quo," it is legitimate to ask whether within certain instances of design education, the impetus to subvert the status quo is precisely what ultimately serves it.

POLITICAL
ECONOMY

> Both in education and in business graphic design is often a case of the blind leading the blind. To make the classroom a perpetual forum for political and social issues for instance is wrong; and to see aesthetics as sociology, is grossly misleading. A student whose mind is cluttered with matters which have nothing directly to do with design; whose goal is to learn doing and making; who is thrown into the fray between learning how to use a computer, at the same time that he or she is learning design basics; and being overwhelmed with social problems and political issues is a bewildered student; this is not what he or she bargained for, nor, indeed, paid for.[470]

---

[469] "Members of the PMC [Professional-Managerial Class] believe themselves to be virtuous vanguardists, floating above historical forms and conditions, transgressing boundaries and inventing new ways of being and seeing. It is hard to argue with them, because they do not accept debate as a meaningful form of the advancement of knowledge. For them, every conflict is moral, not intellectual or political." Liu, *op. cit.*, p. 33.

[470] Paul Rand. "Confusion and Chaos: The Seduction of Contemporary Graphic Design." *AIGA Journal of Graphic Design* 10, no. 1 (1992). https://www.paulrand.design/writing/articles/1992-confusion-and-chaos-the-seduction-of-

CHAPTER 7

Found image. Source unknown.

Here, Paul Rand bitterly laments the over-politicisation of graphic design education. It is Aggie Toppins again who reveals the backstory of this rant. Infuriated by the appointment of Sheila Levrant de Bretteville, a feminist designer associated with postmodernism, as director of Yale's graphic design course, Paul Rand abandoned his position in the department, convincing Armin Hoffman to do the same. Quoting Roger Kimball, Rand bemoaned the apparent predominance of "women's studies, black studies, gay studies" over supposedly "traditional curriculum and modes of intellectual inquiry."[471] It is as if the spirit of Jordan Peterson had retrospectively taken hold of him. Aggie Toppins' critique of this article deserves to be read in full.[472] Here, I will instead extract a grain of truth from this almost irredeemable material. The student bewildered by political issues is no less lost than the student thrown into an indecipherable world described by De Carlo in '68. Unfortunately, politics does not make the world a less complex place, and therein lies its value. As we have seen, the ethical disposition instead risks reducing the political to elementary binarisms and bombastic displays of outrage that serve to produce distinctive skills recognised, perhaps, only by designers themselves. It may be a good show, but do-goodism is not much of an educational offering and may even fuel conservatism.

How can we take advantage of political complexity in the educational context? By acknowledging, among other things, students' legitimate professional aspirations, including the less 'revolutionary' ones. The ornamental inclusion of blatantly political issues, the spectacle of indignation, and the ethical crossroads do not absolve schools from their professionalising shortcomings; on the contrary, they may obscure them. This is why a school that really wants to act

---

[471] contemporary-graphic-design.html. *Ivi.*
[472] Aggie Toppins. "Good Nostalgia/Bad Nostalgia." *Design and Culture* 14, no. 1 (January 2, 2022): 5–29. https://doi.org/10.1080/17547075.2021.2010876.

upon so-called 'complexity' must rather extend the domain of what it understands as political, including the economic dimension of political manifestations. In other words, it must devote itself to *political economy*.

COMPROMISE

Hysteresis. Pierre Bourdieu uses a difficult word to describe an all-too-simple phenomenon, which consists of applying an outdated perspective to a mutated context. The sociologist writes:

> The hysteresis effect is proportionately greater for agents who are more remote from the educational system and who are poorly or only vaguely informed about the market in educational qualifications.[473]

The virulent diffusion of the "ok boomer" expression shows that the hysteresis effect has gone mainstream: the new generations are increasingly convinced that old approaches and perspectives don't work anymore in the mutated context of today. So-called boomers are like Don Quixote, immersed in obsolete world of ideas but – beware! – the boomer category is not strictly related to age. A boomer is whoever is tricked by the hysteresis effect – and the young can be tricked too. There are numerous informal accounts of this effect in both the art and design contexts. Joshua Citarella, a US artist, declares to his audience made up of students and emerging artists that "this education and career path is training you to become part of a professional class that, in reality, no longer exists. Institutions pay below market rates and no longer offer the protections that allowed artists to engage with complex ideas."[474] Roberto Arista, an Italian designer, reiterates the point by claiming that "[o]ur professionalizing studies were based on a model that was already crumbling in the

---

[473] Bourdieu, *Distinction, op. cit.*, p. 147.
[474] Citarella, Instagram story.

THE SCHOOL AS REAL WORLD

"We want to think." Slogan formulated in Italy by protesting students in '68.

nineties, and that in the 2000s was just a faded multiple of the original matrix."[475] The way the art and design school conceives self-design is out of sync. The glue that binds its dated ideals is the concept of autonomy. This manifests itself in various ways: romantic detachment from the things of the world, self-conviction of the social necessity of one's skills, critical repositioning within a context that limits access to problem-solving, a disconnect from the present and therefore from history.

In his text on critical autonomy, Andrew Blauvelt proposed that graphic design be understood as "a discipline capable of generating meaning out of its own intrinsic resources without reliance on commissions, functions, or specific materials or means."[476] As I have attempted to demonstrate, critical autonomy is more effect than cause; it is a dazzle, a nice story to tell in the classroom, at the museum or at a conference. This kind of autonomy is only apparent; it is in fact a symptomatic response to professional estrangement. What can this approach be replaced with? Let us take up Maldonado and Anceschi again:

> [...] the technical intellectual, while practising the stoic and realist art of design compromise is never a neutral manager, indifferent to the thing, the theme, the substance.[477]

Design compromise is the antithesis of critical autonomy. It is an admission of the fact that the designer is, after all, inevitably a *bricoleur* – a person who makes do with what they find, in the conditions in which they find themselves.[478] This doesn't mean that design compromise is docile or victimistic. Rather, it is a critique of compromise, an awareness of the reasons that guide awareness.

---

475 Roberto Arista. "Interfaces Are a Solid Object." *Progetto Grafico* 33 (2018).
476 Blauvelt, "Towards Critical Autonomy," *op. cit.*
477 Anceschi, *op. cit.*, p. 36.
478 Gaspare Caliri. "Cos'è il design-as(-a)-bricolage, la cultura del progetto attraverso le teorie della complessità." *cheFare*, January 19, 2021. https://www.che-fare.com/almanacco/cultura/design/cose-il-design-as-a-bricolage-la-cultura-del-progetto-attraverso-le-teorie-della-complessita/.

It is also historical compromise: the ability and courage to distinguish the past from the present. Honing the art of design compromise means recognising the *compromission* of the school as an integral part of the real world. It means overcoming professional proprioception to come to terms with others' perceptions of one's role, especially when these turn out to be unpleasant. An art and design school that wants to embrace an ethos of compromise must be idealist and materialist at the same time. To do so, it should be able to scrutinise the very ambitions that it produces and the mechanisms, both internal and external, that legitimise those ambitions. If such a school wants to become a space for self-realisation, it has to recognise the processes of professionalisation of the self, and overcome them.

Epilogue:

Ragequit

> "Design is only possible where confidence and hope are united. Where there is resignation, that is, no belief in future prospects, there is no design."
> – Gui Bonsiepe, 1992[479]

> "[T]o turn a problem into a project is not to solve it."
> – Hal Foster, 2002[480]

> "Literature really changes things when it bumps up against its own impotence."
> – Walter Siti, 2021[481]

According to G.H., the tortured protagonist of a quasi-mystical novel by Clarice Lispector, "[p]erhaps disillusionment is the fear of no longer belonging to a system."[482] In this book I've traced the porous boundaries of this system employing a two-fold method: on the one hand, I've revived old forms of disenchantment, some of which have been long forgotten; on the other hand, I've felt the pulse of the present by analysing memes and outbursts found in the informal arena of social media. This endeavour has led to the realisation that the larger the gap between expectations and reality, the more likely is the prospect of generating a dispirited, disillusioned practitioner. And from disillusionment to *ragequit* is but a short step. To avoid quitting in anger one should exercise realism, make a healthy compromise with reality, tame professional narcissism. This is what I call *disillusion,* the progressive

---

[479] Gui Bonsiepe. *The Disobedience of Design.* Edited by Lara Penin. Radical Thinkers in Design. London: Bloomsbury, 2022, p. 237.
[480] Foster, *op. cit.*, p. 121.
[481] Walter Siti. *Contro l'impegno: Riflessioni sul Bene in letteratura.* Milano: Rizzoli, 2021, p. 263.
[482] Clarice Lispector. *A paixão segundo G.H.* Rio de Janeiro: Rocco, 2009, p. 7.

tearing of disciplinary veils to develop a realist understanding of what a designer can do in the world.

What is to be done? Here is usually where the reader expects to be enlightened about the way forward, the path to take, the solution to all the discussed problems. This is where the *pars construens* goes. Let's tear off this last veil. Especially in design literature, conclusions have a rhetorical function: a happy end of sorts engineered to leave the reader energised. At the risk of disappointment, this is not gonna happen in this book. Will the reader be left "in the cynic's hall of mirrors" (as one anonymous reviewer put it), then? Hopefully not. Instead of proposing some half-baked alternatives for the sake of expectations, I want to defend pure criticism, as it is nowadays perceived as tantamount to cynicism. This is a stance that affects literature as a whole (see the triumph of manuals and how-to books) and design in particular, given its intrinsic focus on how things ought to be. Since, as we have seen, design is optimistic by default, I used the Gramscian pessimism of intelligence to criticise design's optimism of the will. The *fil rouge* running throughout this book is that it is not negativity and doubt that lead to cynicism but, instead, it is the false *pars construens*, the chimerical ambition, the appearance of constructiveness that do so. When structural problems (reality) are met with gestural solutions (expectations), disillusionment can only spread. To avoid that, it is crucial to "organise pessimism."[483]

HOW BOOKS CHANGE PEOPLE

From this perspective, it becomes clear that the lack of *discussion* of alternatives is not the same as a lack of alternatives. The misunderstanding derives from our understanding of how books change people. Advocates of the

---

[483] A book with a similar mission is the one written by Portuguese architectural critic Pedro Levi Bismarck, who borrows the expression "organised pessimism" from Walter Benjamin. *Arquitectura e «pessimismo»: Sobre uma condição política em arquitectura*. Porto: Punkto, 2020.

pars construens see change as linear, mechanistic: a book describes a solution which is then implemented by the reader. According to this view, a book without solutions, proposals or 'ways out' is an incomplete, crippled book. But arguing that criticism *per se* is not generative and that a case study is more 'real' than an analysis is misleading. What is really missing nowadays in design literature are texts that definitively place themselves outside of design optimism. In this regard, I would like to mention a person from whom the design field has learned a lot and still has a lot to learn: Salvatore Iaconesi, who together with Oriana Persico formed Art is Open Source. Iaconesi, who passed away last year, was a designer, a hacker and a theorist. He was deeply occupied with the question of tragedy within design practices. What the design field lacks, its great unspoken, is the tragic. Not the blockbuster representation of the tragedy of others (there is plenty of that), but the lived tragedy coming from the misery of everyday life. This story has not yet been sufficiently told. One cannot formulate a how-to for dealing with the tragic, one cannot develop a series of 'best practices' to fix tragedy, for tragedy is not a problem but a *dilemma*. How does a book act in the world? "The only way out of the tragedy is to *change state*," wrote Iaconesi.[484] A book really acts when it is able to transform the subject, and a subject can be transformed even by the least constructive book in the world – I am thinking of authors like Emil Cioran or Albert Caraco. Here, then, is the gap to be filled in the field of design: we have never been pessimists.

While discussing my ideas about disillusion, a friend called me a 'doomer.' Another one christened me 'blackpilled.' Finally, I was deemed hopeless. Can hope sprout from hopelessness? According to Maldonado, designing without hope is that "paradoxical behaviour that

---

[484] Salvatore Iaconesi. "Nuovo Abitare, after COVID." *Counter Arts* (blog), July 15, 2021. https://medium.com/counterarts/nuovo-abitare-after-covid-e85e40e49861..

EPILOGUE

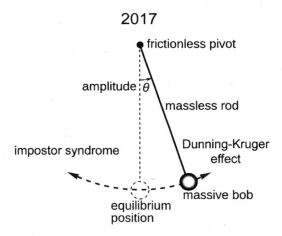

Federico Antonini (2021). The designer's activity as a pendulum between impostor syndrome and the Dunning-Kruger effect, that is, unfounded overconfidence.

→ *Saint Jerome in His Study*, Albrecht Dürer (1514), engraving.

stems from being compelled to design without having anything concrete to design. What's more: without having confidence, without the will."[485] Authentic hope, however, is not to be found *written* in the last pages of a book, but outside it, practised in the affinities and alliances built between the author and the readers, and among the readers themselves. This is why those rare obstinately hopeless books might be the most authentically hopeful ones. For Maldonado, hope is the functional belief in the designer's autonomy:

> When a designer – for example an architect – is persuaded that, as a designer, he can contribute to the transformation of society, he can only act in this sense to the extent that he believes in a relative innovative autonomy of his work. [The designer] will have to act even if this question will always remain open, that is, without knowing whether his autonomy will ultimately prove to be an illusion.[486]

As we see here, this belief in autonomy might prove itself illusory, but the issue is not a either-or one: illusions coexist with autonomy. In this book, I've highlighted the illusory aspects of the design field and described how they affect everyday designers' work and self-perception. Hopefully, this effort shows, in contrast, some of the real autonomy that designers can have, including the ability to disillusion themselves.

SIMPLIFYING ACCORDING TO TRUTH

In the previous chapters I have argued that complexity is not only the condition we inhabit, but also a lobbying instrument for design, a way to positions the designer as the figure who is most suited to dealing with it. The outcome of this situation is a paradoxical one: designers and

---

[485] Maldonado, *La speranza progettuale, op. cit.*, p. 29.
[486] *Ibidem*, p. 124.

design theorists have an incentive to increase complexity in order to reduce it. This way, any attempt at simplification is portrayed as a trivialisation of the issue at hand. The result is a sort of paralysing apophenia, where everything is linked to everything else. Here, drawing any type of boundary, proposing categories, employing models... all of this leads to suspicion.

In 2008, historian Russell Jacoby admitted that "the world is complex, but how did 'complication' turn from an undeniable reality into a desirable goal? How did the act of complicating become a virtue?" He noticed an emphasis on *problematising, contextualising, relativising*, etc.[487] These are valuable endeavours, but boundaries must be drawn, categories need to be produced, models need to be developed. If we don't do that, we will simply be trapped in other people's models, categories and boundaries. This doesn't mean that they should be crystallised once and for all. While designers formalise, they have to look at their formalisations as temporary arrangements. Here, as well, they should act as bricoleurs. The intransigent complexist insists that 'it's not that simple,' to which the cautious simplicist responds: 'exactly: sometimes complexity can be simplistic, and simplicity can be complex.'

That said, designers cannot simplify alone, they do not possess an all-embracing synthetic ability. Synthesis will always be concerted and involve negotiation and conflict: it's a political-epistemic act. But what should be the driving principle of this synthesis? Perhaps designers can embrace the motto of Italian writer and politician Leonardo Sciascia: "simplifying according to truth,"[488] where truth, that unfashionable notion, is the difficult part.

---

[487] Jacoby quoted in Guido Vitiello. "I nuovi complessisti contro il 'pensiero unico'. Esercizi di atletica retorica." *Il Foglio*, April 5, 2022. https://www.ilfoglio.it/societa/2022/04/05/news/i-nuovi-complessisti-contro-il-pensiero-unico-esercizi-di-atletica-retorica-3876461/.

[488] Sciascia quoted in Euclide Lo Giudice. "Sciascia su Sciascia." *Leonardo Sciascia Web*. https://www.amicisciascia.it/leonardo-sciascia/sciascia-su-sciascia.html.

EPILOGUE

COMPROMISSION

In his memoirs, Francesco Borromini includes a disclaimer to explain that when he served a particularly timid patron, it was better to curb his creative impetus and submit to their will.[489] Agreeing with and appreciating the humbleness of such a monumental figure as the Baroque architect means embracing compromise. For, when it comes to actually realising things, designing is neither about synthesis nor autonomy, neither order nor reason, but about compromise. We could speak of interdependence, but while interdependence acknowledges the constrictive and generative relationships that exist beyond autonomy, its essence is passive. Compromise, on the other hand, is an active and political endeavour: it implies mediation, if not *compromission*, that is, the adulteration of pure vision, with hands getting dirty in the messiness of reality. Stretching etymology a bit, compromission includes the word 'mission,' revealing an agency, an intention. As architect Marta Lonzi explains:

> My own experience tells me that there is nothing more exciting than to design accepting the limits that reality reveals and the constraints that the pre-existent imposes in a creative effort of great respect, above all, for the existential expectations that humans seek in order to be happy on this earth: at home, in a city, amid nature that makes them feel worthy of living this life, without upheavals or functional misery.[490]

After all, design is a compromise with the real, that is, a compromise with past things and, therefore, a negotiation of future ones. To design is both to compromise yourself and to compromise things. Design can undermine reality, while reality can jeopardise design. Against the

---

489 Marta Lonzi. *Autenticità e progetto*. Milano: Jaca Book, 2006, p. 12.
490 *Ibidem*, pp. 42-43.

pseudo-scientific rationale of a project as the result of a logical, ineluctable process, we must opt for a political one, which does not necessarily correspond to activism, but it surely involves a compromise between conflicting forces.

THE PRACTICE OF PRACTICES

The first chapter of C. Wright Mills' *The Sociological Imagination* (1959) is entitled "The Promise." This chapter is not, as I suspected, about generic expectations, such as having a house, finding a job or building a career. What Mills talks about is "the promise of social science," ensured by a fundamental skill that a social scientist should muster. This skill is the sociological imagination, the ability to connect the personal and the societal, what Mills calls "the interplay of man and society, of biography and history, of self and world." It is about understanding personal troubles in the light of structural issues. A problem, for Mills, is an adequate formulation of these two scales. This is how he discusses it:

> The sociological imagination enables its possessor to understand the larger historical scene in terms of its meaning for the inner life and the external career of a variety of individuals. It enables him to take into account how individuals, in the welter of their daily experience, often become falsely conscious of their social positions. Within that welter, the framework of modern society is sought, and within that framework the psychologies of a variety of men and women are formulated. By such means the personal uneasiness of individuals is focused upon explicit troubles and the indifference of publics is transformed into involvement with public issues. The first fruit of this imagination – and the first lesson of the social science that embodies it – is the idea that the

> individual can understand his own experience and gauge his own fate only by locating himself within his period, that he can know his own chances in life only by becoming aware of those of all individuals in his circumstances. In many ways it is a terrible lesson; in many ways a magnificent one.[491]

Keeping in mind Mills' terribly magnificent lesson, what I attempted in this book was to turn the lens of sociological imagination to the *milieu* of design. Paraphrasing some of Mills' questions, this book asked:

> What varieties of [practitioners] now prevail in this field and in this period? And what varieties are coming to prevail? In what ways are they selected and formed, liberated and repressed, made sensitive and blunted?[492]

We have seen that part of this selection revolves around a promise of autonomy which implies self-direction. This self-direction is what we call a practice. What do we mean by that? 'Practice' is a term used mainly in the arts to define an artist's poietic activity. It involves the artist's concerns, their method, medium and even their theoretical and ethical ground. Through the decades, design has been considered a style, a craft, a thinking approach, etc. Now, with the notion of practice, we observe an extension of the understanding of the designer's activity as that of an increasingly generic cultural professional. What does this shift mean? Borrowing from programming, one could say that each *constant* of the discipline (methods, techniques, media and products, literacy, topics, ethical issues) is turned into a *variable*. Unavoidably, a degree of specificity is lost as the designer is encouraged to tweak all these variables. But if none of these is shared among peers, how can we call this a field? The liberating potential

---

[491] C. Wright Mills. *The Sociological Imagination*. New York: Oxford University Press, 1959, p. 5.
[492] *Ibidem*, p. 7.

of tweaking the very terms of one's work might also lead to isolation and individualisation. Educational institutions that are aware of this problem partially compensate the atomising drive with participatory and collaborative modes of interaction.

The variable-tweaking process that constitutes a design practice resembles micro-targeted advertising: as specific as to address one person only. It might be that 'at the intersection of' (an expression commonly found in designers' bios) there is no one else other than you. The autonomy of the self-directed professional can adumbrate precarity and insidiously replicate the much-despised design protagonism. In which case, it is not autonomy but wishful thinking. *Fauxtonomy*, if you will. The 'practice' model of the cultural professional is not dissimilar to the subject formation of the contemporary artist, which rarely offers more than a faint sense of belonging. Is this model, then, a weak form of professional, and therefore social, reproduction? The traditional medium-based or problem-based orientation was perhaps more solid for the simple fact that it had at least some fixed variables. The point, however, is not to choose one model over the other, but to raise a specific concern: what effects does the 'practice of practices' have on identification? Are design schools partially responsible for the disintegrating sense of belonging and tangible social isolation that many practitioners, often self-defined as outsiders, feel? By offering an abstract promise of autonomy, are schools uncritically abdicating their role to nurture a recognisable field?

ST. JEROME

The devaluation of skill-specificity is also worrisome because, in a society that cherishes work above all, craft is one of the few stable forms left of identity making: the mastery of a craft goes way beyond a professional title. A job well done for its own sake, the ample definition of a craft offered by Richard Sennett,[493] can be an island of personal stability in a sea of impostor syndrome and self-doubt, punctuated by episodes of megalomania. Furthermore, crafts defy make-believe horizontalism by showing the positive side of hierarchy: a workshop master-apprentice relationship is not in itself an exploitative, abusive one.

Himself a craftsman, C. Wright Mills wrote that "[t]he most fundamental splits in contemporary life occur because of the break-up of the old unity of design, production and enjoyment." In craftsmanship, these three activities are conjoined. Mills also saw his research activity as a form of "intellectual craftsmanship," which we can understand as a mode of operating of the technical intellectual. As Treviño explains:

> "Social science," writes Mills "is the practice of a craft." A craft refers to the manual or mental processes through which workers freely employ their capacities and skills in creating the products of their enjoyment and enjoying the products of their creation. Mills uses the term "intellectual craftsmanship" in referring to a reflective style of work as well as "to the joyful experience of mastering the resistance of the materials with which one works."[494]

I started this book with Dürer's *Melencolia*, a brooding figure that expresses apathy and impotence, as the allegory of the disillusioned designer. I'd like to conclude it with another engraving, also by Dürer. Here, we see St. Jerome diligently occupied with the translation of the Bible into Latin. The scene exudes tranquillity: Jerome's study is well arranged, radiating brightness. The objects in the room are neatly organised, although not rigidly so. Rather than being burdensome, the saint's work is contemplative. He moves at a relaxed pace, undisturbed by the presence of a skull and

---

493   Richard Sennett. *The Craftsman*. London: Penguin, 2009.
494   Treviño, *op. cit.*, pp. 343-4.

an hourglass, symbols of mortality and the passage of time. These reminders do not provoke any sense of urgency or fear within him. Jerome has embraced the inevitability of death, and he focuses intently on his task without anxiety. A lion, the saint's loyal companion, lies quietly at the front of the sunlit room, symbolising the taming of human passions.[495] Jerome's craft seems to give him peace. Whereas *Melencolia* stands for disillusionment and chaos, *St. Jerome* represents a provisional yet fulfilling sense of order.

THE COMING FIELD

To find this provisional sense of order, to avoid succumbing to the multi-layered identity crises driven by fauxtonomy and futurelessness, it is time to put self-design aside and rebuild the design field around different, but not necessarily unprecedented, principles. This field should be a space inhabited by a series of connected communities of practice (where practice is *not* understood as in contemporary art, namely devoid of an authentic communal sense). It shouldn't shy away from problems. Instead, it should constantly redefine its own set of issues and concerns: functional problems, ethical problems, problems of method, access and inclusion. Unavoidably it will deal with complexity, but it won't try to tackle it in its entirety. Through the specialised knowledge it produces and the situated activity it performs, it will look at complexity without being blinded by its frightening, Cthulhu-like appearance.

The design field should be considered a political entity, but not because it regularly issues statements and manifestos. It is political because it is concerned with its own organisational politics, as well as the politics of the artefacts it circulates. Such a design field would be preoccupied with tangible, lower-case futures. The future rests in

---

[495] See https://www.khanacademy.org/humanities/renaissance-reformation/northern/durer/a/durer-melancholia.

its surroundings, but also in the broader effects that interventions on these surroundings have. It thus moves within a gradient of multiple scales. A field such as this is not a 'scene:' its main engine isn't visibility. It might even unconsciously limit the exchange with the outside. But if it's too self-referential, it will become a club.

Nor is it a school: while learning takes place within it, scholastic hierarchies, both implicit and explicit, don't apply there. This doesn't mean that it rejects hierarchy completely: its structure is based on the healthy, reconfigurable hierarchies of apprenticeship, amateurship and curiosity. Design should be informal in nature, but it shouldn't fetishise informality: it should resist character normativity and protect its people from hurtful behaviour. It should be attentive to its flows of social, cultural and economic capital: generous with quoting, crediting and remunerating; mistrustful of impresarios and creative directors; rejectful of inner qualitative distinctions. All the work it needs is essential, interdependent work. Validation comes with effort, helpfulness and mutuality, more than with smartness, talent and bravado. It should believe in expertise, but not worship experts. It should provide an activity-based sense of belonging where people have roles and purposes, but these can be renegotiated. Here, biographical and cultural differences would be understood, but foregrounded only when necessary, so that a designer can blissfully forget themselves.

THE CROSSROAD

Right now, design culture is cohabited by two conflicting sets of values: a culture of smartness and one of contribution. Smart culture – the culture that has shaped my generation of designers – privileges the new idea, the concept that makes you go 'a-ha.' As such, it's based on detachment: worthy of attention is the thing that distances itself from the others, and by extension, the maker that stands out from the crowd. In this sense, it is tragically similar to the operative logic of the neoliberal ethos: relentless reinvention. It is inattentive and uncompromising, as it ignores what's there and forgets what was there. Contribution culture, on the other hand, is humble, it *builds upon*. When a useful idea emerges, it helps it to flourish. Smart culture is uncompromising, intransigent and self-absorbed. Contribution culture is compromissory, tolerant and indulgent. It is realistic, but it doesn't ignore the reality of ideas. Whereas smart culture creates, contributory culture maintains. Smart culture is design, contribution culture is bricolage.

We see smart culture in the celebration of design heroes, in the throwaway solutions to epochal problems, in the pervasiveness of personal branding, in the distinctive performance of kritikaoke. We see contribution culture in the online syllabi put together collaboratively and semi-anonymously, in free and open-source tools, in students' translation of texts they find important into their mother tongue, in artefacts designed 'for and with' specific communities. Exploring design disillusion means venturing into the sorry shadow cast by smart culture, this kitschy relic of our shaky modernity. This book indicates the shadow's contour in the hope that other people, in other contexts, will dissipate it, together.

Acknowledgements

While working on *What Design Can't Do,* I came to realise that to cultivate the perseverance to write a book and get it published, one needs to know at all times that there is one person out there who *gets it*. For me this person was Geert Lovink, and for this reason I thank him immensely. I'm also particularly grateful to Sebastian Schmieg, for our decade-long conversation that shaped the book and sharpened my thinking. My gratitude goes as well to the Centre for Other Worlds, and especially to Francisco Laranjo and Luís Alegre.

Furthermore, I want to thank those who read and commented on the essays: Manetta Berends, Cristina Cochior, Cade Diehm, Clive Dilnot, Caterina Di Paolo, Michele Galluzzo, Sami Hammana, Gui Machiavelli, Pau de Riba, Eduardo Staszowski, Marta Sternberg and the anonymous reviewers. Then, those who gave suggestions and support: Roel Roscam Abbing, Luigi Amato, Federico Antonini, J. Dakota Brown, Georgiana Cojocaru, Alessio D'Ellena, Claudia Doms, Frederico Duarte, Eva Gonçalves, Angelo Gramegna, Gabriele Marino, Afonso Matos, Ruben Pater, Pia Pol, Simone Robutti, Ilaria Roglieri, Eduardo Souza, Raffaele Alberto Ventura, Adriano Vulpio, Thomas Walskaar, the members of Varia and the folks of Scambio Theory.

For many years now, design schools have constituted a large part of my own 'real world.' Teaching in institutions located in various European countries has deeply influenced my understanding of the design field. These are the Lusófona University of Lisbon, the Royal Academy of Art in The Hague, the Sandberg Instituut of Amsterdam, the Design Academy Eindhoven, the Piet Zwart Institute in Rotterdam, the Burg Giebichenstein University of Art and Design in Halle, the Abadir Academy in Catania, the CFP Bauer in Milan.

I'm grateful for the opportunity to present and discuss the ideas that led to this book at the following venues: Pratt Institute (at the invitation of Nida Abdullah, Chris Lee

ACKNOWLEDGEMENTS

and Xinyi Li), Design Academy Eindhoven (Marco Ferrari), Paris College of Art (Lucrezia Russo), Burg (Matthias Görlich, Marion Kliesch and Sanna Schiffler), MAAT Museum, Design Write podcast (Joeri Pruys, Jeroen Deckers, Aynouk Tan), The New Design Congress (Cade Diehm and Benjamin Royer), Merz Akademie (Olia Lialina), Yale School of Art (Julian Bittiner and Paul Bille), Iuav University of Venice (Noemi Biasetton and Pierfrancesco Califano), Iaspis (Mahmoud Keshavarz and Magnus Ericson), The Hague University of Applied Sciences (Alex Zakkas), the Faculty of Fine Arts at the University of Lisbon (Sofia Gonçalves), Abadir Academy (Mauro Bubbico and Giacomo Boffo).

Earlier versions or parts of these essays were published in: my personal blog; *CheFare*; *Extra-curricular*, edited by Jacob Lindgren (Onomatopee, 2018); *Design School: After Boundaries and Discipline*, edited by Paul A. Rodgers and Craig Bremner (Vernon Press, 2019); *Menelique*; *Other Worlds*; *Designers Write*; *Graphic Design in the Post-Digital Age*, edited by Demian Conrad, Rob van Leijsen and David Héritier (Set Margins' 2022); *Who Can Afford to Be Critical?*, edited by Afonso Matos (Set Margins' 2023); *The New Design Congress*; *BookCloud*, edited by Noemi Biasetton.

Over the years, I took notes on social media and tried to make sense of them publicly. In fact, *What Design Can't Do* can be seen as the byproduct of a never-ending Twitter thread.[496] I also discussed it on the Lurk instance of Mastodon. Many users engaged with this work and I want to collectively thank them.

A final thought goes to all the students that I got to know, both as a teacher and as a student myself.

Silvio Lorusso
Lisbon, September 2023

---

[496] https://twitter.com/silvio_lorusso/status/1336248731033882624.

Bibliography

PROLOGUE: STARTER PACK

Adorno, Theodor W. *Minima Moralia: Reflections from Damaged Life*. London: Verso, 1978.

Bridle, James. *New Dark Age: Technology and the End of the Future*. London: Verso, 2018.

Caraco, Albert. *Breviario del caos*. Milano: Adelphi, 1998.

Carstens, Delphi. "Hyperstition." *orphan Drift Archive* (blog), 2010. https://www.orphandriftarchive.com/articles/hyperstition/.

Castoriadis, Cornelius. "The Crisis of Modern Society." *Solidarity Pamphlet*, 1965. https://libcom.org/article/crisis-modern-society-cornelius-castoriadis.

Chayka, Kyle. "How Silicon Valley Helps Spread the Same Sterile Aesthetic Across the World." *The Verge*, August 3, 2016. https://www.theverge.com/2016/8/3/12325104/airbnb-aesthetic-global-minimalism-startup-gentrification.

De Carlo, Giancarlo. *La piramide rovesciata: architettura oltre il '68*. Macerata: Quodlibet, 2018.

Enzensberger, Hans Magnus. "Remarks Concerning the New York Universitas Project." In *The Universitas Project: Solutions for a Post-Technological Society*, edited by Emilio Ambasz. New York: The Museum of Modern Art, 2006.

Gerritzen, Mieke, and Geert Lovink. *Made in China, Designed in California, Criticised in Europe: Design Manifesto*. Amsterdam: BIS Publishers, 2020.

Gramsci, Antonio. *Letters from Prison*. New York: Columbia University Press, 1994.

Green, Penelope. "Mary Catherine Bateson Dies at 81; Anthropologist on Lives of Women." *The New York Times*, January 14, 2021. https://www.nytimes.com/2021/01/14/books/mary-catherine-bateson-dead.html.

Labranca, Tommaso. *Vraghinaroda: Sopravvivendo a hipster situazionisti, santexuperine scalze e mistificatori deleuziani*. Milano: 20090, 2019.

Laranjo, Francisco. "Critical Graphic Design: Critical of What?" *Design Observer*, April 16, 2014. http://designobserver.com/feature/critical-graphic-design-critical-of-what/38416.

Lovink, Geert. "Precarious by Design." In *Entreprecariat: Everyone Is an Entrepreneur, Nobody Is Safe*, by Silvio Lorusso. Eindhoven: Onomatopee, 2019.

Maldonado, Tomás. *La speranza progettuale: ambiente e società*. Torino: Einaudi, 1997.

Mari, Enzo. *25 modi per piantare un chiodo: Sessant'anni di idee e*

progetti per difendere un sogno. Milano: Mondadori, 2011.
Pater, Ruben. *Caps Lock: How Capitalism Took Hold of Graphic Design, and How to Escape from It*. Amsterdam: Valiz, 2021.
Popova, Maria. "'Frankenstein' Author Mary Shelley on Creativity." *The Marginalian* (blog), June 25, 2018. https://www.themarginalian.org/2018/06/25/mary-shelley-creativity-franksenstein-1831/.
Potter, Norman. *What Is a Designer: Things, Places, Messages*. London: Hyphen Press, 2006.
Rittel, Horst W. J., and Melvin M. Webber. "Dilemmas in a General Theory of Planning." *Policy Sciences* 4, no. 2 (June 1, 1973): 155–69. https://doi.org/10.1007/BF01405730.
Till, Jeremy. *Architecture Depends*. Cambridge, MA: MIT Press, 2013.

CHAPTER 1.
IN THE MIDDLE

Agamben, Giorgio. *Nudities*. Stanford: Stanford University Press, 2011.
Benjamin, Walter. *Selected Writings Vol. 1, 1913-1926*. Cambridge, MA: Belknap, 2004.
Berlant, Lauren. *Cruel Optimism*. Durham, NC: Duke University Press, 2011.
Blosch, Marcus, and Jackie Fenn. "Understanding Gartner's Hype Cycles." *Gartner*, August 20, 2018. https://www.gartner.com/en/documents/3887767/understanding-gartner-s-hype-cycles.
Buchanan, Richard. "Design Research and the New Learning." *Design Issues* 17, no. 4 (October 1, 2001): 3–23. https://doi.org/10.1162/07479360152681056.
Castoriadis, Cornelius. *Postscript on Insignificance: Dialogues with Cornelius Castoriadis*. London: Bloomsbury, 2011.
Clifton, Jim. "The World's Broken Workplace." *Gallup*, June 13, 2017. https://news.gallup.com/opinion/chairman/212045/world-broken-workplace.aspx.
Colomina, Beatriz, and Mark Wigley. *Are We Human? The Archaeology of Design*. Zürich: Lars Müller, 2016.
De Martin, Paola. "Breaking Class: Upward Climbers and the Swiss Nature of Design History." In *Design Struggles: Intersecting Histories, Pedagogies, and Perspectives*, edited by Claudia Mareis and Nina Paim. Amsterdam: Valiz, 2021.
Fluzin, Baptiste. "Designers, Designers, Designers." *Tumblr* (blog), October 11, 2016. https://bfluzin.tumblr.com/post/152990139318.
Franklin, Ursula M. *The Real World of Technology*. Toronto: Anansi, 1999.
Garrett, Jesse. "Ux Design Is More Successful Than Ever, but Its Leaders Are Losing Hope. Here's Why." *Fast Company*, June 3,

2021. https://www.fastcompany.com/90642462/ux-design-is-more-successful-than-ever-but-its-leaders-are-losing-hope.

Giddens, Anthony. *The Consequences of Modernity*. Cambridge, UK: Polity Press, 2015.

Grievink, Hendrik-Jan. "Template Culture." *Mediamatic*, 2009. http://www.mediamatic.net/en/page/116348/template-culture.

Heller, Steven. "The Evolution of Design." *The Atlantic*, April 9, 2015. https://www.theatlantic.com/entertainment/archive/2015/04/a-more-inclusive-history-of-design/390069/.

International Design Conference in Aspen: The First Decade, 1961. https://www.youtube.com/watch?v=8MxCGKicSfg.

Irwin, Terry, Gideon Kossoff, and Cameron Tonkinwise. "Transition Design Provocation." *Design Philosophy Papers* 13, no. 1 (January 2, 2015): 3–11. https://doi.org/10.1080/14487136.2015.1085688.

Julier, Guy. *Economies of Design*. Los Angeles: SAGE Publications, 2017.

Klibansky, Raymond, Erwin Panofsky, and Fritz Saxl. *Saturn and Melancholy: Studies in the History of Natural Philosophy, Religion and Art*. Nendeln: Kraus Reprint, 1979.

Le Goff, Jacques, ed. *L'uomo medievale*. Bari: Laterza, 2013.

Lunardi, Flavia. "Grafica Italia 2018." ISIA, 2018.

Maldonado, Tomás. *La speranza progettuale: ambiente e società*. Torino: Einaudi, 1997.

Manzini, Ezio. *Design, When Everybody Designs*. Cambridge, MA: MIT Press, 2015.

Margolin, Victor. *The Politics of the Artificial: Essays on Design and Design Studies*. Chicago: University of Chicago Press, 2018.

Metahaven. *Can Jokes Bring down Governments?* Moscow: Strelka Press, 2014.

Mills, C. Wright. "Man in the Middle: The Designer." In *Power, Politics and People*, edited by Irving L. Horowitz. London: Oxford University Press, 1969.

Moholy-Nagy, László. *Vision in Motion*. Chicago: P. Theobald, 1947.

Pater, Ruben. *Caps Lock: How Capitalism Took Hold of Graphic Design, and How to Escape from It*. Amsterdam: Valiz, 2021.

Peters, Tom. *Re-Imagine!* London: DK, 2006. https://archive.org/details/reimagineoooopete.

Petroni, Marco. *Il progetto del reale: il design che non torna alla normalità*. Milano: Postmedia Books, 2020.

Pownall, Augusta. "'We Don't Have the Power to Stop Our Extinction' Says Paola Antonelli." *Dezeen*, February 22, 2019. https://www.dezeen.com/2019/02/22/paola-antonelli-extinction-milan-triennale-broken-nature-exhibition/.

Roberts, Lucienne, Rebecca Wright, and Jessie Price, eds. *Graphic

Designers Surveyed. London: GraphicDesign&, 2015.

Simon, Herbert A. *The Sciences of the Artificial*. Cambridge, MA: MIT Press, 2019.

Suchman, Lucy. "Anthropological Relocations and the Limits of Design." *Annual Review of Anthropology* 40, no. 1 (2011). https://www.academia.edu/19545153/Anthropological_Relocations_and_the_Limits_of_Design.

The Invisible Committee. *The Coming Insurrection*. New York: Autonomedia, 2009.

The National Gallery. "Albrecht Dürer, Melencolia I, 1514." https://www.nga.gov/collection/highlights/durer-melencolia.html/.

Treviño, A. Javier. "C. Wright Mills as Designer: Personal Practice and Two Public Talks." *The American Sociologist* 45, no. 4 (December 1, 2014): 335–60. https://doi.org/10.1007/s12108-014-9196-y.

Twemlow, Alice. "'A Guaranteed Communications Failure:' Consensus Meets Conflict at the International Design Conference in Aspen, 1970." In *Aspen Complex*, edited by Martin Beck. London: Sternberg Press, 2013. https://alicetwemlow.com/a-guaranteed-communications-failure-consensus-meets-conflict-at-the-international-design-conference-in-aspen-1970/.

Whyte, William H. *The Organization Man*. Philadelphia: University of Pennsylvania Press, 2002.

Williams, Raymond. *The Long Revolution*. London: Penguin Books, 1965.

Wizinsky, Matthew. *Design After Capitalism: Transforming Design Today for an Equitable Tomorrow*. Cambridge, MA: MIT Press, 2022.

Zohn, Harry. *Karl Kraus*. New York: Ungar, 1971.

CHAPTER 2.
EVERYTHING EVERYONE ALL AT ONCE

Antonelli, Paola. "Foreword." In Alexandra Midal. *Design by Accident: For a New History of Design*. Berlin: Sternberg Press, 2019.

Benjamin, Ruha. *Race After Technology: Abolitionist Tools for the New Jim Code*. Cambridge, UK: Polity, 2020.

Blackler, Alethea, Levi Swann, Marianella Chamorro-Koc, Wathsala Anupama Mohotti, Thirunavukarasu Balasubramaniam, and Richi Nayak. "Can We Define Design? Analyzing Twenty Years of Debate on a Large Email Discussion List." *She Ji: The Journal of Design, Economics, and Innovation* 7, no. 1 (March 1, 2021): 41–70. https://doi.org/10.1016/j.sheji.2020.11.004.

Blauvelt, Andrew. "Towards Critical Autonomy or Can Graphic Design Save Itself?" *Emigre*, 2004.

Colomina, Beatriz, and Mark Wigley. *Are We Human? The Archaeology of Design*. Zürich: Lars Müller, 2016.

Franklin, Ursula M. *The Real World of Technology*. Toronto: Anansi, 1999.

Gerritzen, Mieke, and Geert Lovink. *Everyone Is a Designer in the Age of Social Media*. Amsterdam: BIS, 2010.

–––. *Everyone Is a Designer! Manifest for the Design Economy*. Amsterdam: BIS, 2001.

Giddens, Anthony. *The Consequences of Modernity*. Cambridge, UK: Polity Press, 2015.

Gramsci, Antonio. *The Antonio Gramsci Reader: Selected Writings, 1916-1935*. Edited by David Forgacs. New York: New York University Press, 2000.

Heller, Steven. "The Evolution of Design." *The Atlantic*, April 9, 2015. https://www.theatlantic.com/entertainment/archive/2015/04/a-more-inclusive-history-of-design/390069/.

Hills, Thomas. "Can Animals Imagine Things That Have Never Happened?" *Psychology Today*, October 22, 2019. https://www.psychologytoday.com/intl/blog/statistical-life/201910/can-animals-imagine-things-have-never-happened.

Hollein, Hans. "Alles Ist Architektur." *Bau*, 1968. https://socks-studio.com/2013/08/13/hans-holleins-alles-ist-architektur-1968/.

Latour, Bruno. "A Cautious Prometheus? A Few Steps Toward a Philosophy of Design (with Special Attention to Peter Sloterdijk)." edited by Fiona Hackne, Jonathan Glynne, and Viv Minto, 2–10. Falmouth: Universal Publishers, 2009.

Levin, Golan, and Tega Brain. *Code As Creative Medium: A Handbook for Computational Art and Design*. Cambridge, MA: MIT Press, 2021.

Maldonado, Tomás. *Disegno industriale: un riesame*. Milano: Feltrinelli, 2008.

Manzini, Ezio. *Design, When Everybody Designs*. Cambridge, MA: MIT Press, 2015.

Marx, Karl. *Capital*. Vol. 1. Marx/Engels Internet Archive, 1999. https://www.marxists.org/archive/marx/works/1867-c1/index.htm.

Mau, Bruce, Jennifer Leonard, and Institute without Boundaries. *Massive Change*. London, New York: Phaidon, 2004. http://archive.org/details/massivechange0000maub.

Mitcham, Carl. "In Memoriam Ivan Illich: Critic of Professionalized Design." *Design Issues* 19, no. 4 (October 1, 2003): 26–30. https://doi.org/10.1162/074793603322545037.

Moles, Abraham A. "Objet et communication." *Communications* 13, no. 1 (1969): 1–21. https://doi.org/10.3406/comm.1969.1183.

Munari, Bruno. *Good Design*. Mantova: Corraini, 2010.

Murtaugh, Michael. "Torn at the Seams: Considering Computational Vernacular." In *Vernaculars Come to Matter*, edited by Cristina Cochior, Sofia Boshat-Thorez, and Manetta Berends, 93–110. Rotterdam: Everyday Technology Press, 2021.

Potter, Norman. *What Is a Designer: Things, Places, Messages*. London: Hyphen Press, 2006.

Poynor, Rick. "First Things Next." In *Obey the Giant: Life in the Image World*. Boston, MA: Birkhauser Verlag AG, 2007.

Rodgers, Paul A., and Craig Bremner. "The Design of Nothing: A Working Philosophy." In *Advancements in the Philosophy of Design*, edited by Pieter E. Vermaas and Stéphane Vial, 549–64. Design Research Foundations. Cham: Springer International Publishing, 2018. https://doi.org/10.1007/978-3-319-73302-9_25.

Ruskin, John. *The Nature of Gothic: A Chapter of the Stones of Venice*. Hammersmith: Kelmscott Press, 1892.

Secomandi, Fernando, and Dirk Snelders. "Interface Design in Services: A Postphenomenological Approach." *Design Issues* 29, no. 1 (January 1, 2013): 3–13. https://doi.org/10.1162/DESI_a_00192.

Stewart, Susan. "And So to Another Setting...." In *Design and the Question of History*, edited by Tony Fry and Clive Dilnot, 275–301, 2020. https://doi.org/10.5040/9781474245890.

Suchman, Lucy. "Keywords for Ethnography and Design: Design." *Society for Cultural Anthropology*, March 29, 2018. https://culanth.org/fieldsights/design.

Treviño, A. Javier. "C. Wright Mills as Designer: Personal Practice and Two Public Talks." *The American Sociologist* 45, no. 4 (December 1, 2014): 335–60. https://doi.org/10.1007/s12108-014-9196-y.

United Nations, Department of Social and Economic Affairs. "Measures for the Economic Development of Under-Developed Countries," 1951. http://digitallibrary.un.org/record/708544.

Von Foerster, Heinz, and Francisco Varela. "Introduction." In *Observing Systems*, XVI. Systems Inquiry Series. Seaside CA: Intersystems Publications, 1984.

Willis, Anne-Marie. "Ontological Designing." *Design Philosophy Papers* 4, no. 2 (June 1, 2006): 69–92. https://doi.org/10.2752/144871306X13966268131514.

Zuccari, Federico. *L'Idea de' Pittori, Scultori Ed Architetti*, 1607.

CHAPTER 3.
A COMPLEX RELATIONSHIP

Abdulla, Danah. "Disciplinary Disobedience." In *Design Struggles:*

Intersecting Histories, Pedagogies, and Perspectives, edited by Claudia Mareis and Nina Paim. Amsterdam: Valiz, 2021.

Bayer, Herbert, Ilse Gropius, and Walter Gropius, eds. *Bauhaus 1919-1928*. New York: The Museum of Modern Art, 1938. https://www.moma.org/documents/moma_catalogue_2735_300190238.pdf.

Beegan, Gerry, and Paul Atkinson. "Professionalism, Amateurism and the Boundaries of Design." *Journal of Design History* 21, no. 4 (2008): 305–13.

Bonsiepe, Gui. "Design and Democracy." *Design Issues* 22, no. 2 (2006): 27–34.

———. "Design e Sottosviluppo." *Casabella*, 1974.

Bremner, Craig, and Paul A. Rodgers. "Design Without Discipline." *Design Issues* 29 (July 1, 2013): 4–13. https://doi.org/10.1162/DESI_a_00217.

Brown, J. Dakota. "American Graphic Design in the 1990s: Deindustrialization and the Death of the Author." *Post45*, January 10, 2019. https://post45.org/2019/01/american-graphic-design-in-the-1990s-deindustrialization-and-the-death-of-the-author.

———. *The Power of Design as a Dream of Autonomy*. Chicago: Green Lantern Press, 2019.

Cross, Nigel. "Designerly Ways of Knowing: Design Discipline versus Design Science." *Design Issues* 17, no. 3 (2001): 49–55.

"Design Thread 2 – Excess of Everything," 2022. https://www.designthreads.report/thread2.

Dunne, Anthony, and Fiona Raby. *Speculative Everything: Design, Fiction, and Social Dreaming*. Cambridge, MA: MIT Press, 2013.

Eco, Umberto. "Critical Essay." In *The Universitas Project: Solutions for a Post-Technological Society*, edited by Emilio Ambasz. New York: The Museum of Modern Art, 2006.

Escobar, Arturo. *Designs for the Pluriverse: Radical Interdependence, Autonomy, and the Making of Worlds*. London: Duke University Press, 2018.

Franke, Björn, and Hansuli Matter, eds. *Not at Your Service: Manifestos for Design*. Zurich, Basel: Zurich University of the Arts, 2021.

Frearson, Amy. "Max Siedentopf Suggests Alternative Masks to Protect Against Coronavirus." *Dezeen*, February 17, 2020. https://www.dezeen.com/2020/02/17/alternative-coronavirus-masks-max-siedentopf/.

Gedenryd, Henrik. "How Designers Work – Making Sense of Authentic Cognitive Activities." *Lund University Cognitive Studies*. Doctoral thesis, Lund University, 1998. http://lup.lub.lu.se/record/18828.

Glanville, Ranulph. "Designing Complexity." *Performance Improvement Quarterly* 20, no. 2 (June 2007): 75–96. https://doi.org/10.1111/j.1937-8327.2007.tb00442.x.

Gordon, Lewis R. "Shifting the Geography of Reason in an Age of Disciplinary Decadence." *Transmodernity* 1, no. 2 (2011). https://doi.org/10.5070/T412011810.

Graeber, David. *The Utopia of Rules: On Technology, Stupidity, and the Secret Joys of Bureaucracy*. Brooklyn: Melville House, 2015.

Grant, Donald P. "Design Methodology and Design Methods." *Design Methods and Theories* 13, no. 1 (1979).

Heinlein, Robert A. *Time Enough for Love: The Lives of Lazarus Long*. New York: Ace, 2003.

Ito, Joi. "Antidisciplinary." *Joy Ito's Web* (blog), October 2, 2014. https://joi.ito.com/weblog/2014/10/02/antidisciplinar.html.

Krippendorff, Klaus. "A Dictionary of Cybernetics." *Departmental Papers (ASC)*, 1986. https://repository.upenn.edu/asc_papers/224.

LaRossa, Brian. "Design as a Third Area of General Education." *Medium* (blog), January 23, 2021. https://brianlarossa.medium.com/design-as-a-third-area-of-general-education-80bc59875e45.

Latour, Bruno. "A Cautious Prometheus? A Few Steps Toward a Philosophy of Design (with Special Attention to Peter Sloterdijk)." edited by Fiona Hackne, Jonathan Glynne, and Viv Minto, 2–10. Falmouth: Universal Publishers, 2009.

Lorusso, Silvio. *Entreprecariat: Everyone Is an Entrepreneur, Nobody Is Safe*. Eindhoven: Onomatopee, 2019.

Lucentini, Paolo, ed. *Il libro dei ventiquattro filosofi*. Milano: Adelphi, 1999.

McGuirk, Justin. "Designs for Life Won't Make You a Living." *The Guardian*, April 18, 2011. https://www.theguardian.com/artanddesign/2011/apr/18/designs-milan-furniture-fair.

Mejias, Ulises A. "The Limits of Networks as Models for Organizing the Social." *New Media & Society* 12, no. 4 (June 1, 2010): 603–17. https://doi.org/10.1177/1461444809341392.

Norman, Don. "Opening Speech." Koç University, October 4, 2012. https://www.youtube.com/watch?v=z_7G053Zc-Y.

———. "What Is Humanity-Centered Design?" *The Interaction Design Foundation*, 2022. https://www.interaction-design.org/literature/topics/humanity-centered-design.

Ozenc, Kursat. "The 3 Most Unconventional Designers of 21st Century – Starting with Design Shaman." *Ritual Design Lab* (blog), April 4, 2016. https://medium.com/ritual-design/a-new-breed-of-21st-century-designers-b73712963b4.

Potter, Norman. *What Is a Designer: Things, Places, Messages*. London: Hyphen Press, 2006.

Rame, Sergio. "Gli sprechi di Vendola: un corso per formare gli sciamani (digitali)." *ilGiornale.it*, July 18, 2014. https://www.ilgiornale.it/news/politica/sprechi-vendola-corso-formare-sciamani-digitali-1038689.html.

Rancière, Jacques. *Et tant pis pour les gens fatigués*. Paris: Éditions Amsterdam, 2009.

Reinfurt, David. *A *New* Program for Graphic Design*. Los Angeles: Inventory Press, 2019.

Rock, Michael. "On Unprofessionalism." *2x4* (blog), August 5, 1994. https://2x4.org/ideas/1994/on-unprofessionalism/.

Schön, Donald A. *The Reflective Practitioner: How Professionals Think in Action*. London, New York: Routledge, 2016.

Shaner-Bradford, Nikki. "What Do You Do? I'm a Podcaster-Vlogger-Model-Dj." *The Outline*, November 25, 2019. https://theoutline.com/post/8301/everyone-you-know-is-a-multi-hyphenate.

Smith, Adam. *The Wealth of Nations. Books 1-3*. London: Penguin, 2003.

Varela, Francisco. *Ethical Know-How: Action, Wisdom, and Cognition*. Stanford: Stanford University Press, 1999.

Ventura, Raffaele Alberto. *Radical choc: ascesa e caduta dei competenti*. Torino: Einaudi, 2020.

Vet, Annelys de, ed. *Design Dedication: Adaptive Mentalities in Design Education*. Amsterdam: Valiz + Sandberg Instituut Design Department, 2020.

Vinsel, Lee. "Design Thinking Is Kind of Like Syphilis — It's Contagious and Rots Your Brains." *Medium* (blog), August 3, 2020. https://sts-news.medium.com/design-thinking-is-kind-of-like-syphilis-its-contagious-and-rots-your-brains-842ed078af29.

Wagner, Kate. "Coronagrifting: A Design Phenomenon." *McMansion Hell* (blog), May 23, 2020. https://mcmansionhell.com/post/618938984050147328/coronagrifting-a-design-phenomenon.

Wild, Lorraine. "The Macramé of Resistance." *Emigre*, no. 47 (1998).

CHAPTER 4.
FLIPPING THE TABLE

Adamson, Glenn. "The Communist Designer, the Fascist Furniture Dealer, and the Politics of Design." *The Nation*, February 20, 2021. https://www.thenation.com/article/culture/enzo-mari-ikea-design/.

Antonelli, Paola. "MoMA curator: '[Humanity] will become extinct. We need to design an elegant ending.'" Interview by Suzanne LaBarre, January 8, 2019. https://www.fastcompany.com/90280777/moma-curator-we-will-become-extinct-we-need-to-design-an-elegant-ending.

Appadurai, Arjun. *The Future as Cultural Fact: Essays on the Global Condition*. London: Verso, 2013.
Bateson, Gregory, Don D. Jackson, Jay Haley, and John Weakland. "Toward a Theory of Schizophrenia." *Behavioral Science* 1, no. 4 (1956): 251–64. https://doi.org/10.1002/bs.3830010402.
Bent, Shaun, Marina Posniak, and Geerit Kaiser. "Reimagining Design Systems at Spotify." *Spotify Design*, September 2020. https://spotify.design/article/reimagining-design-systems-at-spotify.
Boer, Gijs de. "Between Fox Traps and Hero Bait." *Design Drafts*, no. 1 (2023).
Bødker, Susanne, and Morten Kyng. "Participatory Design That Matters – Facing the Big Issues." *ACM Transactions on Computer-Human Interaction* 25, no. 1 (February 13, 2018): 4:1-4:31. https://doi.org/10.1145/3152421.
Burka, Daniel. "Mission Accomplished? The Hard Work of Design Is Still Ahead of Us." *Thinking Design* (blog), July 9, 2020. https://medium.com/thinking-design/mission-accomplished-the-hard-work-of-design-is-still-ahead-of-us-a4e47e5a0c8c.
Campanella, Thomas J. "The True Measure of Robert Moses (and His Racist Bridges)." *Bloomberg*, July 9, 2017. https://www.bloomberg.com/news/articles/2017-07-09/robert-moses-and-his-racist-parkway-explained.
Colomina, Beatriz, and Mark Wigley. *Are We Human? The Archaeology of Design*. Zürich: Lars Müller, 2016.
Deleuze, Gilles. *Spinoza: Practical Philosophy*. City Lights Books, 1988.
Dunne, Anthony, and Fiona Raby. "Dunne & Raby," 2009. http://dunneandraby.co.uk/content/bydandr/36/0.
Easterling, Keller. "On Political Temperament." *The Double Negative*, January 18, 2021. http://www.thedoublenegative.co.uk/2021/01/on-political-temperament-keller-easterling/.
Flusser, Vilém. "Ethics in Industrial Design?," March 20, 1991.
Ford, Henry, and Samuel Crowther. *My Life and Work*. Garden City, NY: Doubleday, Page & Co., 1922. https://college.cengage.com/history/primary_sources/us/henry_ford_discusses.htm.
Forrester. "The $162 Billion Design Industry Won't Stop Growing." *Forbes*, March 25, 2021. https://www.forbes.com/sites/forrester/2021/03/25/the-162-billion-design-industry-wont-stop-growing/.
Foster, Hal. *Design and Crime*. London: Verso, 2002.
Gerritzen, Mieke, and Geert Lovink. *Made in China, Designed in California, Criticised in Europe: Design Manifesto*. Amsterdam: BIS Publishers, 2020.

Harnett, JP. "Ontological Design Has Become Influential in Design Academia – But What Is It?" *Eye on Design*, June 14, 2021. https://eyeondesign.aiga.org/ontological-design-is-popular-in-design-academia-but-what-is-it/.

Haug, Wolfgang Fritz. *Critique of Commodity Aesthetics: Appearance, Sexuality, and Advertising in Capitalist Society*. Cambridge, UK: Polity Press, 1986.

Heller, Steven. "'Design Is One of the Most Powerful Forces in Our Lives.'" *The Atlantic*, March 13, 2014. https://www.theatlantic.com/entertainment/archive/2014/03/design-is-one-of-the-most-powerful-forces-in-our-lives/284388/.

Heskett, John. *Design: A Very Short Introduction*. Oxford: Oxford University Press, 2005.

Julier, Guy. *Economies of Design*. Los Angeles: SAGE Publications, 2017.

Kenedi, Aaron. "Marks Men: An Interview With Ivan Chermayeff, Tom Geismar, and Sagi Haviv of Chermayeff & Geism." *Print*, September 14, 2011. https://www.printmag.com/designer-interviews/marks-men-an-interview-with-ivan-chermayeff-tom-geismar-and-sagi-haviv-of-chermayeff-geismar/.

Laranjo, Francisco. "We Don't Need Speculative Design Education, Just Better Design Education." *SpeculativeEdu*, November 17, 2020. https://speculativeedu.eu/interview-francisco-laranjo/.

Latour, Bruno. "Technology Is Society Made Durable." *The Sociological Review* 38, no. 1 (May 1, 1990): 103–31. https://doi.org/10.1111/j.1467-954X.1990.tb03350.x.

Lee, Chris, and Ali S. Qadeer. "Editorial." *C Mag*, 2019.

Maldonado, Tomás. *La speranza progettuale: ambiente e società*. Torino: Einaudi, 1997.

Mari, Enzo. "Inserzione a Pagamento." *Domus*, April 2004.

Marx, Karl. *Capital*. Vol. 1. Marx/Engels Internet Archive, 1999. https://www.marxists.org/archive/marx/works/1867-c1/index.htm.

Masure, Anthony. Interview by Karl Pineau, August 2019. https://livre-ethique-numerique.designersethiques.org/content/interviews/interview-anthony_masure.html.

Mensvoort, Koert van, and Hendrik-Jan Grievink. *Next Nature: Nature Changes Along With Us*. Barcelona: Actar, 2015.

Monteiro, Mike. *Ruined by Design: How Designers Destroyed the World, and What We Can Do to Fix It*. San Francisco: Mule Design, 2019.

Norman, Don. "Email to the PhD-Design Mailing List," August 9, 2020. https://www.jiscmail.ac.uk/cgi-bin/wa-jisc.exe?A2=ind2008&L=PHD-DESIGN&P=R7343.

———. "Email to the PhD-Design Mailing List," March 18, 2021. https://www.jiscmail.ac.uk/cgi-bin/wa-jisc.

exe?A2=ind2103&L=PHD-DESIGN&P=R110555.
Oliver, Richard L. "Effect of Expectation and Disconfirmation on Postexposure Product Evaluations: An Alternative Interpretation." *Journal of Applied Psychology* 62, no. 4 (1977): 480–86. https://doi.org/10.1037/0021-9010.62.4.480.
Osherow, Evan. "Designers, Stop Asking for a 'Seat at the Table.'" *UX Collective* (blog), March 7, 2020. https://uxdesign.cc/designers-stop-asking-for-a-seat-at-the-table-4ab933d7037f.
Richardson, Adam. "The Death of the Designer." *Design Issues* 9, no. 2 (1993): 34. https://doi.org/10.2307/1511672.
Roberts, Lucienne, Rebecca Wright, and Jessie Price, eds. *Graphic Designers Surveyed*. London: GraphicDesign&, 2015.
Rogan, Kevin. "Keller Easterling's Medium Design Ignores the Role of Power in Design." *The Architect's Newspaper*, February 22, 2021. https://www.archpaper.com/2021/02/keller-easterling-medium-design-review/.
Schmitt, Carl. *Dialogo sul potere*. Milano: Adelphi, 2012.
Schwab, Katharine. "John Maeda: 'In Reality, Design Is Not That Important.'" *Fast Company*, March 15, 2019. https://www.fastcompany.com/90320120/john-maeda-in-reality-design-is-not-that-important.
———. "Take The Survey: Do Designers Have A Seat At The Table?" *Fast Company*, April 25, 2018. https://www.fastcompany.com/90169455/take-the-survey-do-designers-have-a-seat-at-the-table.
Shaughnessy, Adrian. *How to Be a Graphic Designer Without Losing Your Soul*. New York: Princeton Architectural Press, 2005.
Tharp, Bruce, and Stephanie Tharp. "The 4 Fields of Industrial Design." *Core77*, January 5, 2009. https://www.core77.com/posts/12232/The-4-Fields-of-Industrial-Design-No-not-furniture-trans-consumer-electronics-n-toys-by-Bruce-M-Tharp-and-Stephanie-M-Tharp.
"The Power of Design." Arte, 2021.
Tsing, Anna Lowenhaupt. *The Mushroom at the End of the World: On the Possibility of Life in Capitalist Ruins*. Princeton, NJ: Princeton University Press, 2021.
Velden, Daniel van der. "Lyrical Design." In *Design Dedication: Adaptive Mentalities in Design Education*, edited by Annelys de Vet. Amsterdam: Valiz + Sandberg Instituut Design Department, 2020.
Vignelli, Massimo, and Lella Vignelli. "Emigranti di lusso." Interview by Barbara Radice. *Modo*, March 1981.
Weber, Max. *Typen der Herrschaft*. Ditzingen: Reclam, 2019.
Willis, Anne-Marie. "Ontological Designing." *Design Philosophy*

Papers 4, no. 2 (June 1, 2006): 69–92. https://doi.org/10.2752/144871306X13966268131514.

Winner, Langdon. "Do Artifacts Have Politics?" *Daedalus* 109, no. 1 (1980): 121–36.

Wizinsky, Matthew. *Design After Capitalism: Transforming Design Today for an Equitable Tomorrow*. Cambridge, MA: MIT Press, 2022.

CHAPTER 5.
FORM FOLLOWS FORMAT

Ackermann, Rebecca. "Design Thinking Was Supposed to Fix the World. Where Did It Go Wrong?" *MIT Technology Review*, February 9, 2023. https://www.technologyreview.com/2023/02/09/1067821/design-thinking-retrospective-what-went-wrong/.

Alessi, Chiara. *Design senza designer*. Bari: Laterza, 2016.

Andreessen, Marc. "Why Software Is Eating the World." *Andreessen Horowitz* (blog), August 20, 2011. https://a16z.com/2011/08/20/why-software-is-eating-the-world/.

Atkinson, Rhys, and Clara Balaguer. "Learning from the Vernacular." *Futuress*, June 16, 2021. https://futuress.org/stories/learning-from-the-vernacular/.

Basu, Ritupriya. "Algorithms Are a Designer's New BFF – Here's Proof." *Eye on Design*, December 19, 2019. https://eyeondesign.aiga.org/algorithms-are-a-designers-new-bff-heres-proof/.

Beegan, Gerry, and Paul Atkinson. "Professionalism, Amateurism and the Boundaries of Design." *Journal of Design History* 21, no. 4 (2008): 305–13.

Bratteteig, Tone, and Guri Verne. "Does AI Make PD Obsolete? Exploring Challenges from Artificial Intelligence to Participatory Design." In *Proceedings of the 15th Participatory Design Conference - Volume 2*, 1–5. PDC '18. New York, NY, USA: Association for Computing Machinery, 2018. https://doi.org/10.1145/3210604.3210646.

Brown, J. Dakota. *Typography, Automation, and the Division of Labor: A Brief History*. Chicago: Other Forms, 2019.

Brown, Tim. *Change by Design: How Design Thinking Transforms Organizations and Inspires Innovation*. New York: Harper Business, 2009.

Colomina, Beatriz, and Mark Wigley. *Are We Human? The Archaeology of Design*. Zürich: Lars Müller, 2016.

Cooley, Mike. *Architect or Bee? The Human Price of Technology*. Nottingham: Spokesman, 2016.

Corneliux. "Everyone Used to Be a Designer." *UX*

Planet, February 13, 2023. https://uxplanet.org/everyone-used-to-be-a-designer-530aa762e415.

Edgerton, David, Hugo Palmarola, and Pedro Álvarez Caselli. "Some Problems with the Concept of 'Technology' in Design: Interview with David Edgerton." *Diseña*, no. 18 (January 29, 2021): 2–8. https://doi.org/10.7764/disena.18.Interview.2.

Foster, Hal. *Design and Crime*. London: Verso, 2002.

Frey, Carl Benedikt, and Michael A. Osborne. "The Future of Employment: How Susceptible Are Jobs to Computerisation?" *Technological Forecasting and Social Change* 114, no. C (2017): 254–80.

Fuller, Jarrett. "Design Criticism Is Everywhere – Why Are We Still Looking For It?" *Eye on Design*, August 19, 2020. https://eyeondesign.aiga.org/design-criticism-is-everywhere-why-are-we-still-looking-for-it/.

Garrett, Jesse. "Ux Design Is More Successful Than Ever, but Its Leaders Are Losing Hope. Here's Why." *Fast Company*, June 3, 2021. https://www.fastcompany.com/90642462/ux-design-is-more-successful-than-ever-but-its-leaders-are-losing-hope.

Gerritzen, Mieke, and Geert Lovink. *Everyone Is a Designer in the Age of Social Media*. Amsterdam: BIS, 2010.

Giampietro, Rob, and Rudy VanderLans. "Default Systems in Graphic Design." *Emigre*, 2003. https://linedandunlined.com/archive/default-systems-in-graphic-design/.

Gold, Jon. "Taking The Robots To Design School." *Jon Gold* (blog), May 25, 2016. https://web.archive.org/web/20160525193649/http://www.jon.gold/2016/05/robot-design-school/.

Gray, Mary L., and Siddharth Suri. *Ghost Work: How to Stop Silicon Valley from Building a New Global Underclass*. Boston: Houghton Mifflin Harcourt, 2019.

Groten, Anja. "The Workshop and Cultural Production." *Open!*, June 1, 2019. https://www.onlineopen.org/the-workshop-and-cultural-production.

———. "Towards a Critical Collaborative Practice." In *Design Dedication: Adaptive Mentalities in Design Education*, edited by Annelys de Vet. Amsterdam: Valiz + Sandberg Instituut Design Department, 2020.

Groys, Boris. "Under the Gaze of Theory." *E-Flux*, May 2012. https://www.e-flux.com/journal/35/68389/under-the-gaze-of-theory/.

Hawley, Rachel. "Don't Worry, These Gangly-Armed Cartoons Are Here to Protect You From Big Tech." *Eye on Design*, August 21, 2019. https://eyeondesign.aiga.org/dont-worry-these-gangley-armed-cartoons-are-here-to-protect-you-from-big-tech/.

Heller, Steven. "Cult of the Ugly." *Eye Magazine*, 1993. https://www.

eyemagazine.com/feature/article/cult-of-the-ugly.

Julier, Guy. *Economies of Design*. Los Angeles: SAGE Publications, 2017.

Laranjo, Francisco. "Ghosts of Designbots yet to Come." *Eye Magazine*, December 21, 2016. https://www.eyemagazine.com/blog/post/ghosts-of-designbots-yet-to-come.

Lorusso, Silvio. "Learn to Code vs. Code to Learn: Creative Coding Beyond the Economic Imperative." In *Graphic Design in the Post-Digital Age*, edited by Demian Conrad, Rob van Leijsen, and David Héritier. Eindhoven: Onomatopee, 2021. https://silviolorusso.com/publication/learn-to-code-vs-code-to-learn/.

Lupton, Ellen. *D.I.Y. Design It Yourself*. New York: Princeton Architectural Press, 2006.

McVarish, Emily. *Inflection Point*. Berkeley, CA: Emigre, 2017.

Monteiro, Mike. *Design Is a Job*. New York: A Book Apart, 2012.

Neuburg, Klaus, Sven Quadflieg, and Simon Nestler. "Will Artificial Intelligence Make Designers Obsolete?" Berlin, 2020.

Oh, Jasmine. "Yes, AI Will Replace Designers." *Microsoft Design* (blog), August 22, 2019. https://medium.com/microsoft-design/yes-ai-will-replace-designers-9d90c6e34502.

Pater, Ruben. *Caps Lock: How Capitalism Took Hold of Graphic Design, and How to Escape from It*. Amsterdam: Valiz, 2021.

Peart, Rob. "Automation Threatens to Make Graphic Designers Obsolete." *Eye on Design*, October 25, 2016. https://eyeondesign.aiga.org/automation-threatens-to-make-graphic-designers-obsolete/.

Poynor, Rick. *No More Rules: Graphic Design and Postmodernism*. London: Laurence King, 2003.

Press, Alex. "On the Origins of the Professional-Managerial Class: An Interview with Barbara Ehrenreich." *Dissent Magazine*, October 22, 2019. https://www.dissentmagazine.org/online_articles/on-the-origins-of-the-professional-managerial-class-an-interview-with-barbara-ehrenreich.

Rittel, Horst W. J., and Melvin M. Webber. "Dilemmas in a General Theory of Planning." *Policy Sciences* 4, no. 2 (June 1, 1973): 155–69. https://doi.org/10.1007/BF01405730.

Rock, Michael. "On Unprofessionalism." *2x4* (blog), August 5, 1994. https://2x4.org/ideas/1994/on-unprofessionalism/.

Rodgers, Paul A., and Craig Bremner. "The Design of Nothing: A Working Philosophy." In *Advancements in the Philosophy of Design*, edited by Pieter E. Vermaas and Stéphane Vial, 549–64. Design Research Foundations. Cham: Springer International Publishing, 2018. https://doi.org/10.1007/978-3-319-73302-9_25.

Roth, Bernard. *The Achievement Habit: Stop Wishing, Start Doing, and*

Take Command of Your Life. New York: Harper Business, 2015.
Sarmah, Harshajit. "5 AI-Powered Home And Interior Designing Tools." *Analytics India Magazine*, July 26, 2019. https://analyticsindiamag.com/5-ai-powered-home-and-interior-designing-tools/.
Schön, Donald A. *The Reflective Practitioner: How Professionals Think in Action*. London, New York: Routledge, 2016.
Sfligiotti, Silvia. "This Is Auto-Tune Typography." *Medium* (blog), August 19, 2020. https://silviasfligiotti.medium.com/this-is-auto-tune-typography-3953e74cc2ac.
Snook, Tanya. "UX Design Has a Dirty Secret." *Fast Company*, October 18, 2021. https://www.fastcompany.com/90686473/ux-design-has-a-dirty-secret.
Stinson, Liz. "John Maeda: If You Want to Survive in Design, You Better Learn to Code." *Wired*, March 2017. https://www.wired.com/2017/03/john-maeda-want-survive-design-better-learn-code/.
Taylor, Astra. "The Automation Charade." *Logic*, August 1, 2018. https://logicmag.io/failure/the-automation-charade/.
Ullman, Ellen. *Life in Code: A Personal History of Technology*. New York: Picador, 2018.
Velden, Daniel van der. "Lyrical Design." In *Design Dedication: Adaptive Mentalities in Design Education*, edited by Annelys de Vet. Amsterdam: Valiz + Sandberg Instituut Design Department, 2020.
———. "Research and Destroy." *Metropolis M*, 2006. http://indexgrafik.fr/daniel-van-der-velden-metahaven-research-and-destroy/.
Ventura, Raffaele Alberto. *Radical choc: ascesa e caduta dei competenti*. Torino: Einaudi, 2020.
Vinsel, Lee. "Design Thinking Is Kind of Like Syphilis — It's Contagious and Rots Your Brains." *Medium* (blog), August 3, 2020. https://sts-news.medium.com/design-thinking-is-kind-of-like-syphilis-its-contagious-and-rots-your-brains-842ed078af29.

CHAPTER 6.
KRITIKAOKE

Adamson, Glenn. "The Communist Designer, the Fascist Furniture Dealer, and the Politics of Design." *The Nation*, February 20, 2021. https://www.thenation.com/article/culture/enzo-mari-ikea-design/.
Alinsky, Saul D. *Rules for Radicals: A Practical Primer for Realistic Radicals*. New York: Vintage Books, 1989.
Amin, Kadji. "We Are All Nonbinary." *Representations* 158, no. 1 (May 1, 2022): 106–19. https://doi.org/10.1525/rep.2022.158.11.106.
Baudrillard, Jean. "Design and the Environment: Or, The Inflationary Curve of Political Economy." In *The Universitas Project: Solutions*

for a Post-Technological Society, edited by Emilio Ambasz. New York: The Museum of Modern Art, 2006.

Berry, Anne H., Kareem Collie, Penina Acayo Laker, Lesley-Ann Noel, Jennifer Rittner, and Kelly Walters, eds. *The Black Experience in Design: Identity, Expression & Reflection*. New York: Allworth Press, 2022.

Bourdieu, Pierre. *Distinction: A Social Critique of the Judgement of Taste*. Cambridge, MA: Harvard University Press, 1984.

———. "The Forms of Capital." In *Handbook of Theory and Research for the Sociology of Education*, edited by J. Richardson, 241–58. New York: Greenwood, 1986. https://www.marxists.org/reference/subject/philosophy/works/fr/bourdieu-forms-capital.htm.

Bratton, Benjamin. *Revenge of the Real: Politics for a Post-Pandemic World*. London: Verso, 2022.

Brillon, James. "Instagram Account Dank.Lloyd.Wright Aims to 'Amplify Narratives That Are Excluded from Architecture's Official Consensus.'" *Dezeen*, August 30, 2022. https://www.dezeen.com/2022/08/30/instagram-dank-lloyd-wright-interview/.

Budds, Diana. "9 Ideas Shaping The Future Of Design, According To Ideo, Microsoft, Autodesk, MIT, And More." *Fast Company*, September 12, 2017. https://www.fastcompany.com/90139617/9-ideas-shaping-the-future-of-design-according-to-ideo-microsoft-autodesk-mit-and-more.

Cuninghame, Patrick. "'A Laughter That Will Bury You All': Irony as Protest and Language as Struggle in the Italian 1977 Movement." *Libcom*, January 5, 2012. https://libcom.org/article/laughter-will-bury-you-all-irony-protest-and-language-struggle-italian-1977-movement.

Dunne, Anthony, and Fiona Raby. "A/B." *Dunne & Raby*, 2009. https://dunneandraby.co.uk/content/projects/476/0.

Ebbesen, Toke Riis. "Why Critical Design Is Useless: Criteria." Sursock Museum, Beirut, Lebanon, 2017.

e-janestudio. "Nope." *Tumblr* (blog). https://e-janestudio.tumblr.com/post/132335744305/i-am-not-an-identity-artist-just-because-i-am-a.

Fuller, Jarrett. "The Auto-Ethnographic Turn in Design." *Design and Culture*, April 27, 2022, 1–3. https://doi.org/10.1080/17547075.2022.2061138.

Garbutt, Schessa. "Black Lives Matter Is Not a Design Challenge." *Design Toast* (blog), July 14, 2020. https://medium.com/design-toast/black-lives-matter-is-not-a-design-challenge-f6e452ff7821.

Gebrayel, Imad. "The Design Exit: Don't Look Behind!" In *Unununimimimdededesign*, edited by Joannette van der Veer.

Eindhoven: Onomatopee, 2022.

Gerritzen, Mieke, and Geert Lovink. *Everyone Is a Designer in the Age of Social Media*. Amsterdam: BIS, 2010.

Giampietro, Rob. "School Days." In *Graphic Design: Now in Production*, edited by Ellen Lupton and Andrew Blauvelt. New York, 2012. https://linedandunlined.com/archive/school-days/.

Goldstein, Mitch. *How to Be a Design Student (and How to Teach Them)*. New York: Princeton Architectural Press, 2023.

Groten, Anja. "Towards a Critical Collaborative Practice." In *Design Dedication: Adaptive Mentalities in Design Education*, edited by Annelys de Vet. Amsterdam: Valiz + Sandberg Instituut Design Department, 2020.

Harney, Stefano, and Fred Moten. *The Undercommons: Fugitive Planning & Black Study*. Wivenhoe: Minor Compositions, 2013.

Holm, Nicholas. "Critical Capital: Cultural Studies, the Critical Disposition and Critical Reading as Elite Practice." *Cultural Studies* 34, no. 1 (January 2, 2020): 143–66. https://doi.org/10.1080/09502386.2018.1549265.

hooks, bell. *Teaching to Transgress: Education as the Practice of Freedom*. New York: Routledge, 1994.

Horkheimer, Max, and Theodor W. Adorno. *Dialectic of Enlightenment*. London: Verso, 1997.

Labranca, Tommaso. *Vraghinaroda: Sopravvivendo a hipster situazionisti, santexuperine scalze e mistificatori deleuziani*. Milano: 20090, 2019.

Laranjo, Francisco. "Critical Everything." *Modes of Criticism*, August 4, 2015. https://modesofcriticism.org/critical-everything/.

Lasch, Christopher. *The Culture of Narcissism: American Life in an Age of Diminishing Expectations*. New York, NY: W. W. Norton & Company, 1991.

Lier, Bas van. "If Things Are Bad, That's Good." *What Design Can Do*, March 28, 2017. https://www.whatdesigncando.com/stories/things-bad-thats-good/.

Liu, Catherine. *Virtue Hoarders: The Case Against the Professional Managerial Class*. Minneapolis: University of Minnesota Press, 2021.

Lorusso, Silvio. "We, the Doers: Fiverr's Entrepreneurial Populism and a 3-Days Workweek." *Entreprecariat* (blog), March 20, 2017. https://networkcultures.org/entreprecariat/we-the-doers/.

Lupton, Ellen. "Designer as Producer." In *Graphic Design: Now in Production*, edited by Ellen Lupton and Andrew Blauvelt. New York, 2012.

Lupu, Alina. "The Palestinian Conflict Rippling Across Dutch Art Educational Institutions." *The Office of Alina Lupu* (blog), 2022.

https://theofficeofalinalupu.com/printed-matter/the-palestinian-conflict-rippling-across-dutch-art-educational-institutions/.

Maldonado, Tomás. *La speranza progettuale: ambiente e società*. Torino: Einaudi, 1997.

Mattioli, Valerio. "RIP Club Culture (finalmente)." *Not*, June 15, 2021. https://not.neroeditions.com/rip-club-culture-finalmente/.

Mclaughlin, Aimee. "Nelly Ben Hayoun on Her Theory of Total Bombardment." *Creative Review*, June 27, 2018. https://www.creativereview.co.uk/nelly-ben-hayoun-on-her-theory-of-total-bombardment/.

Medium. "UUGH! Or: Issues Regarding University of the Underground," September 22, 2017. https://medium.com/@uugh/issues-regarding-the-university-of-the-underground-and-the-sandberg-instituut-fe58dbbf889b.

Mr. Keedy. "Graphic Design in the Postmodern Era." *Emigre*, 1998. https://www.emigre.com/Essays/Magazine/GraphicDesigninthePostmodernEra.

Nelson, Tara-Nicholle. "What Transformational Brands Do: Manifesto Marketing." *Ad Age*, April 25, 2017. https://adage.com/article/agency-viewpoint/transformational-brands-manifesto-marketing/308572.

O'Flynn, Brian. "Class Struggle: When Did 'Unemployed' Become a T-Shirt Slogan?" *The Guardian*, May 3, 2018, sec. Fashion. https://www.theguardian.com/fashion/2018/may/03/class-struggle-working-class-unemployed-become-t-shirt-slogans.

Pater, Ruben. "Treating the Refugee Crisis as a Design Problem Is Problematic." *Dezeen*, April 21, 2016. https://www.dezeen.com/2016/04/21/ruben-pater-opinion-what-design-can-do-refugee-crisis-problematic-design/.

Rock, Michael. "Designer as Author." *2x4* (blog), August 5, 1996. https://2x4.org/ideas/1996/designer-as-author/.

———. "Mad Dutch Disease." 2x4, August 9, 2003. https://2x4.org/ideas/2003/mad-dutch-disease/.

Rule, Alix, and David Levine. "International Art English." *Triple Canopy*, 2013. https://canopycanopycanopy.com/contents/international_art_english.

Táíwò, Olúfẹ́mi O. *Elite Capture: How the Powerful Took Over Identity Politics (and Everything Else)*. Chicago: Haymarket Books, 2022.

Thorpe, Ann. "Defining Design as Activism." In *Journal of Architectural Education*, 2011.

Ventura, Raffaele Alberto. "La cattiva notizia è che la cancel culture esiste eccome." *Wired Italia*, May 10, 2021. https://www.wired.it/play/cultura/2021/05/10/

cancel-culture-esiste-debunker-politicamente-corretto/.
Wallace, David Foster. "E Unibus Pluram: Television and U.S. Fiction." *Review of Contemporary Fiction* 13, no. 2 (1993). http://jsomers.net/DFW_TV.pdf.

CHAPTER 7.
THE SCHOOL AS REAL WORLD

Anceschi, Giovanni. *Tomás Maldonado intellettuale politecnico*. Milano: Edizioni del Verri, 2020.

Arista, Roberto. "Interfaces Are a Solid Object." *Progetto Grafico* 33 (2018).

Blauvelt, Andrew. "Towards Critical Autonomy or Can Graphic Design Save Itself?" *Emigre*, 2004.

Bourdieu, Pierre. *Distinction: A Social Critique of the Judgement of Taste*. Cambridge, MA: Harvard University Press, 1984.

Brown, J. Dakota. *The Power of Design as a Dream of Autonomy*. Chicago: Green Lantern Press, 2019.

Caliri, Gaspare. "Cos'è il design-as-(a)-bricolage, la cultura del progetto attraverso le teorie della complessità." *cheFare*, January 19, 2021. https://www.che-fare.com/almanacco/cultura/design/cose-il-design-as-a-bricolage-la-cultura-del-progetto-attraverso-le-teorie-della-complessita/.

Clarke, Alison J. "Design for the Real World: Contesting the Origins of the Social in Design." In *Design Struggles: Intersecting Histories, Pedagogies, and Perspectives*, edited by Claudia Mareis and Nina Paim. Amsterdam: Valiz, 2021.

Dawood, Sarah. "Design Most Popular University Choice – but Graduates Aren't Becoming Designers." *Design Week*, February 15, 2018. https://www.designweek.co.uk/issues/12-18-february-2018/design-popular-university-choice-graduates-arent-ending-designers/.

De Carlo, Giancarlo. *La piramide rovesciata: architettura oltre il '68*. Macerata: Quodlibet, 2018.

De Martin, Paola. "Breaking Class: Upward Climbers and the Swiss Nature of Design History." In *Design Struggles: Intersecting Histories, Pedagogies, and Perspectives*, edited by Claudia Mareis and Nina Paim. Amsterdam: Valiz, 2021.

Dunne, Anthony, and Fiona Raby. "A/B." *Dunne & Raby*, 2009. https://dunneandraby.co.uk/content/projects/476/0.

———. *Speculative Everything: Design, Fiction, and Social Dreaming*. Cambridge, MA: MIT Press, 2013.

Falcinelli, Riccardo. *Critica portatile al visual design: da Gutenberg ai social network*. Torino: Einaudi, 2014.

BIBLIOGRAPHY

Freire, Paulo. *Pedagogy of the Oppressed*. London: Penguin Books, 2017.

Galbraith, John Kenneth. *The New Industrial State*. Princeton: Princeton University Press, 2015.

Gerritzen, Mieke, and Geert Lovink. *Made in China, Designed in California, Criticised in Europe: Design Manifesto*. Amsterdam: BIS Publishers, 2020.

hooks, bell. *Teaching to Transgress: Education as the Practice of Freedom*. New York: Routledge, 1994.

Illich, Ivan. *Deschooling Society*. London: Calder & Boyars, 1971.

Lorusso, Silvio. "No Problem: Design School as Promise." *Entreprecariat* (blog), December 7, 2020. https://networkcultures.org/entreprecariat/no-problem-design/.

Lorusso, Silvio and @wdka.teachermemes. "'May the Bridges We Burn Light the Way': Five Questions to a Dutch Design School's Meme Page." *Other Worlds*, no. 3 (July 26, 2021). https://buttondown.email/otherworlds/archive/ow-3-may-the-bridges-we-burn-light-the-way-five/.

Maldonado, Tomás. *Che cos'è un intellettuale? Avventure e disavventure di un ruolo*. Milano: Feltrinelli, 2010.

Mari, Enzo. *25 modi per piantare un chiodo: Sessant'anni di idee e progetti per difendere un sogno*. Milano: Mondadori, 2011.

Moholy-Nagy, László. *Vision in Motion*. Chicago: P. Theobald, 1947.

Monteiro, Mike. *Ruined by Design: How Designers Destroyed the World, and What We Can Do to Fix It*. San Francisco, CA: Mule Design, 2019.

Pater, Ruben. *Caps Lock: How Capitalism Took Hold of Graphic Design, and How to Escape from It*. Amsterdam: Valiz, 2021.

Rand, Paul. "Confusion and Chaos: The Seduction of Contemporary Graphic Design." *AIGA Journal of Graphic Design* 10, no. 1 (1992). https://www.paulrand.design/writing/articles/1992-confusion-and-chaos-the-seduction-of-contemporary-graphic-design.html.

Roberts, Lucienne, Rebecca Wright, and Jessie Price, eds. *Graphic Designers Surveyed*. London: GraphicDesign&, 2015.

Rock, Michael. "On Unprofessionalism." *2x4* (blog), August 5, 1994. https://2x4.org/ideas/1994/on-unprofessionalism/.

Roose, Kevin, and Stefan Becket. "Meet the Real-Life 'Old Economy Steve.'" *Intelligencer*, May 30, 2013. https://nymag.com/intelligencer/2013/05/meet-the-real-life-old-economy-steve.html.

Schön, Donald A. *The Reflective Practitioner: How Professionals Think in Action*. London, New York: Routledge, 2016.

Siang, Teo Yu. "How to Change Your Career from Graphic Design to UX Design." *Interaction Design Foundation*, September 12, 2020. https://www.interaction-design.org/literature/article/

how-to-change-your-career-from-graphic-design-to-ux-design.

Toppins, Aggie. "Good Nostalgia/Bad Nostalgia." *Design and Culture* 14, no. 1 (January 2, 2022): 5–29. https://doi.org/10.1080/17547075.2021.2010876.

———. "We Need Graphic Design Histories That Look Beyond the Profession." *Eye on Design*, June 10, 2021. https://eyeondesign.aiga.org/we-need-graphic-design-histories-that-look-beyond-the-profession/.

Zweege, Tessel ten. "Calling Out Dutch Art Institutions." *Futuress*, February 26, 2021. https://futuress.org/stories/calling-out-dutch-art-institutions/.

EPILOGUE: RAGEQUIT

Bonsiepe, Gui. *The Disobedience of Design*. Edited by Lara Penin. London: Bloomsbury, 2022.

Foster, Hal. *Design and Crime*. London: Verso, 2002.

Iaconesi, Salvatore. "Nuovo Abitare, after COVID." *Counter Arts* (blog), July 15, 2021. https://medium.com/counterarts/nuovo-abitare-after-covid-e85e40e49861.

Levi Bismarck, Pedro. *Arquitectura e «pessimismo»: Sobre Uma Condição Política Em Arquitectura*. Porto: Punkto, 2020.

Lispector, Clarice. *A paixão segundo G.H.* Rio de Janeiro: Rocco, 2009.

Lo Giudice, Euclide. "Sciascia su Sciascia." *Leonardo Sciascia Web*. Accessed June 28, 2023. https://www.amicisciascia.it/leonardo-sciascia/sciascia-su-sciascia.html.

Lonzi, Marta. *Autenticità e progetto*. Milano: Jaca Book, 2006.

Maldonado, Tomás. *La speranza progettuale: ambiente e società*. Torino: Einaudi, 1997.

Mills, C. Wright. *The Sociological Imagination*. New York: Oxford University Press, 1959.

Sennett, Richard. *The Craftsman*. London: Penguin, 2009.

Siti, Walter. *Contro l'impegno: Riflessioni sul Bene in letteratura*. BUR (Series). Milano: Rizzoli, 2021.

Treviño, A. Javier. "C. Wright Mills as Designer: Personal Practice and Two Public Talks." *The American Sociologist* 45, no. 4 (December 1, 2014): 335–60. https://doi.org/10.1007/s12108-014-9196-y.

Vitiello, Guido. "I nuovi complessisti contro il 'pensiero unico'. Esercizi di atletica retorica." *Il Foglio*, April 5, 2022. https://www.ilfoglio.it/societa/2022/04/05/news/i-nuovi-complessisti-contro-il-pensiero-unico-esercizi-di-atletica-retorica-3876461/.

Index of Names

*foundationClass, 209
Abdulla, Danah, 113
Accademia del lusso, 275
Ackermann, Rebecca, 195
Adamson, Glenn, 133, 136, 225
Ader, Bas Jan, 42
Adorno, Theodor W., 20, 209, 230
Agamben, Giorgio, 33, 63, 64
Airbnb, 27, 209
Al-Hawajri, Mohammed, 229
Alessi, Chiara, 177
Alinsky, Saul D., 213
Ambasz, Emilio, 13, 116, 227
American Institute of Graphic Arts (AIGA), 40
Amin, Kadji, 230
Anceschi, Giovanni, 274, 288
Andreessen, Marc, 97
Anti-Design, 119, 209, 227, 228
Antonelli, Paola, 62, 78, 139, 140
Antonini, Federico, 294
Appadurai, Arjun, 153, 154, 155
Apple, 33, 34, 163, 177, 178
Archer, Bruce, 112
Arista, Roberto, 286, 288
Aronowitz, Kate, 151
Art is Open Source, 293
Ashworth, Chris, 258
Atkinson, Paul, 115, 203
Atkinson, Rhys, 206
Augusta, Pownall, 62
boysfirm, @, 260
Balaguer, Clara, 206
Balasubramaniam, Thirunavukarasu, 84
Barry, Ben, 135
Barthes, Roland, 148, 202, 211
Bass, Saul, 41, 134
Basu, Rituprya, 180
Bateson, Mary Catherine, 20
Bateson, Gregory, 158
Baudelaire, Charles, 64
Baudrillard, Jean, 105, 240
Bauhaus, 97, 118, 183
Bayer, Herbert, 97, 118
Beck, Martin, 41
Beck, Ulrich, 230
Becker, Gary, 247
Beegan, Gerry, 115, 203
Belonax, Tim, 135
Ben Hayoun, Nelly, 209, 210, 211
Benjamin, Walter, 46, 292
Benjamin, Ruha, 78, 82

Bent, Shaun, 132
Berends, Manetta, 83
Bergson, Henri, 20
Berlant, Lauren, 40
Berry, Anne H., 228
Beuys, Joseph, 76
Bierut, Michael, 24, 209
Blackler, Alethea, 84
blank_gehry, @, 79
Blauvelt, Andrew, 84, 123, 124, 125, 221, 231, 288
Blosch, Marcus, 38
Bødker, Susanne, 161
Boehnert, Joanna, 59
Boer, Gijs de, 156
Bonsiepe, Gui, 90, 92, 97, 98, 103, 105, 122, 126
Borromini, Francesco, 298
Boshat-Thorez, Sofia, 83
Bourdieu, Pierre, 211, 213, 214, 245, 252, 256, 263, 272, 274, 276, 286
Brain, Tega, 83
Bratteteig, Tone, 179
Bratton, Benjamin, 232
Bremner, Craig, 78, 101, 112, 113, 122, 197
Breuer, Marcel, 22
Bridle, James, 18
Brillon, James, 220
Brown, J. Dakota, 114, 124, 125, 127, 194, 195, 238, 279, 281
Brown, Tim, 195
Bruinsma, Max, 85
Buchanan, Richard, 51
Buchanan, Lisa, 134
Budds, Diana, 219
Bürger, Manuel, 182, 203
Burka, Daniel, 151
Caliri, Gaspare, 288
Campanella, Thomas J., 136
Caraco, Albert, 15, 293
Cardan, Paul, 15
Caronia, Antonio, 89, 92
Carstens, Delphi, 24
Caselli, Pedro Álvarez, 189
Castoriadis, Cornelius, 15, 64
Certeau, Michel de, 155
Cervantes, Miguel de, 273
Chamorro-Koc, Marianella, 84
Chayka, Kyle, 27
Chermayeff & Geismar, 159
CIA, 21
Cioran, Emil, 293

Citarella, Joshua, 286
Clarke, Alison J., 278
clayhor, @, 201
Clifton, Jim, 58
Cochior, Cristina, 83
Collie, Kareem, 228
Collins, Anastasia, 217, 232
Colomina, Beatriz, 64, 73, 87, 162, 195, 196
Conrad, Demian, 189
Content y Contenido, 253
Cooley, Mike, 181, 187
Cooper, Muriel, 83
Corneliux, 186
Corporate Memphis, 186, 201
Critical Design, 119, 211, 218, 225, 239, 277
Critical Graphic Design, 19, 24, 25, 104, 157
Cross, Nigel, 107, 108
Crowther, Samuel, 132
Cthulhu, 303
Culkin, John M., 87
Cuninghame, Patrick, 215
Dadaism, 215
dank.lloyd.wright, @, 21, 29, 220
Davidson, Stephanie, 61
Davis, Dantley, 228
Dawood, Sarah, 265
De Carlo, Giancarlo, 20, 251, 285
De Martin, Paola, 59, 265
de Mattia, Giuseppe, 271
Defaultism, 174, 176, 177, 179, 181, 185, 188, 205
Deira, Yessica, 262
Deleuze, Gilles, 163
Design Thinking, 48, 78, 82, 120, 138, 195, 196, 218, 233
Dettmer-Finke, Reinhild, 163
Dewey, John, 25
Diehm, Cade, 160, 161
Dilnot, Clive, 82
Don Quixote, 286
Dunne, Anthony, 125, 126, 149, 211, 216, 277
Dürer, Albrecht, 65, 68, 294, 302
Dutch Design, 240
Dutch Design Week, 21, 221
Dwiggins, W. A., 194
Easterling, Keller, 142, 152, 153
Eatock, Daniel, 174, 176, 204
Ebbesen, Toke Riis, 239
Eco, Umberto, 116

Edgerton, David, 118, 189
Engelhardt, Lukas, 262
Enzensberger, Hans Magnus, 13
Erasmus, 273
Escobar, Arturo, 105, 124
ethicaldesign69, @, 142, 152, 222
Experimental Jetset, 24
Falcinelli, Riccardo, 263
Fawkes, Guy, 24
Fenn, Jackie, 38
Fiverr, 21, 184, 185, 198
Fleming, Billy, 146
Flusser, Vilém, 160, 161
Fluzin, Baptiste, 38
Ford, Henry, 132
Forrester, 140
Foster, Hal, 132, 200, 291
Foucault, Michel, 155
Franke, Björn, 126
Franklin, Ursula M., 46, 90, 148
Frearson, Amy, 109
Freelance Studio, 43
Freeman, Jo, 266
Freire, Paulo, 25, 245
Frey, Carl Benedikt, 179
Fry, Tony, 82, 87, 136, 137, 283
Fuller, Buckminster, 99, 110
Fuller, Jarrett, 169, 226
G.H., 291
Galbraith, John Kenneth, 277
Gallet, Alix, 75
Galluzzo, Michele, 143
Gantz, Carroll, 131, 132
Garbutt, Schessa, 221
Garland, Ken, 35, 216, 279
Garrett, Jesse, 34, 186
Gartner, 38, 67
Gebrayel, Imad, 236, 237
Gedenryd, Henrik, 108
Gelberg, Justus, 262
Gerritzen, Mieke, 22, 24, 93, 159, 195, 220, 276
Giampietro, Rob, 172, 176, 177, 179, 186, 207, 230, 263
Gibson, Mel, 153
Giddens, Anthony, 68, 69, 90, 95
Gideon, Kossoff, 35
Glanville, Ranulph, 119
Gold, Jon, 179
Goldstein, Mitch, 74, 230
Gonçalves, Sofia, 221
Gordon, Lewis R., 97, 113
Goya, Francisco, 201

INDEX OF NAMES

Graeber, David, 120
Gramsci, Antonio, 13, 92, 153, 273, 292
Grant, Donald P., 107, 108
Gray, Mary L., 187
Greater Good Studio, 133
Green, Penelope, 20
Greiman, April, 170
Grid, The, 169, 180
Grievink, Hendrik-Jan, 139, 174
Gropius, Walter, 97, 118
Gropius, Ilse, 97
Groten, Anja, 196
Groys, Boris, 196, 197
Guest, David, 105
Guevara, Che, 221
Habermas, Jürgen, 199
Hackers and Designers, 194, 210
Haley, Jay, 158
Harnett, JP, 137
Harney, Stefano, 232
Hartjes, Nathalie, 206
Haug, Wolfgang Fritz, 140, 156
Hawley, Rachel, 186
Heidegger, Martin, 273
Heinlein, Robert A., 101, 102
Heller, Steven, 54, 140, 172, 177, 266
Héritier, David, 189
Heskett, John, 143, 144
Hills, Thomas, 43
Hollein, Hans, 76, 80
Holm, Nicholas, 223, 224, 237
hooks, bell, 238, 252, 256, 261
Horkheimer, Max, 209, 230
Horowitz, Irving L., 41
Iaconesi, Salvatore, 89, 293
IDEO, 195, 196
IKEA, 21, 92, 136, 180
Illich, Ivan, 25, 89, 92, 252, 273
Indiani metropolitani, 215
Institute without Boundaries, 73
Invisible Committee, The, 58
Irwin, Terry, 35
Ito, Joi, 106, 107
Izenour, Steven, 203
Jackson, Don D., 158
Jacoby, Russell, 297
Jane, E., 229
Julier, Guy, 34, 46, 50, 55, 57, 62, 114, 119, 120, 161, 196
Kaiser, Gerrit, 132
Kalman, Tibor, 203, 205, 276
Kamprad, Ingvar, 136
Kasparov, Garry, 209

Keedy, Mr., 221, 223
Kenedi, Aaron, 159
Keys, Zak, 24
Kimball, Roger, 285
Klibansky, Raymond, 68
Knake, Dennis, 212
Koolhaas, Rem, 200, 216
Kopcke, Nikandre, 40
Kraus, Karl, 52
Krippendorff, Klaus, 101
ktsuski, @, 169
Kubrak, Anastasia, 220
Kyng, Morten, 161
Labedz, Celeste, 112
Labranca, Tommaso, 27, 239
Laker, Penina Acayo, 228
Land, Nick, 24
Laranjo, Francisco, 24, 25, 149, 187, 188, 213
LaRossa, Brian, 115
Lasch, Christopher, 68, 229, 230
Latour, Bruno, 77, 99, 154
Le Corbusier, 64
Le Goff, Jacques, 65, 68
Lee, Chris, 165
Leijsen, Rob van, 189
Leonard, Jennifer
Levi Bismarck, Pedro, 292
Levin, Golan, 83
Levine, David, 239, 240
Levrant de Bretteville, Sheila, 285
Licko, Zuzana, 170, 172
Lier, Bas van, 218
Lille, Alain de, 97
Lim, Adelia, 53
Linz, Max, 282
Lispector, Clarice, 291
Liu, Catherine, 225, 283
Lo Giudice, Euclide, 297
Lonergan, Guthrie, 175
Long, Lazarus, 101
Lonzi, Marta, 298
Lorusso, Silvio, 18, 189, 215, 246, 247, 272
Lovink, Geert, 18, 22, 24, 93, 159, 195, 220, 276
Lucentini, Paolo, 97
Luhmann, Niklas, 199
Lunardi, Flavia, 40
Lupton, Ellen, 188, 221, 231, 266, 273
Lupu, Alina, 236
M&CO, 203
Maeda, John, 141, 192

337

maetl, @, 152
Maldonado, Tomás, 20, 45, 46, 82, 93, 94, 127, 131, 144, 156, 207, 221, 273, 274, 288, 293, 296
Malpass, Matt, 228
Manzini, Ezio, 54, 55, 57, 93, 109, 122, 261
Mareis, Claudia, 59, 113, 279
Margolin, Victor, 54, 55, 85, 88
Mari, Enzo, 28, 136, 140, 141, 246, 265
Marx, Karl, 85, 139
Masure, Anthony, 145
Matos, Afonso, 268
Matter, Hansuli, 126
Mattioli, Valerio, 235, 238
Mau, Bruce, 73, 76, 77, 91, 94, 200, 218
McArdle, Jack, 254
McGuirk, Justin, 122
McKinsey, 33
Mclaughin, Aimee, 209
McLuhan, Marshall, 87
McVarish, Emily, 170, 172
Mejía, Mauricio, 100
Mejias, Ulises A., 98
Mensvoort, Koert van, 137, 139
Metahaven, 24, 39
Microsoft, 181, 188
Midal, Alexandra, 78
Mignolo, Walter, 105
Mills, C. Wright, 41, 44, 45, 46, 51, 55, 299, 300, 302
Mitcham, Carl, 89, 92
Moholy, Lucia, 254
Moholy-Nagy, László, 33, 35, 38, 113, 254, 276, 283
Mohotti, Wathsala Anupama, 84
Moles, Abraham A., 77
Montaigne, Michel de, 273
Monteiro, Mike, 156, 158, 169, 279
Moses, Robert, 136
Moten, Fred, 232
Munari, Bruno, 78, 86
Murtaugh, Michael, 83
Nayak, Richi, 84
Nelson, Tara-Nicholle, 366
Nestler, Simon, 180
Neuburg, Klaus, 180
neurotic_arsehole, @, 152
Nicoletti, Valerio, 164
Noel, Lesley-Ann, 228, 233, 234
Norman, Don, 102, 103, 141, 143
O'Flynn, Brian, 215
Obrist, Hans Ulrich, 209

Oh, Jasmine, 181
Oliver, Richard L., 159
OM Graphic, 182
Open Set, 210
Oroza, Ernesto, 93
Osborne A., Michael, 179
Osherow, Evan, 150, 151
Ozenc, Kursat, 116
Paepke, Walter, 194
Paim, Nina, 59, 113, 279
Palmarola, Hugo, 189
Panofsky, Erwin, 68
Papanek, Victor, 15, 84, 87, 88, 98, 102, 103, 105, 141, 145, 216, 278, 279
Parallel School, 210
Parco Studio, 190
Pater, Ruben, 27, 59, 62, 181, 184, 185, 187, 199, 218, 266
Peart, Rob, 179
Penin, Lara, 291
Persico, Oriana, 89
Peters, Tom, 33
Peterson, Jordan, 143
Petroni, Marco, 63
Pineau, Karl, 145
Platform BK, 270
Popova, Maria, 17
Posavec, Stefanie, 40
Posniak, Marina, 132
Potter, Norman, 15, 90, 112, 128, 202
Potter, Peter de, 173
Poynor, Rick, 84, 203, 205
Press, Alex, 199
Price, Jessie, 40
Qadeer, Ali S., 165
Quadflieg, Sven, 180
Raby, Fiona, 125, 126, 149, 211, 216, 277
Radical Design, 64, 119, 228
Radice, Barbara, 143
Rame, Sergio, 117
Rancière, Jacques, 106
Rand, Paul, 283, 285
Rawsthorn, Alice, 140, 226
Re:Publica, 209, 212, 214, 216, 221
Reinfurt, David, 106
Relearn, 210
Richardson, Adam, 145, 148
Richardson, J., 211
Rittel, Horst W. J., 17, 18, 21, 199
Rittner, Jennifer, 228
Roberts, Lucienne, 40, 59, 192
Rock, Michael, 115, 117, 169, 170, 226,

INDEX OF NAMES

227, 240, 270
Rodgers, Paul A., 78, 101, 112, 113, 122, 197
Rodina, The, 280
Rogan, Kevin, 153
Rohde, Charlotte, 183
Roth, Bernard, 195
Rule, Alix, 239
Ruskin, John, 65
Sagmeister, Stefan, 22
Sarmah, Harshajit, 180
Saxl, Fritz, 68
Schmieg, Sebastian, 177
Schmitt, Carl, 133, 150, 163
Schön, Donald A., 108, 109, 117, 119, 120, 121, 199, 266, 270
School for Poetic Computation, 194
Schouwenberg, Louise, 226
Schwab, Katharine, 141, 151
Sciascia, Leonardo, 297
Scott Brown, Denise, 203
Scuola Open Source, 117, 210
Scuro, Enrico, 250
Secomandi, Fernando, 92
Sennett, Richard, 302
Seyp, Vera van de, 183
Sfligiotti, Silvia, 174
Shaner-Bradford, Nikki, 113
Shaughnessy, Adrian, 131
Shaw, George Bernard, 199
Shelley, Mary, 17
Siang, Teo Yu, 270
Siedentopf, Max, 109
Simon, Herbert A., 63
Siti, Walter, 291
Slimer, 77
Sloterdijk, Peter, 99
Smith, Adam, 101
Smith, J, 135
Smiths, The, 211
Snelders, Dirk, 92
Snook, Tanya, 196
Social Design, 162, 219
Sottsass, Ettore, 116
Speculative Design, 126, 149, 150, 218, 227, 233, 277
Spiderman, 156
Spools, Jared, 158
Spotify, 132
Stewart, Susan, 82
Stilinović, Mladen, 241
Stinson, Liz, 192
Studio at the Edge of the World, 101
Suchman, Lucy, 55, 88
Sunday, Mike, 264
Suri, Siddharth, 187
suwuuuuu, @, 62
Swann, Levi, 84
Swift, Jonathan, 273
Táíwò, Olúfẹ́mi, 221, 266
Taylor, Astra, 184
Tharp, Bruce, 149
Tharp, Stephanie, 149
Thorpe, Ann, 225, 226, 227
tiffanyton, @, 131
Till, Jeremy. 18, 20
Tonkinwise, Cameron, 35
Toorn, Jan van, 52
Toppins, Aggie, 265, 285
Trend List, 197
Treviño, Javier A., 45, 51, 302
Trevisani, Luca, 42
Troemel, Brad, 113, 224, 237
Trump, Donald, 20
Tsing, Anna Lowenhaupt, 154
Twemlow, Alice, 41
Ugly Design, 176
Ullman, Ellen, 170
Ulm, Elliott, 60
United Nations, 83
University of the Underground (UUG), 210, 211, 213, 216, 242, 243
Upwork, 184
VanderLans, Rudy, 114, 170, 176, 177, 179, 207
Varela, Francisco, 84, 124
Veerman, Yuri, 269
Velden, Daniel van der, 150, 179, 185, 202
Ventura, Raffaele Alberto, 99, 199, 223
Venturi, Robert, 203
Vermaas, Pieter E., 78
Verne, Guri, 179
Vet, Annelys de, 117, 150, 196, 220
Vial, Stéphane, 78
Vignelli, Massimo, 141, 143
Vignelli, Lella, 141, 143
Vinsel, Lee, 120, 195
Virilio, Paul, 94
Vitiello, Guido, 219, 297
Von Foerster, Heinz, 84
Vonnegut, Kurt, 174, 176
Wagner, Kate, 109
Wallace, David Foster, 215, 216
Walters, Kelly, 228

wdka.teachermemes, @, 259, 267
Weakland, John, 158
Webber, Melvin M., 17, 18, 21
Weber, Max, 132, 139
West, Kanye, 173
What Design Can Do, 147, 162, 218
Whyte, William H., 44
Wigley, Mark, 64, 73, 87, 162, 196
Wilde, Lorraine, 125
Williams, Raymond, 18
Willis, Anne-Marie, 87, 88, 137
Winner, Langdon, 136, 143, 155
Wizinsky, Matthew, 62, 132, 228
Wright, Rebecca, 40
young_agamben, @, 66
Zohn, Harry, 52
Zuccari, Federico, 85
Zuckerberg, Mark, 191
Zweege, Tessel ten, 247

NOTES

NOTES

NOTES

NOTES

NOTES

NOTES

NOTES